Planting Fields

Planting Fields

A Place on Long Island

EDITED BY
Gina J. Wouters and Jerome E. Singerman

ESSAYS BY
Jennifer L. Anderson, John Dixon Hunt,
Arleyn A. Levee, Patricia M. O'Donnell,
and Witold Rybczynski

PHOTOGRAPHS BY
David Almeida

Introduction
Gina J. Wouters
17

A Country Place and
Its Makers
Witold Rybczynski
21

Before the Gold Coast:
The Early History
of Planting Fields
Jennifer L. Anderson
59

PORTFOLIO
Planting Fields:
The House and the
Landscape
David Almeida
83

On Planting Fields and
the Making of Place
John Dixon Hunt
135

Planting Fields
and Olmsted Brothers
on Long Island
Arleyn A. Levee
151

A Historic Landscape
Evolving Sustainably
Patricia M. O'Donnell
175

NOTES 198

INDEX 206

CONTRIBUTORS 212

Gina J. Wouters

Introduction

THE STORY OF PLANTING FIELDS IS ONE OF PEOPLE SHAPING PLACE. EVER SINCE the melting Laurentide glacial sheet sculpted Long Island and deposited a plethora of organic riches on its surfaces, this land has been defined by human activity. Originally in the ancestral homeland of the Matinecock, the area was named in their native tongue for its greatest attribute, the *planting fields*. After centuries of shifting ownership and land use, the Coe era that began in 1913 defines our experience of Planting Fields today. William Robertson Coe's legacy ensured that all 409 acres became a public asset. In 1971, the site became part of the New York State Parks system and classified as an arboretum; it was added to the National Register of Historic Places in 1979. With the completion of the *Planting Fields Cultural Landscape Report* (CLR) in 2019, it became apparent just how interesting and abundant the Olmsted Brothers contributions at Planting Fields were. Recent scholarship has revealed that the site exists as one of the most intact residential projects by the Olmsted firm. This awareness ushered in a focus on the reinvigoration and celebration of the historic landscape design of the site and public engagement with it. As we revitalize the Olmsted firm's various landscapes at Planting Fields in a process that is informed by historic plans and precedent, our strategic approach is underscored by environmental sustainability.

With more than 250,000 visitors each year, it is evident that the beauty and impact of Planting Fields is universal. To sustain this appeal, we steward the site with equal consideration of its preservation as well as its place in an evolving world. Through cultural and seasonal festivals, 5K races along the six miles of trails, exhibitions by leading contemporary artists, dynamic tours, and youth engagement, the site is activated all year long for the public. Planting Fields also serves as both a catalyst and a backdrop to milestones such as weddings, quinceañeras, engagements, birthdays, first dates, and more, fostering an inherent affection for the place. Social media influencers flock to the site to document and celebrate the seasonal wonders in posts that send Planting Fields out into the digital world. These patrons create a new meaning for Planting Fields, in a way that is emblematic of how people shape its value. I don't think the Coe family could ever have imagined Planting Fields having such an impact on the exceptionally diverse communities of Long Island, but I'm certain they would be pleased.

In an era when analogous sites were demolished, developed, or otherwise broken up, it is remarkable that Planting Fields survives with astonishing integrity. This prompts the question, is Planting Fields special because it exists, or does it exist because it is special? The essays in this book emphasize how rare it is—and how fortunate we are—to retain the original footprint of this place and to have much of the architecture intact, but that did not happen by chance or without foresight. Established in 1952 by W. R. Coe, Planting Fields Foundation works in tandem with the New York State Office of Parks, Recreation, and Historic Preservation to steward the acres of Planting Fields in a manner that honors the site's past, activates it in the present, and sustains it for the future. While the story of Planting Fields began long before the Coes laid eyes on the land, the place that exists today is the result of their vision and generosity. Gifted by them to the people of the State of New York in 1955, the site is a cultural and natural asset in public hands.

This publication is the culmination of a group of distinguished landscape and architecture historians and preservationists thinking deeply about Planting Fields. The pages take the reader on a nonlinear journey, introducing the site through a new entry point with each chapter. Together, the authors have given readers five distinct vantage points in one place. Witold Rybczynski's essay, "A Country Place and Its Makers," lays the foundation for the book. After years of deep immersion into the Planting Fields story, Rybczynski has unraveled the many layers of the site's twentieth-century existence. Piecing together decades of a blurry past, he situates the protagonists of the Planting Fields we know today, underscoring the distinct role each owner, designer, and caretaker played. Because of Rybczynski's relentless sleuthing, so many questions have been answered and a small, yet essential detail was unearthed: Planting Fields was originally created with a view to the waters of Oyster Bay. Jennifer Anderson looks at the centuries that preceded the Coe era. She starts with the Matinecock—one of the original thirteen tribes of Long Island—and traces the sequence of their dispossession by newly arrived Europeans. The chapter takes us through the colonial era, the development of Oyster Bay, the agricultural land uses of the nineteenth century, and ends where Rybczynski starts, with the wealthy industrialists who found new recreational pleasures in the storied grounds of the North Shore. John Dixon Hunt's essay "On Planting Fields and the Making of Place" contextualizes the ethos of Planting Fields within a broader narrative of English landscape design and the connected concept of placemaking, which he argues to be a more suitable term for landscape architecture. Hunt traces Olmstedian design found at the site within a *longue durée* and emerging from a tradition of garden design by historical figures such as Lancelot "Capability" Brown, William Kent, and Humphrey Repton and best considered within the ideologies of Alexander Pope and Le Corbusier among others.

Focusing directly on Long Island itself, Arleyn Levee places the landscape that Olmsted Brothers designed for the Coes in the context of the firm's other Long Island projects. While recognizing that the firm provided singularity to each design, Levee identifies patterns in landscape design typologies that connect each of these Gold Coast estates. She foregrounds the leadership of Olmsted Brothers partner James

Frederick Dawson throughout the firm's nearly twenty-year engagement with Planting Fields and gives color to his relationship with a demanding client in W. R. Coe.

The book concludes as it should, with thinking about the legacy of Planting Fields beyond our present time. Patricia O'Donnell positions the stewardship of Planting Fields today within broader narratives of sustainability and global responsibility. Applying the United Nations Sustainable Development Goals and considering principles of preservation and rehabilitation to a historic designed landscape, O'Donnell challenges us to think about what Planting Fields can and should offer the next generation.

Many individuals made this book possible, and I'd like to thank those who contributed to its production. First and foremost, this book would not be possible without the generosity of the Robert David Lion Gardiner Foundation. The prescience of Kathryn Curran, executive director of the Foundation, has benefited Planting Fields Foundation, and we are deeply appreciative for her steadfast support. I am indebted to the essayists, Jennifer Anderson, John Dixon Hunt, Arleyn Levee, Patricia O'Donnell, and Witold Rybczynski, for their contributions to this book. Their immersion in the site provides us with new ways of understanding Planting Fields that will shape experiences for generations to come. The idea for this publication emerged in 2020, and since shortly after its inception, Jerome Singerman has been my trusted co-editor to whom I am grateful. His wisdom, editorial expertise, and grasp of the content have been a decisive factor in doing justice to the Planting Fields story. Elizabeth White, editor-at-large at Monacelli, is a hero for recognizing that Planting Fields deserved to be introduced to the world in book form. We are so lucky to have the site memorialized in a stunning Monacelli/Phaidon creation. Additional thanks to David Almeida for his multiyear process of photographing the site in every season and from every angle, and whose photographs capture the *genius loci* of Planting Fields in two-dimensions; to Marie Penny for her diligent uncovering of archival content that yielded troves of new information, both fascinating and mundane, and for her careful selection of archival images; to Yve Ludwig for her thoughtful and creative design; and lastly, to the enduring leadership of the Planting Fields Foundation Board of Trustees and the partnership of New York State Office of Parks, Recreation, and Historic Preservation.

Planting Fields blurs the boundaries between binaries. It is both an archetype and a replica, natural and artificial, historic and relevant, traditional and vanguard, familiar and surprising, enduring and evolving, and everything in between. These tensions have captivated me for years and this book is an exciting step in sharing the multi-dimensionality of Planting Fields with the world. Let the perspectives shared within these pages propel you to make your first-ever visit or to come again and see Planting Fields with new eyes. It is a place to experience, waiting for you to make it your own.

Witold Rybczynski

A Country Place and Its Makers

THE COUNTRY PLACE ERA IS A LANDSCAPE HISTORY TERM THAT REFERS TO A period from roughly the late nineteenth century to the Depression, when wealthy Americans built country estates that were noted for their exceptional gardens.[1] Country places were found along the North Shore of Long Island, in the Massachusetts Berkshires, on Mount Desert Island in Maine, along Philadelphia's Main Line, in Ohio's Lake County, and bordering Wisconsin's Lake Geneva. The gardens surrounded mansions modeled on European precedents—English manors, French chateaux, and Italian villas. The Gilded Age and the Roaring Twenties were prosperous periods, but as the contemporary writer and architect Geoffrey Scott observed, "Prosperity is a condition of great achievements; it is not their cause."[2] The great wealth of industrialists, financial moguls, and corporate lawyers was happily allied with gifted architects and landscape architects, assisted by artists, craftsmen, and small armies of skilled artisans. In this regard, Planting Fields is both exemplary and unusual. The house and its garden, unlike most country places, were not the result of a concentrated building campaign but of three decades that involved two sets of owners, two separate houses, three architects, four landscape architects, and several artistic talents, each reinforcing and expanding the work of their predecessors.

HELEN MACGREGOR BYRNE AND JAMES BYRNE
GROSVENOR ATTERBURY AND JAMES LEAL GREENLEAF
1904–13

The modern story of Planting Fields began in December 1904, when Helen Macgregor Byrne (1869–1945) bought a farm in the township of Oyster Bay on Long Island's North Shore. This area was readily accessible from Manhattan—the North Shore Railroad ran to Port Washington, and the Long Island Rail Road operated a branch to Oyster Bay. Thanks to its natural setting and proximity to the city, since the end of the nineteenth century the western portion of the North Shore had attracted wealthy New Yorkers, who built lavish rural retreats. This was where F. Scott Fitzgerald situated the fictional West Egg, the site of Jay Gatsby's fabulous mansion—"a factual imitation of some Hôtel de Ville in Normandy."[3] There would be so many such grand country places between Great Neck and Oyster Bay that the area became known as the Gold Coast.[4] In 1974 the *New York Times* estimated that "at its peak the Gold Coast contained more than 500 estates of 50 or more acres with appropriately scaled mansions."[5]

Helen Byrne was what today would be called an early adopter; Locust Valley had only recently become fashionable. The first Manhattanite to build a country house in the area—four years earlier—had been Paul D. Cravath, a prominent corporate lawyer, whose estate, Veraton, encompassed 600 acres overlooking Long Island Sound. Cravath was the originator of the meritocratic Cravath System for recruiting, training, and remunerating young attorneys, and the founder of a venerable firm that still bears his name. It is possible that he bought and sold land on his own account, for it is recorded that Byrne was advised by one W. Burling Cocks, a local real estate lawyer who has been described as "a land speculator with the Cravath syndicate."[6]

The property that Byrne purchased from John M. Sammis consisted of two parcels, Upper Planting Fields Farm (164 acres), and the smaller Nine Partners Lot (13 acres). The name Planting Fields is said to be derived from an old Matinecock tribal name.[7] The octogenarian merchant and leading local landowner drove a hard bargain; she paid $123 per acre at a time when the agricultural value of land on western Long Island was about $75 per acre.[8] But Helen Byrne did not stop there. Over the next two years, she acquired three more adjoining parcels, large and small, increasing the size of her holding to slightly more than 300 acres. The total cost of Planting

Helen Macgregor Byrne. Arnold Genthe, 1917.

James Byrne. *Courtesy of Harvard Alumni Bulletin.*

Fields, as she christened the estate, was about $50,000, a considerable sum, more than $1.6 million today.

Helen Byrne was familiar with the world of business. Her father, James C. McGregor (Helen spelled the name Macgregor), the son of Scottish immigrants and a Yale graduate, was a successful Terre Haute, Indiana, entrepreneur with real estate holdings in his native Cincinnati. Her mother, Elizabeth, part Scot, was a Daughter of the American Revolution, thanks to French Huguenot ancestors. We know nothing of Helen's early life or how she made her way to New York, but by the time of her 1896 wedding to attorney James Byrne, she was described in the announcement as a New Yorker. It was no spring romance—she was twenty-seven; Byrne was thirty-nine. Her letters suggest an intelligent, educated, and independent-minded person. An original member of the Colony Club, the first women's social club in the city, she was an art patron and a serious collector of prints and drawings—there are records of her lending works to the Metropolitan Museum, including a large Puvis de Chavannes triptych. Her 1917 portrait by Arnold Genthe, a noted German American photographer of politicians, celebrities, and artists, shows a handsome woman, stylishly dressed and wearing a long wraparound pearl necklace, hardly a flapper—she is 48—but clearly a modern woman.

Helen Byrne could have met Paul Cravath through her husband. James Byrne (1857–1942) was born in Springfield, Massachusetts, of Irish immigrant parents, graduated from Harvard College, and worked as a private tutor in Philadelphia before putting himself through Harvard Law School, where he graduated cum laude.[9] He was recruited by the New York law firm of Walter S. Carter, a legendary spotter of legal talent; Cravath, who joined the office a few years later, was another "Carter kid." In 1900 Byrne, now a partner in a white-shoe Wall Street firm, served as lead lawyer in a sensational trial involving litigation of a disputed inheritance that led to the founding of Rice University and made Byrne something of a legal celebrity. He was described as an "idol of the young lawyers," and top Harvard Law School graduates flocked to his office.[10] As an Irish-Catholic, Byrne had to overcome formidable social barriers, and he did so successfully—by 1913 he and Helen were listed in the Social Register. Byrne served as president of the New York Bar Association and as chancellor of the University of the State of New York; he was a founder of the philanthropic Irish Industrial Society of America. He was also a member of the Harvard Corporation, the board governing the university—the first Roman Catholic to hold that position. "He was warm, and violent, and unjust [sic]. He was keen, and sparkling, and exciting. His voice was clear and pleasant," wrote one of his former employees. "On the whole the conclusion of those who worked for Byrne is that to associate with him on *any* terms was a privilege."[11]

Shortly after purchasing Upper Planting Fields Farm, the Byrnes began planning their future country home. Their architect was Grosvenor Atterbury, who five years earlier had renovated their West 59th Street townhouse. Atterbury (1869–1956), born in Detroit, grew up in New York, where his father practiced corporate law. While Grosvenor was a student at Yale, which both his father and grandfather had attended, his parents built a country house on eastern Long Island in Shinnecock Hills. The charming, shingled cottage was designed with the advice of Stanford White, a family friend who likely influenced young Grosvenor's choice of profession. After graduating from Yale, Atterbury enrolled in architecture classes at Columbia (though not

West wing of Planting Fields. Atterbury's design, with its shingled half-hip roofs and rough-adzed timber frame filled with red-brown burnt brick, respected tradition but did not follow a historical style. August H. Patzig, 1906–8. *Planting Fields Foundation Archives.*

long enough to receive a degree), took painting lessons in William Merritt Chase's art school in Shinnecock Hills, apprenticed with McKim, Mead & White, and spent a year in Paris in an atelier of the École des Beaux-Arts. Obviously a young man in a hurry, he opened an office immediately on his return to New York in 1895 and soon established a reputation as an up-and-coming designer of townhouses in Manhattan and country houses on Long Island. Atterbury was not a typical society architect. A few years after the Byrne house, he was commissioned by the Russell Sage Foundation, which was led by a former client, to be the architect of the model community of Forest Hills Gardens in Queens, a project in which he collaborated with the landscape architect and planner Frederick Law Olmsted Jr. The success of Forest Hills, for which Atterbury developed an ingenious prefabricated concrete building system, was the beginning of a lifelong active interest in social housing.

But that was in the future. At the time of the Planting Fields commission, Atterbury's practice was focused on residences for the well-to-do. Although his city houses were generally Georgian revival, the country houses were ahistorical: low-slung, covered in cedar shingles, stucco, or brick—he pioneered the use of overburnt or "lammie" brick, which gave his houses a rough appearance. It is hard to characterize their style; although Atterbury was influenced by the Arts and Crafts movement, he was his own man. All in all, he represented an adventurous choice for Helen Byrne, for it appears that it was she, rather than her husband, who took the lead in the building project.[12]

"The true answer to a problem," Atterbury once said, "must be derived from its own premises and conditions."[13] The chief condition of the Byrne property was

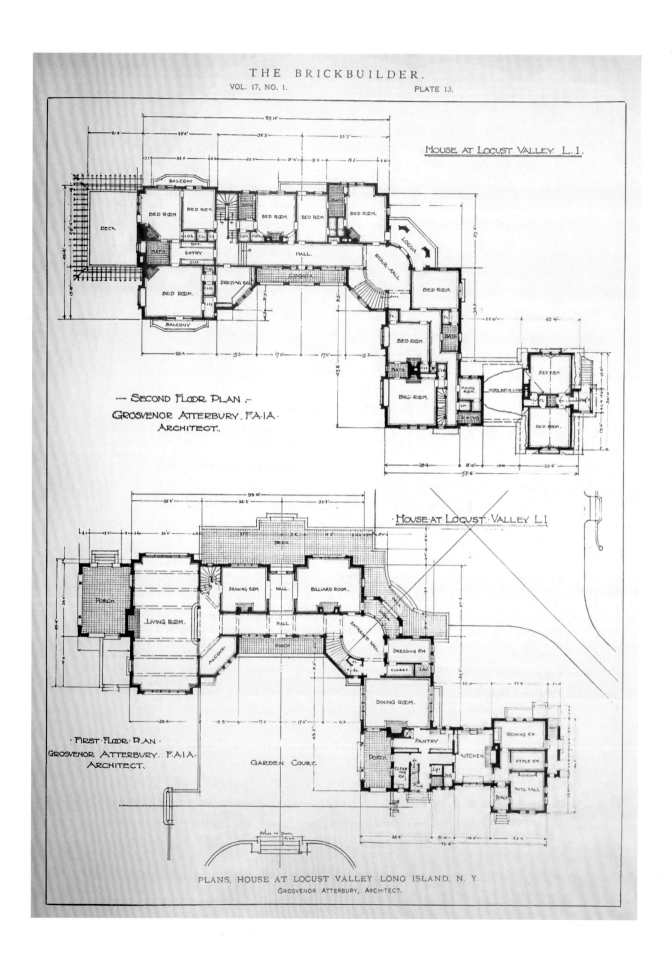

the beautiful setting, heavily wooded on the east and west, open fields on the north and south. "In planning this house photographs were taken at every part of the site beforehand, in order that the house might blend with the landscape as far as possible, a result which was successfully achieved," Atterbury explained in a magazine article.[14] He located the house well back from Planting Fields Road, on the edge of a plateau that provided a distant view of the "brilliant blue waters" of Long Island Sound, a view that has long since disappeared as open fields have turned into woodland and trees have grown.[15] The large house—eleven bedrooms, not including staff quarters— consisted of three narrow wings in a dogleg arrangement, a common plan type that architectural historian Mark Alan Hewitt has described as "modern picturesque," to distinguish it from earlier shingle style houses, and from Georgian and colonial revival plans, which tended to follow a more regular geometry.[16]

The long narrow plan sheltered the private garden from the public arrival area and the service court. The asymmetrical arrangement, which broke down the scale of the architecture, also allowed rooms to respond to views and solar orientation. That did not mean that the house was not rigorously organized. "The first principle of good planning," Atterbury stated, "[is] simple and obvious circulation."[17] The main rooms were located along several lines of movement. A diagonal led from the exterior arrival area into an octagonal entrance hall containing the stair. From there, a wide hallway passed by a billiard room and a drawing room and stepped down into a large, beamed living room that was centered on a prominent brick fireplace; in the other direction lay the paneled dining room. Upstairs, the primary bedrooms were at the west end, next to the children's bedrooms—three daughters—with two guest bedrooms on the far side of the stair hall.

Grosvenor Atterbury, House at Locust Valley, first and second floor plans. *The Brickbuilder*, 17 (January 1908). *Planting Fields Foundation Archives*.

The provision of an after-dinner drawing room for the ladies and a billiard room for the gentlemen followed old-fashioned custom, but the intimate connection to the outdoors was a modern feature. The living room opened onto a porch overlooking the lawn; a short hall between the drawing room and the billiard room led to a stone terrace that offered views of the lawn and the Sound; on the south side, the long hallway opened onto a porch overlooking the garden with its circular pool. A glazed porch off the dining room similarly overlooked the garden and provided an opportunity for sheltered outdoor dining. Most of the family bedrooms had access to balconies or loggias, and the primary bedrooms were provided with a large roof deck and a sleeping porch. A loggia off the upstairs corridor overlooked the garden. The south-facing loggias, balconies, and windows were shaded by striped canvas awnings, and many had planting boxes, which produced an overall effect of cheerful domesticity.

The eastern end of the dogleg contained the kitchen, pantry, ironing room, refrigerator room, and servants hall; staff bedrooms were in the attic.* The far end of the service wing included two second-floor guest bedrooms with their own outdoor access. These seem to have been what were called "bachelor bedrooms," which, according to the nineteenth-century British novelist Wilkie Collins, were "familiar to everybody who owns a country house, and to everybody who has stayed in a country house."[18] Byrne sometimes invited young lawyers from his office to spend the

---

* According to the 1910 Census, the Byrnes employed ten staff, including a dressmaker, two nannies, a houseman, and a poultryman. The butler was Scottish, as was the dressmaker, the nannies were French, and the rest were Irish; James Byrne was known for hiring Irish staff, both at home and in his office.

A long hall extended from the grand Living Room to the entrance. August H. Patzig, 1906–8. *Planting Fields Foundation Archives.*

Billiard Room. August H. Patzig, 1906–8. *Planting Fields Foundation Archives.*

Drawing Room. August H. Patzig, 1906–8. *Planting Fields Foundation Archives.*

weekend, and these isolated bedrooms allowed for smoking, drinking, and late-night card games without disturbing the family or other guests.

Atterbury's site plan showed a freestanding garage, although it is unclear if that was ever built. On the far side of the court stood an L-shaped stable—the Oyster Bay area was known for its extensive riding trails, maintained by a neighborhood Country Lane Committee. The stable contained ten horse stalls (with a hay loft above), as well as a carriage house, a carriage washing area, a harness room, and quarters for the stableman. The construction drawings were titled "Stable for Mrs. J. Byrne," further underlining her role as Atterbury's client.

The stable, like the house, was built with a rough-adzed timber frame infilled with red brown lammie brick. This sounds like Elizabethan half-timbering, but the effect of the rustic materials, irregular massing, and shingled half-hip roofs was picturesque rather than historical—the "style of the English farm house," according to Atterbury.¹⁹ That is an odd description as there was nothing particularly English or rustic about the most imposing feature, an octagonal tower that contained the entrance hall and the main staircase. The exact function of the fifth-floor room, which was ringed by windows and would have made an excellent lookout, is unclear—it was accessed via the attic and a servant's stair. Perhaps the octagonal tower room was a "secret" playroom for the girls?

The tower room was not included in the views of the house that the Byrnes commissioned from the Jersey City architectural photographer August H. Patzig, whose photographs show elegantly furnished rooms with chestnut paneling and stylish woodwork.²⁰ Oriental carpets abounded; the wide downstairs hall between the entrance and the living room functioned as a picture gallery and was hung floor-to-ceiling with Helen Byrne's collection of prints, which were all over the house. The furniture was an eclectic mixture: antiques, carved chests, slip-covered easy chairs, rockers, a Chinese settee in the entrance hall. The attractive decor was her doing. Gardner Cox, a noted Boston portraitist who married the youngest Byrne daughter, called his mother-in-law "a born architect and a brilliant decorator."²¹

The chief feature of the beamed living room was a brick fireplace with a large circular plaque of a Madonna and Child. James Byrne was a devout Catholic, and a secluded alcove off the living room was "arranged so that, if desired, this can be used as a private chapel," Atterbury wrote.²² We have a vignette of life at Planting Fields from one of Byrne's young lawyers. "Naturally, being himself, he married a Protestant, and when you went out to stay with him over the weekend, Byrne and all the maids and the children would get up very early and go to Mass, while Mrs. Byrne and Potter, the butler, and distinguished guests would have the opportunity to rest rather late."²³

Responsibility for the design of the garden rested with James Leal Greenleaf (1857–1933). The wonderfully named Greenleaf had an unusual background for a landscape architect. Born to a prominent New York City family, he studied civil engineering at Columbia University, where he eventually held a teaching post. After a dozen years, he stepped down to devote himself to practice, eventually specializing in garden design, for which he showed exceptional ability. He was responsible for landscaping the grounds of no fewer than thirty large estates in New Jersey, Connecticut, and Long Island, including the Italian garden at Hyde Park, the Frederick W. Vanderbilt mansion by McKim, Mead & White in the Hudson Valley.²⁴ Greenleaf's professional career later included laying out battlefield cemeteries in France and Belgium, advising on the grounds of the Lincoln Memorial, and participating in the movement to establish national parks. He became a prominent figure in his chosen field, serving on the U.S. Commission of Fine Arts, and succeeding Frederick Law Olmsted Jr. as president of the American Society of Landscape Architects.

Greenleaf's domestic masterpieces are generally considered to be the gardens of two Gold Coast estates, The Braes in Glen Cove and Killenworth in Oyster Bay, both completed in 1912. His earlier work for the Byrnes was less elaborate, but his landscape decisions would influence the evolution of Planting Fields for decades to come. He laid out a winding access road through the woodland and an octagonal arrival court next to the house. He turned the sloping fields in front into lawns. On the south side, he created an intimate garden that consisted of a sunken grassy circle whose edges were defined by seating on one side and a brick pergola on the other, with a large circular pool in the center. The garden accentuated the north-south axis

that was a key element of Atterbury's design, which Greenleaf extended in the form of a long walk—later named Vista Path—and a parallel rose-arbor walk farther west.

West of the house, beside an east-west path, Atterbury designed two small cottages. The identical buildings, 19 by 13 feet in plan, were framed in wood and stuccoed on the exterior. The first was next to a wooden tennis court; the second, 150 feet farther along the path, was distinguished by its chimney. The interior, simply finished with exposed studs and rafters, was dominated by a massive brick fireplace with patterned brick, corbels, and two niches for storing firewood. The cottages were a picturesque sight, adorned with climbing roses, and with shingled half-hip roofs and an eyebrow over the door, features common in Atterbury's architecture.

On the site plan, the first cottage is called a "Play House," and it was perhaps a place where the three Byrne girls could play house while the adults played tennis. The function of the second cottage, with its massive fireplace, is unclear. It sat next to a flat grassy area that could have been used for lawn games—croquet, badminton, and volleyball—in which case the cottage could have served as a sort of field house.* If the lawn were flooded in the winter to make a skating rink, the cottage would have made a good warming hut. Or it might have been a Teahouse. Teahouses were a fashionable garden accessory in the Country Place Era, and the fireplace opening was large enough to hang a kettle and toast crumpets.

Tall red cedars around the house replicated the effect of Italian cypress trees. Greenleaf's pastime was landscape painting, and he had a painterly approach to garden design—"building up pictures," as he described it.[25] Patzig's photographs, taken between 1906 and 1908, illustrate how effectively Greenleaf's heavy planting complemented Atterbury's picturesque architecture, shrouding the house with climbing vines. The southern portion of the property, which included fields and pastures and several existing agricultural buildings, was left largely untouched, as were the heavily wooded areas on the east and west.

Greenleaf's densely layered planting complemented Atterbury's architecture. August H. Patzig, 1906–8. *Planting Fields Foundation Archives.*

A view of the pool and garden from the upstairs loggia. Features such as the long north-south walk (seen through the opening through the plantings) would influence the evolution of Planting Fields for decades to come. August H. Patzig, 1906–8. *Planting Fields Foundation Archives.*

---

* American "backyard" croquet became popular in the mid-nineteenth century. The exclusive New York Badminton Club was founded in 1878. Volleyball, an American invention, originated in Massachusetts in 1895.

The cottage/playhouse, designed by Grosvenor Atterbury, before Everett Shinn converted it into a Teahouse for Mai Coe. *Planting Fields Foundation Archives.*

The house and garden were completed by 1906. Planting Fields appears to have been the Byrnes' year-round home. Oyster Bay was a good place to raise three young girls—some of the stable stalls would have held ponies. Two more children were born in the house, a girl in 1907, and two years later, a boy. Yet in 1911, the Byrne family was back in the city. What happened? Helen Byrne had put Planting Fields on the market. Her agent was S. Osgood Pell & Co., a leading Manhattan real estate brokerage house that specialized in leasing and selling large country estates.[26] During the summers of 1911 and 1912, Planting Fields was leased to the Coe family, wealthy New Yorkers who the previous summer had rented a house in the fashionable seaside resort of Elberon, New Jersey.[27] They must have enjoyed their stay on the North Shore, because in February 1913 William Robertson Coe made an offer to purchase Planting Fields—which Helen Byrne accepted. Coe had to wait until the end of the year to take possession, because the estate had already been leased for the summer, first by Robert Livingston and subsequently by C. K. G. Billings, a celebrated industrial tycoon, who was building his own country house nearby. The closing of the sale of Planting Fields took place on December 1, 1913, at 24 Broad Street in Lower Manhattan, in the law office of Byrne & Cutcheon. Helen Byrne was represented by one Mr. O'Leary from her husband's firm. Earlier that year the whole family had sailed to Europe for an extended tour: London, Paris, the French Riviera, and a long stay in Florence.

What was the reason for the sale? It was not financial; in September 1912, while Planting Fields was rented, Helen Byrne had purchased yet another farm, adding 70 acres to the property and providing a useful "back door" to Mill River Road. Did she plan the sale all along? Or did Coe simply make an offer that she couldn't refuse? A somewhat cryptic letter that she later wrote to him is not much help. "You see, perhaps foolishly, I wasn't half as keen on the sale as Mr. Dennis was for me. He has always underestimated the value of Long Island holdings & could never be persuaded that there were many people who were ready to invest at what seemed to him fictitious values. But perhaps you've talked to him & know his views, with which I disagree."[28] "Mr. Dennis" may have been an agent with S. Osgood Pell & Co.

Helen Byrne sounds like a seasoned businesswoman, and it is possible that with her family background in real estate, and perhaps aided by an inheritance (her father died in 1890), she was building up the family fortune by buying, improving, and re-selling houses—or building anew in the case of Planting Fields. That would explain the Byrnes' frequent moves. After marrying, they had lived on Central Park South for five years before moving to the townhouse renovated by Atterbury on West 59th Street; while Planting Fields was rented the family lived on East 71st Street.

Four months after the sale, Helen Byrne, who was in Cap Martin on the Cote d'Azur, wrote to Coe's wife, Mai. The letter ended on a poignant note. "I think we shall all of us find it difficult to go back to America & face the fact that Planting Fields is no longer waiting for us. I wish you much happiness there & I shall always have the warmest interest in the place. It is possible of such great beauty—& I was able to do so little! With remembrances to your husband & many regrets before me."[29] Whatever regrets Helen Byrne had would have been offset by the $625,000 selling price of Planting Fields, a considerable sum, almost $19 million today.

MAI HUTTLESTON ROGERS COE AND WILLIAM ROBERTSON COE
WALKER & GILLETTE AND GUY LOWELL
1913–18

The new owners of Planting Fields were a formidable couple. Mary Huttleston Rogers Coe (1875–1924)—known as Mai—was the youngest daughter of Henry Huttleston Rogers, a self-made entrepreneur and one of the richest men in the country. Born in the small seaside town of Fairhaven, Massachusetts, he made his fortune in the Pennsylvania oil fields, and after selling his refining business to John D. Rockefeller, became his partner in the Standard Oil trust. Rogers was active in many fields including oil pipelines, copper mining, natural gas, and the construction of urban trolley systems and railroads, including the immensely profitable Virginian Railway, widely known as the "richest little railroad in the world," which hauled coal from West Virginia to Hampton Roads. Known as Hell Hound Rogers for his aggressive business practices, he was an unusual character whose closest friend was Samuel Clemens and whose circle included George Washington Carver, Helen Keller, and the muckraking journalist Ida Tarbell.

Rogers had five children, but Mai was his favorite. She grew up in privileged circumstances, privately educated abroad and interested in the arts, but at age seventeen, she shocked her family by eloping. It was reported that the twenty-year-old Joseph Cooper Mott gave Mai a diamond bracelet said to be worth $22,000 ($600,000 today), so he does not sound like a fortune hunter or "scalawag," as Henry Rogers would have it.[30] Whatever the details, the two-year marriage ended when Rogers, acting as his underage daughter's legal guardian, engineered an annulment.[31] Mai was sent to Europe, with her older sister as chaperone, until the scandal died down.

It was on a later transatlantic voyage that Mai met her future husband, William Robertson Coe (1869–1955). Coe, thirty-one and recently widowed, was born in England. His ancestors were in domestic service, and his father rose to be manager of an ironworks before emigrating to the United States when William—the fifth of eleven

William Robertson Coe, Mai Rogers Coe, and their children (from left) Robert, Natalie, Henry, and William Jr., c. 1911, when the Coes first rented Planting Fields for the summer. *Planting Fields Foundation Archives.*

children—was fourteen. The family settled in New Jersey outside Philadelphia. It was in that city that Coe went to work a year later as an office boy in what would become a branch of Johnson & Higgins, one of the world's largest marine insurers. In a career worthy of a Horatio Alger tale, Coe worked his way up the company ladder, and by the time he met Mai, he was in the New York head office running the claims department. A widowed immigrant* with a modest family background hardly sounds like an ideal suitor at a time when American heiresses were marrying British nobility, but Mai, now twenty-five, had the elopement and an annulled marriage in her past. The pair were married in 1900. Thanks in part to the fortuitous Rogers connection, Johnson & Higgins prospered, and Coe rose to be president and later chairman of the board. A dramatic increase in the Coe family fortune occurred in 1909 when Henry Rogers died, leaving an estate of $40 million (more than $1 billion today), to be divided equally among his four surviving children. Mai received an annual income that in the 1920s was estimated to be about $425,000 ($7 million today)—her husband's not inconsiderable salary was about a quarter of that—and when she turned forty—in 1915—she would inherit $5 million and an equal amount as a life estate.[32] At the time they purchased Planting Fields, William and Mai had four children: William, Robert, Henry, and Natalie.

Coe had big plans for his new country home. Shortly after acquiring the property, he started constructing farm buildings in the southern portion of the estate: a house for the estate superintendent, a six-car garage, and an imposing, five-hundred-foot-long, cupola-topped building that was called the Hay Barn but which included not only a stalls for riding horses and ponies and Coe's thoroughbreds, a hay loft, and a tack room, but also a wagon house, milking stalls, and a creamery.

A tower at one end housed a grain silo, and an entire wing was a bunk-house for estate workers. The building was half-timbered with lammie brick to match the main house. The architects of the monumental Hay Barn and the other farm buildings were Stewart Walker and Leon Gillette. Coe had engaged the New York firm in 1911, when he bought a 492-acre ranch near Cody, Wyoming, from the famous showman Colonel William F. "Buffalo Bill" Cody, with whom he had become friends. Walker

---

* When he was 24, Coe married Janie Hutchinson Falligant (1868–1899), the daughter of a Savannah judge and state senator. She died only five years later of "inflammation of the brain" according to the *Savannah Morning News*.

The equestrian family: William Robertson Coe with Natalie, William, Robert, and Henry, in front of the entrance to the house, 1915. *Planting Fields Foundation Archives.*

& Gillette designed a sprawling ranch house cum hunting lodge that resembled an Adirondack camp, brown shingles with white trim.*

Walker & Gillette is not celebrated today, but the firm was highly regarded in its day. A. Stewart Walker (1876–1952) and Leon N. Gillette (1878–1945) had joined forces in 1906. The two met while working for Warren & Wetmore, a New York firm known for its large hotels and railroad terminals, including the Ritz-Carlton Hotel and Grand Central Terminal. Walker, a graduate of Harvard, had married well and had the social connections, and Gillette, a University of Pennsylvania graduate who was born in Massachusetts, had the design skills—he had placed second in the highly competitive entrance exam of the École des Beaux-Arts of which he was a *diplomé*. Although the pair later specialized in banks and office buildings, they began as residential architects, initially in Tuxedo Park, where Walker's father-in-law owned properties, and later in Manhattan and on Long Island, where they were responsible for sixteen large country houses. A 1920 article in the British magazine *Country Life* featured nine American "distinguished architects who have made a specialty of designing successful country houses" and included Walker & Gillette alongside such celebrated practitioners as John Russell Pope, Charles A. Platt, and Delano & Aldrich.[33] Walker & Gillette country houses bore no signature style. Clients sought out Grosvenor Atterbury because they liked his personal approach; they went to Walker & Gillette because they knew they would get an accomplished design in whatever historical style they chose—American colonial, Georgian revival, or Mediterranean.

---

* The ranch house was completely destroyed by fire in 1940. Coe rebuilt the house the following year, commissioning the architect John Walter Wood (1900–1958), an Oxford and Harvard classmate and friend of his son Robert.

The Hay Barn. Harry G. Healy, 1916. *Planting Fields Foundation Archives.*

"Mrs. Byrne had done very little in the shape of landscaping," Coe later recalled, somewhat unfairly.[34] He wanted something more impressive. Something like Billings's magnificent estate, Farnsworth, which was in its final stage of completion just across Chicken Valley Road, the west boundary of Planting Fields. The Georgian revival mansion and its surrounding Italian gardens were the work of the architect Guy Lowell, and when Lowell offered his services to Coe, the latter agreed. Guy Lowell (1870–1927) was a successful architect who was also an accomplished landscape architect. After graduating from Harvard College, he received a degree in architecture from the Massachusetts Institute of Technology and spent five years abroad, studying horticulture at the Royal Botanic Garden, Kew, and landscape architecture at the École des Beaux-Arts. The Lowells were an established Boston Brahmin family, and when Guy Lowell started his practice, he had no difficulty securing commissions and soon opened a branch office in Manhattan.

Lowell was influential in the nascent landscape architecture field. He wrote several books on gardens, and in 1900 he was responsible for establishing a landscape architecture program at MIT—one of the first such programs in the country, and the first to accept women.[35] His approach to garden design was pragmatic. "We may borrow, then, details and ideas from Italy, France, and England, but we must adapt them skillfully to our own needs, and give them the setting which they require. Our gardens need not, when adapted to this country, follow any recognized style," he wrote in his popular book *American Gardens* (1902).[36] Lowell was responsible for the gardens of several prominent North Shore estates, not only Farnsworth, but also Cravath's Veraton, and Harbor Hill, an immense French chateau designed for the business magnate Clarence H. Mackay by Stanford White.

In 1913, when he was hired by Coe, Lowell had just won an important competition to design the New York County Courthouse in Manhattan.* Thus the day-to-day work at Planting Fields was in the hands of Lowell's associate A. Robeson Sargent (1876–1918). Sargent—nicknamed Bobo—was the son of the renowned botanist Charles Sprague Sargent, the founder and director of the Arnold Arboretum at Harvard University, which he had laid out with Frederick Law Olmsted. Although Robeson Sargent did not have formal training in horticulture or landscape architecture, he shared his father's interest in arboriculture. After graduating from Harvard College in 1900, he had accompanied him and the naturalist John Muir on a five-month round-the-world tour to study botanical species and to collect specimens for the Arboretum. Robeson's sister, Henrietta, was married to Guy Lowell, and on his return to Boston, Robeson joined his brother-in-law's firm. The young Sargent is best described as a landscape gardener rather than landscape architect, and it was in that capacity that he assisted Lowell at Harbor Hill, Veraton, and Farnsworth. By the time of Planting Fields, he and architect Benjamin B. F. Russell were listed as associates on the firm's stationery.

One of Sargent's tasks at Planting Fields was completing and refining existing landscape features. He extended Greenleaf's arbor walk and turned the entrance drive into a proper allée with sodded shoulders and two staggered rows of European beeches. He also added red pine and Scotch pine seedlings to the boundary of the estate along Planting Fields Road to create a more effective screen. West of Vista Path he laid out a vegetable garden with cold frames and fruit trees. Sargent introduced the Coes to the pleasures of plant collecting. On his advice, Coe purchased 2,000 rhododendrons from a British nursery, and during a trip to California, where the family wintered, Coe himself selected a large number of specimen plants. In 1917, again advised by Sargent, Coe purchased a large number of camellias from a nursery on the island of Guernsey. To shelter them during Long Island's harsh winters, Sargent designed a greenhouse, which included flower beds and a round pool, to be built into the angle of the L-shaped Atterbury stable. Much of his work was at the farm, which was anchored by Walker & Gillette's monumental barn. Sargent designed a U-shaped greenhouse that functioned as a palm house and winter garden, and south of that building he laid out another large vegetable garden. The following year, he expanded the palm house to include an orchid house, a melon house, and a vegetable house.

Mai Coe put her own stamp on the grounds. She had two mature copper beeches transported from the Rogers family home in Fairhaven. With great difficulty—it was mid-winter—the giant trees, with twelve-foot root balls, were barged across Long Island Sound to a specially built dock in Oyster Bay. From there they were carted to Planting Fields, towed by a team of seventy-two horses. The beeches were planted in the lawn, although only one survived. The plans for the garden were equally ambitious. The Byrnes' wooden tennis court was dismantled and replaced by an unusual sunken flower garden. The focus of the garden, which measured about 75 by 125 feet, was a striking, turquoise-tiled pool adorned with statuary and surrounded by a grass terrace and low brick walls containing beds with a variety of flowering plants including Japanese cherry trees.

---

* The Bostonian Lowell prevailed over prominent New York architects McKim, Mead & White, Cass Gilbert, Carrère & Hastings, and George B. Post.

The sunken Blue Pool Garden with the Olmsted Brothers augmented planting. Frances Benjamin Johnston, 1929. *Courtesy of the National Park Service, Frederick Law Olmsted Historic Site.*

The Planting Fields sunken garden is sometimes described as inspired by Italian gardens. In fact, the first American book on Italian gardens, Charles A. Platt's *Italian Villas and Their Gardens* (1894), does not include any sunken gardens, nor does Edith Wharton's *Italian Villas and Their Gardens* (1904), or Lowell's *Smaller Italian Villas and Farmhouses* (1916), which is illustrated with his travel sketches and photographs. Wharton did create a so-called Italian garden at her country house, The Mount in Lenox, Massachusetts, but it is quite unlike Planting Fields, not sunken but walled, with gravel paths and complicated turfed parterres around a small circular basin.

What then was the inspiration? Guy Lowell regularly visited England, and the Planting Fields garden bears a marked resemblance to two British gardens that had been completed in 1908. One was built for Edward VII at Kensington Palace, and the other was part of William Waldorf Astor's restoration of Hever Castle in Kent. Both are sunken and rectangular, with stepped flower beds and large pools edged by grass or paving. Such geometrical flower gardens, whether sunken or walled, were known in England as "Dutch gardens," and originated in the Netherlands.

A 1929 photograph of the sunken garden at Planting Fields by Frances Benjamin Johnston is titled "Blue Pool Garden," and there is evidence that this was what the Coes called it.³⁷ The enchantment of the garden was enhanced by a lovely little Teahouse overlooking the south end. The interior was the creation of the artist Everett Shinn (1876–1953). Shinn was a mercurial talent. An original member of the gritty Ashcan School, he was known for his realist paintings of the popular theater, but his extravagant lifestyle led him to accept many sorts of commissions. The contemporary painter and art critic Guy Pène Du Bois described Shinn as "a man perpetually busy, with irons scattered here and there in all the fires of the arts and all heating at once."³⁸ He designed magazine covers and illustrations, theater sets and costumes, and spent three years working as art director for the film mogul Samuel Goldwyn. Shinn was also a sought-after muralist—his work survives in the Oak Bar of the Plaza Hotel and in the lobby of the Belasco Theater in New York. He painted frescoes for another Walker & Gillette residential project, so it is likely that it was the architects who introduced him to the Coes.³⁹

The Teahouse interior was a whimsical rococo fantasy: two lunette murals, one at each end of the room, depicting cavorting maidens in idyllic settings. Shinn's decor included a suite of specially painted furniture and hanging light fixtures in the form of flower baskets. Fitted mirrors enlarged the little room whose walls and ceiling were covered in sky-blue trelliswork. In her popular book *The House in Good Taste* (1913), the celebrated society decorator Elsie de Wolfe described the advantages of a "gay garden room, with a few screens of trellis."⁴⁰ Although she and Shinn occasionally worked together, there is no documentary evidence that she was involved in the project, and a 1916 *Town & Country* article on the Planting Fields Teahouse credits Shinn alone.⁴¹

Interior of the Teahouse as decorated by Everett Shinn, c. 1926. *Planting Fields Foundation Archives.*

The original plan had been to house the Teahouse in the Atterbury-designed cottage that stood nearby. Shinn didn't think much of the plain structure; "it seems now as if we had a string of pearls stored in a shoe box," he informed Coe, and he proposed a new Teahouse of his own design, so "the outside will be as beautiful as the inside."[42] He built a model of a theatrical two-story building decorated with exterior murals but was unable to convince his clients. Coe later recalled that the old cottage "was on a lower level, and we raised it and veneered it with Lamay [sic] brick."[43] The roof was tiled, a fireplace was added as well as pergolas at each end. The architectural work was probably overseen by Gillette—the lammie brickwork pattern is the same as that of the Hay Barn. The second cottage was left unaltered and continued to be used, either as a recreational pavilion or as a children's playhouse. There is a 1918 site plan that shows a tennis court on the grassy lawn, although it is unclear if this was built.

1918 was the Planting Fields *annus horribilis*. In March Robeson Sargent, who was recuperating from pneumonia, died unexpectedly in his sleep. He was forty-two years old. In addition to the human tragedy, this deprived the Coes of a knowledgeable and supportive advisor. And only two weeks later, a second calamity. The Coes were in California, and work was being done on the house that included constructing a "new sun parlor in the west wing," complete with leaded painted glass and a mural.[44] In a telegram to Coe's son Robert, Coe's secretary, Noel McVickar, described a "man waterproofing with blow torch outside your father's den over porch," which suggests that the sun parlor was a modification—or replacement—of the sleeping porch on the second floor deck outside what was now Coe's bedroom suite.[45] The blow torch started the fire. The flames moved to the house and attempts to put out the blaze proved futile due to insufficient water pressure. The fire spread so slowly that the servants were able to remove most of the artwork and furniture, but by the time that the firemen arrived and ran hoses from a pond on the neighboring Billings estate, it was too late. The Coes, wintering in Santa Monica, were due to return the following week. McVickar telegrammed the bad news: "Strong wind fanned flames and firemen unable to put them out. House burnt right to ground only one chimney standing. Nearly all contents saved."[46] Although the planting immediately surrounding the house was destroyed, most of the garden was intact. The Coes had an estate with a splendid barn, two greenhouses, a beautiful sunken garden, and a bijou Teahouse—but no home.

MAI HUTTLESTON ROGERS COE AND WILLIAM ROBERTSON COE
WALKER & GILLETTE AND OLMSTED BROTHERS
1918–24

William Robertson Coe was not a man to be disheartened. He immediately had an old farmhouse at the south end of the property renovated to use as a temporary residence, complete with an attractive front garden planted with privet hedges and specimen shrubs. Two months after the fire, he commissioned Walker & Gillette to design a new residence. But in what style? Two years earlier, the firm had completed a beachfront house for Mai's younger brother, Henry, in Southampton. The prize-winning Black Point was a picturesque Tuscan villa, a romantic style that would have suited Planting Fields. But Coe had something else in mind. He retained

North facade, based on Moyns Park, a sixteenth-century Elizabethan country house in Essex. Mattie Edwards Hewitt, c. 1926. *Planting Fields Foundation Archives.*

a pronounced accent all his life, and he had a personal stake in underlining his English—albeit humble—roots. As he recounted in a 1954 interview: "I was a little bit tired of colonial and Georgian architecture—there was so much of it around—that I told Walker & Gillette that I wished a Tudor house."[47]

Despite Coe's claim, Tudor was hardly an original choice. As Mark Hewitt observes: "At the peak of its popularity around 1910, almost 30 percent of the country houses being published in the leading journals could be grouped under this heading, making the Tudor house a close second to the Colonial in popularity."[48] The Tudor revival arrived in America in the late nineteenth century in the form of replicas of picturesque English manor houses, with half-timbering, steep roofs, and tall chimneys. More recent Tudor-inspired houses incorporated Elizabethan features, but they were modern reinterpretations rather than historic facsimiles; two prominent examples in Oyster Bay were Killenworth (1913), designed by the New York firm Trowbridge & Ackerman, and Ormston (1913–18), the work of Bertram Grosvenor Goodhue, one of the leading architects of the day. Walker & Gillette, perhaps responding to Coe's wishes, took the more old-fashioned approach and sent him books with photographs and engravings of historic Elizabethan manor houses. Coe was drawn to Moyns Park in Essex, which became the model for the north facade; Athelhampton, a fifteenth-century country house in Dorset, which served for the south side; and St. Catherine's Court, an Elizabethan manor whose later additions influenced the entrance facade and the porch.

Mixing and matching might sound like an odd way to design a house, but Gillette, who seems to have been in charge, faced an unusual challenge. The new house had to be in the original location to take advantage of the surviving garden.

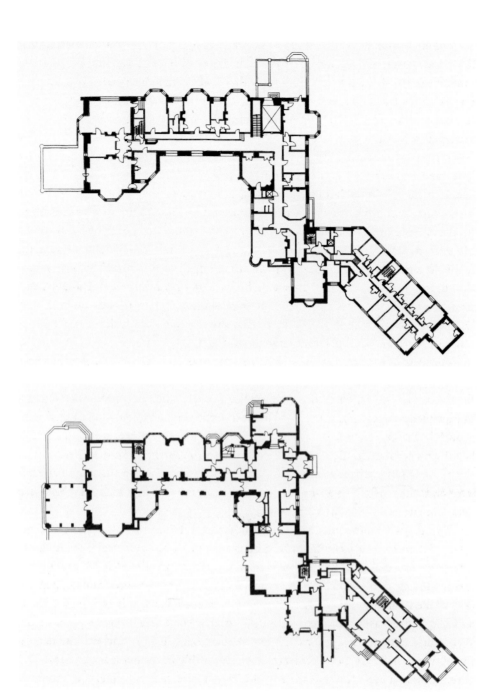

Walker & Gillette, First and second floor plans. *Planting Fields Foundation Archives.*

Moreover, he had to take into account not only the axis of the circular pool and the north-south walk, but also the access drive and Atterbury's stable building, which was untouched by the fire. There were also views to consider, the prime east and west views across the sloping lawn and the long view to Long Island Sound. Walker asked Coe to request a copy of the plans of the earlier house from Atterbury's office. Gillette sensibly duplicated the dogleg arrangement with the living room and porch at the west end, the entrance roughly in the same location as before, and a large kitchen wing, whose second floor contained the staff quarters, at the east end, extending into what had been the service court.* Considerably larger than its predecessor, the new house did not reuse the existing foundations.

42

Gillette's approach to the Tudor style was scenographic. He had the masons give the stone walls tooling marks to produce the impression of age, and he designed the different parts of the house to look as if they had been added gradually over time. For example, the service wing was half-timbered to appear older than the rest of the house, the arcade overlooking the garden court had Gothic vaults, the round arches and Doric columns of the porch were chastely classical, while the spiral columns and broken pediment of the relatively modest entrance pavilion recalled baroque designs by Christopher Wren. There were many evocative details: antique fireplace mantels in the important rooms; Elizabethan grotesques and carved woodwork; and a bas-relief panel of a sailing ship on the porch to honor Coe's maritime insurance métier. The arched pediment over the front door contained a cornucopia with a carved scroll inscribed PLANTING FIELDS—the Coes had kept the name. The exterior of the house, which was intended to be lammie brick to match the surviving stable, changed after Gillette located a ready supply of Indiana limestone that had been stockpiled by Bertram Goodhue when he was designing St. Bartholomew's Church in Manhattan.[49] The stone became available when Goodhue settled on a Byzantine style and switched to brick.

Construction of the house started in June 1918, and despite postwar material shortages, progressed relatively quickly, so that the Coes were able to move in by the fall of 1920. The interior repeated the theme of historical accretion, with a mazelike arrangement of large and small rooms to underline the impression of piecemeal growth. "The entrance hall is Norman, as if it were the remains of an old feudal keep," observed an admiring cover article in *The Architectural Record*. "The bulk of the house is Elizabethan, as if the place had been extended and made more habitable later; and the dressing rooms and den are eighteenth century, as if they had been added in later and more formal days."[50]

The largest public room, lined with bookcases and family portraits, is called the Living Room on the architect's plan and served for formal entertaining. Adjacent was a more casual space, the equivalent of a modern family room. Called the Gallery, it resembled a medieval hall, with a massive fireplace, large bay windows, a paneled and vaulted ceiling, and a minstrel gallery. The mounted heads of bighorn sheep and elk, as well as a six-point elk in the entrance hall, were Coe's trophies from Wyoming hunts; the origin of the South African oryx head is unclear. The den off the entrance hall was Coe's preserve, with an outside door and a secret panel that gave access to a bar—this was the Prohibition era. The den was paneled to resemble an eighteenth-century gentleman's study, although a few years later Coe had the Adamesque decor replaced by Tudor paneling.

Mai's domain was on the opposite side of the entrance hall: a reception room decorated in the French style. Jacques Seligmann (1858–1923), a prominent Parisian antiquarian and art dealer with whom Coe had an account, was critical of the room. "The house is a marvel and this little room I consider a failure," he advised Coe. "First of all it is too green, and secondly the decoration is too rich and it is really not in the

---

* The 1915 Census listed twenty live-in staff at Planting Fields, a mixture of English, Irish, and Japanese. The Census did not detail occupations, but judging from the 1925 Census, the house staff included a butler, housekeeper, valet, governess, cook, and assorted maids. The estate workers included a superintendent, three stablemen, a poultryman, chauffeur, and an engineer, as well as a large number of farm laborers who were not resident and were not included in the census.

Entrance Hall. Mattie Edwards Hewitt, 1927. *Planting Fields Foundation Archives.*

Mai Coe's Reception Room decorated by L. Alavoine & Cie., a leading Parisian *décorateur*. Mattie Edwards Hewitt, 1927. *Planting Fields Foundation Archives.*

French taste."[51] Seligmann asked a leading Parisian *décorateur*, L. Alavoine & Cie., which had a branch in New York City, to present an alternative design to the Coes.[52] Seligmann assured Coe that Alavoine's proposal would be "something most delicious and I do not need to tell you that the room will be something marvelously beautiful."[53] The redo was approved, and the result was an octagonal salon with a domed ceiling whose delicate paneling was painted canary yellow with contrasting trim. The color was suggested by Seligmann, who also provided a suite of Louis XVI furniture, six chairs and a small sofa.

The breakfast room, off the dining room, was an equally sharp contrast to the Tudor decor. The walls and ceiling were covered in gilded and heavily painted murals that depicted the plains and mountain peaks of Wyoming, with Native American hunters on horseback, herds of buffalo and deer, and soaring vultures on the vaulted ceiling. The scene was Mai's tactful acknowledgment of her husband's fascination with the American West—he had an extensive collection of rare books, maps, manuscripts, and art. Stewart Walker, who had established a personal relationship with Coe, diplomatically referred to the murals as "very amusing."[54]

The artist responsible for what inevitably became known as the "Buffalo Room" was Robert Winthrop Chanler (1872–1930), who had earlier been engaged by Mai Coe to paint windows and murals in the ill-fated sunroom. The two may have met in the 1890s during Mai's forced "exile" in Paris, where he was studying art. He was no struggling artist; born to a wealthy family and related to the Astors and the Dudley-Winthrops, he hobnobbed with New York's elite. An outsize personality, he

Breakfast Room murals by Robert Winthrop Chanler. Mattie Edwards Hewitt, c. 1927. *Planting Fields Foundation Archives.*

is remembered today for his vivid painted screens, but he was also an accomplished muralist who decorated Gertrude Vanderbilt Whitney's studio in Greenwich Village, the loggia in Delano & Aldrich's new Colony Club, and a fanciful indoor-outdoor swimming pool in the palatial Floridian villa, Vizcaya. In addition to the breakfast room, Chanler decorated Mai Coe's bedroom, whose walls and ceiling he covered in jungle scenery teeming with birds and overlaid with a shimmering lace-like material.[55] The fantastic result conveys the frothy ambience of French rococo without being historical. The adjacent dressing room was decorated by Shinn in a similarly lighthearted vein. Elsie de Wolfe's showroom supplied "2 Venetian Hanging Baskets and 2 Glass Bowls," according to an invoice for $60.30.[56]

The Louis XVI furniture in Mai Coe's bedroom came from André Carlhian, a Parisian dealer and decorator, but most of the house was furnished by the London antiquarian Charles J. Duveen (1871–1940), a younger brother of the celebrated art dealer Joseph Duveen. Charles Duveen, known as Charles of London, had a showroom

Chanler was also responsible for the murals in Mai Coe's bedroom, photographed in 1922, before the room was furnished. *Nassau County Department of Parks, Recreation, and Museums Photo Archive Center.*

in New York and is credited with introducing Americans to Tudor and Elizabethan furnishings. The furniture, carpets, tapestries, paintings, stained glass, even a suit of armor—some antiques, many reproductions—that he provided to Coe were chosen to heighten the impression of an old English manor house. Although the Coes' Tudor mansion resembled a British country house, it was not a year-round residence. The family, who had a Manhattan apartment on 83rd Street near the Metropolitan Museum, occupied Planting Fields in the fall and spring, spent winters in Southern California, and in the summer, the entire household, including nannies, chambermaids, and cook, migrated to Wyoming.

While Walker & Gillette were designing the house, work continued on the landscaping. Without Sargent, Coe chose to not continue with Lowell and instead engaged Olmsted Brothers, presumably on the advice of Walker, who had collaborated with the firm on three Long Island estates, not only Black Point, but also Mayhasit in Glen Cove and Big Tree Farm in Oyster Bay. Olmsted Brothers had been founded in 1898 by John Charles Olmsted (1852–1920) and Frederick Law Olmsted Jr. (1870–1957), continuing the practice begun by their stepfather and father, Frederick Law Olmsted, who had retired from active practice in the mid 1890s. Based in Brookline, Massachusetts, the Olmsted firm was a national practice, the largest landscape office in the country with as many as sixty employees working on urban parks and college campuses, as well as suburban communities and regional plans. Olmsted *père* had created the splendid gardens of Biltmore House in Asheville, North Carolina—the Country Place par excellence—and a large part of the Olmsted Brothers practice was country estates and private gardens. At the time of Planting Fields, the firm was completing the grounds of nearby Oheka, a spectacular chateau designed for the financier Otto Kahn by Delano & Aldrich, and would soon start on Caumsett, the expansive estate of Marshall Field III, whose Georgian mansion was designed by John Russell Pope.

John C. Olmsted was the senior partner of Olmsted Brothers; his involvement in Planting Fields was short-lived since he would die of cancer in 1920. Frederick Law Olmsted Jr. focused on the firm's town planning projects—the previous year he had been elected the first president of the American City Planning Institute, which he helped found. The firm's far-flung residential projects were overseen by its two associates, James Frederick Dawson (1874–1941) and Percival Gallagher (1874–1934). Although Gallagher had previously worked with Walker & Gillette on Black Point, it was Dawson who was put in charge of the Planting Fields commission, probably in part because he had known Robeson Sargent. Fred Dawson had grown up in the Arnold Arboretum, where his English-born father, Jackson, was superintendent until his death in 1916. In 1896, after graduating from the Bussey Institution, Harvard's school of agriculture and horticulture, Fred Dawson joined Olmsted Brothers, where his apprenticeship included travel to England and Europe to study parks and gardens. His mentor was John C. Olmsted, with whom he worked on the firm's Western projects: public parks in Seattle, Tacoma, and Portland; a palatial hotel and resort in Colorado Springs; expositions in Seattle and San Diego; and the new state capitol in Olympia, Washington. He spent his entire career with Olmsted Brothers, becoming its first associate in 1904 and its first partner in 1922.

Dawson was experienced in North Shore estate gardens, having overseen the magisterial Oheka. Unlike that estate, however, the Coe project was not a tabula rasa. Like Gillette, Dawson had to consider many existing features: Greenleaf's entrance allée, garden court, and Vista Path, and Sargent and Lowell's Blue Pool Garden, camellia house, and palm house, as well as the farm. Dawson's mandate was to complete the work of his predecessors, integrate new elements, and—the greatest challenge—ensure that all these various parts formed a cohesive whole.

The job got off to a rocky start. In September 1918, only two months after starting to work on Planting Fields, Dawson was seconded by the U.S. Housing Corporation, a federal wartime agency charged with building communities for new military factories and shipyards. Because Olmsted Jr. served on a committee that selected landscape architects for Housing Corporation projects, Dawson was required to temporarily sever his connection with the firm, which meant he abruptly withdrew from the Planting Fields project. His place was taken by Percival Gallagher. "Mr. Gallagher has been very busy 'clearing the decks' as it were, so as to be able to take up your work," John C. Olmsted assured Coe.[57] As it happened, an armistice was declared that November, and Dawson was soon released, rejoining the firm and resuming his work on Planting Fields.

Although Frederick Law Olmsted is often associated with the British naturalistic landscape tradition, he worked in a variety of styles: the grounds of Lawrenceville School in New Jersey were naturalistic, the Chicago World's Fair layout was classical, and Biltmore was both French and naturalistic. The residential work of Olmsted Brothers was similarly eclectic. The focus at Oheka, for example, was a large sunken parterre with water basins in the French manner, while the Italian garden of Black Point suited the Tuscan villa. What would suit Planting Fields? There was no popular tradition of Tudor gardens—no sixteenth-century gardens had survived. Partly for that reason, and partly because of the many pre-existing landscape elements, Olmsted Brothers' work at Planting Fields lacks the stylistic consistency of Ormston and Black Point and the operatic sweep of Oheka—it is more like a collection of landscape tableaux. A collection of short stories rather than an epic novel.

Dawson began by completing the planting of the entry drive and redesigning the arrival area to fit the new house. He densified the planting of the Blue Pool Garden (which is called the Flower Garden in his drawing), and replanted the garden court, now called the Cloister Court in the spirit of Walker & Gillette's medieval arcade. New landscapes included a secluded Heather Garden on the far side of the lawn, and a winding azalea-lined walk beside the Vista Path. Immediately below the new balustraded terrace outside the porch, Dawson created an unusual feature: rough stone steps leading down to a secluded circular pool, which he called the Surprise Pool. This below-grade rock garden is a sort of folly, not unusual in Olmsted Brothers gardens of that period.

In 1920 Dawson suggested to Coe that he engage Mattie Edwards Hewitt (1869–1956), a well-regarded photographer who specialized in buildings and gardens, to document Planting Fields in different seasons. Hewitt's evocative photographs illustrate the pronounced effect of Dawson's interventions. A view of the house from Greenleaf's circular pool shows the arcaded facade almost completely obscured by a screen of climbing roses, columnar junipers, shrubs, and trees. The stone coping of the pool is smothered in ground cover, and the lawn is ringed by a low boxwood hedge in front of blooming rhododendrons and flowering trees. Olmsted Brothers specialized in dense and reverberative horticultural orchestration; crescendos of specimen trees, fanfares of flowering shrubs, carpets of annuals. For example, the small area flanking the winding path that led from the Cloister Court to the Blue Pool Garden included almost one hundred trees and shrubs, as well as boxwood hedges and a variety of heather ground cover, and for good measure, twenty stone pads for potted specimen plants. The planting list featured more than forty varieties; the resulting layering, lushness, and sheer diversity would be almost overwhelming to modern eyes.

Dawson's work included fine-tuning the earlier planting and creating transitions between various elements, but there were also new landscape interventions, such as the great lawn that swept down from the house on the east and west sides. He planted the far edges in classic Olmstedian layers: first low azaleas and rhododendrons, then flowering cherries and crab apples, finally a backdrop of deciduous trees and large conifers. At the same time, he introduced an original variation to a familiar theme: building on the surviving Fairhaven copper beech, he dotted the undulating west lawn with specimen trees and exposed a mammoth rock outcropping. The resulting play of light and shadow, especially in the late afternoon, enlarged the vista and further enriched the landscape experience. Another of Dawson's projects was the camellia greenhouse. He proposed adding a domed conservatory, complete with an indoor swimming pool, lockers, and changing rooms.[58] That grand project fell by the wayside, but he did design an innovative shading and heating system, and in 1922 added two wings to accommodate acacias, hibiscus, and oleanders, as well as Coe's growing camellia collection.

Some landscape features were contingent. During a 1921 visit to England, Coe wrote to Dawson: "I have seen some groups of English beeches with an occasional

The Cloister Court, with Dawson's lush planting enhancing Greenleaf's pool and the porch arcade. Mattie Edwards Hewitt, c. 1920. *Planting Fields Foundation Archives.*

Dawson dotted the West Lawn with specimen trees. In spring, crocus groundcover created the impression of a magic carpet. Harry G. Healy, c. 1926. *Planting Fields Foundation Archives.*

Aerial view taken while Dawson was enlarging the Camellia House (right). Lowell and Sargent's Blue Pool Garden is on the left. Aiglon Aerial Photo Company, c. 1924. *Courtesy of the National Park Service, Frederick Law Olmsted Historic Site.*

copper beech planted say about 25 trees in a group about 15 to 20 feet apart, very effective."[59] He was describing a copse, or small stand of trees, and Dawson dutifully created a beech copse at the eastern end of the lawn. "I never dreamed there were such trees & shrubs in existence as over here," Coe wrote in the same letter. "It makes me feel those on Long Island are a joke, Oaks Elms Beeches Sycamores etc, as for rhododendrons they are beyond description."[60] This heartfelt admission is revealing. Unlike some of his more conventional gentlemanly pursuits, such as horse racing, hunting, and an Anglophile home, Coe's involvement with horticulture was more original—and more personal. The avocation was starting to define the man.

The Olmsted Brothers contract effectively put the firm on retainer, submitting monthly bills for expenses and services rendered. Dawson regularly visited Long Island, where he oversaw several on-going residential projects (he stayed at the Harvard Club in New York), and his responsibilities at Planting Fields involved a variety of tasks beyond landscape design. He advised Mai Coe on the flower gardens, he helped Coe find a new superintendent and head gardener, he arranged for deliveries of peat, loam, and horse manure, and he purchased trees and shrubs, some supplied by the Arnold Arboretum. Dawson supervised the construction of a mushroom house and a henhouse, as well as a "Secret Wine Cellar" to store 1,500 cases of wine and 2,000 bottles (private individuals were permitted to stockpile liquor before Prohibition began in 1920). When *The Garden* magazine wanted to publish an article on the spectacular camellia collection—110 plants and 52 varieties—dealing with the journalist landed in Dawson's lap, too. All this, while dealing with an opinionated and sometimes testy client. Judging from the correspondence, Coe was budget-conscious despite his great wealth, although, after grumbling, he generally followed Dawson's advice.

In January 1924, Planting Fields experienced a second major fire. "It started in the old stable and badly damaged the Camellia house," Coe wrote to his daughter, Natalie. "I am afraid I am going to lose a lot of Camellias."⁶¹ Characteristically, Coe was undeterred, and he informed Stewart Walker that he was considering reviving the idea of a swimming pool, to be built on the site of the destroyed stable. "My mind has been running to a squash racket court on the eastern end and a large swimming pool in the middle of a tropical house in the center, and perhaps on the west end some bachelors' rooms."⁶² Walker & Gillette prepared drawings, but neither the bachelor rooms nor the swimming pool were built. That same year, three days after Christmas Day 1924, Mai Coe died of bronchopneumonia accompanied by chronic perihepatitis; she was forty-nine. Coe had a family mausoleum built in the cemetery of St. John's Episcopal Church in Laurel Hollow, five miles from Planting Fields. He suggested that Gillette take a look at the Rogers mausoleum in Fairhaven. Gillette, not impressed, designed a lovely octagonal temple; the landscaping was by Olmsted Brothers.

William Robertson Coe and Caroline Coe in the rose garden at Planting Fields, c. 1950. *Planting Fields Foundation Archives.*

CAROLINE GRAHAM SLAUGHTER COE AND WILLIAM ROBERTSON COE
WALKER & GILLETTE AND OLMSTED BROTHERS
1924–55

Among the routine local and national stories on the front page of the *New York Times* Sunday edition of December 5, 1926, one headline stood out: "W. R. Coe, Sportsman, Weds Suddenly at 57; Bride Mrs. Slaughter, 49, Recently Divorced." The *Times* identified Coe as a racehorse owner but made no reference to his profession nor to his horticultural interests. There was a whiff of scandal in the article, which mentioned Mai Coe's recent passing. "Only a few close friends were at the marriage ceremony... No previous announcement of an engagement had been made and news of the marriage came as a surprise."⁶³ E. Dick Slaughter,* a prominent

---

* E. Dick Slaughter was the son of C. C. Slaughter, the legendary "Cattle King of Texas," whose ranch lands encompassed more than a million acres. He and Caroline were married around 1901 and had one son.

Dallas businessman, and Alabama-born Caroline Graham Slaughter (1877–1960) had indeed been divorced "recently"—barely a month earlier. But she and Coe had known each other for three years, and their frequent public appearances had been the subject of gossip columns.[64]

"Caroline must have had a hard row to hoe, as she never won the hearts of her stepchildren, least of all that of my mother," recollected Coe's grandson Michael D. Coe. "Nonetheless she was a good wife for my grandfather, for she knew exactly how to handle him. A very intelligent woman with a wicked sense of humor, she often laughed at his pontifications and, I think, made him a better person."[65] Caroline, who shared her husband's love of gardening, made her presence felt at Planting Fields. She had Chanler's murals in Mai's bedroom paneled over, and in the 1940s, probably under her influence, the dining room was converted into an intimate living room, and the breakfast room henceforth became the dining room.

Olmsted Brothers' work on the estate was almost done. Since the early 1920s, Dawson's visits to Planting Fields had become less frequent. He was now based in Redondo Beach, California, overseeing the firm's largest commission, the planned community of Palos Verdes Estates. Coe complained to Olmsted about Dawson's absences: "This kind of thing has been going on now for about four years and I wonder if you realize how unfair it is to your old clients."[66] Coe was particularly chagrined because he was about to undertake a major project. He had wanted to mark the entrance to the estate with a set of antique gates, and years earlier he had asked Charles Duveen to find a suitable specimen. The dealer located an exceptional example that had been made in 1711 for Carshalton Park, a country estate in Surrey belonging to one Thomas Scawen, a London merchant and financier. The ironwork was attributed to the master smith Thomas Robinson, and the monumental gates included seventeen-foot-high Portland stone piers topped by lead statues of the mythic hunters Diana and Actaeon.[67] In the early 1900s, when the Carshalton estate had been subdivided into residential lots, the gates had been removed and sold to Denison Faber, the 1st Baron Wittenham, who planned to use them on his own estate but later changed his mind. Coe saw the dismantled gates during his 1921 English visit and bought them for £3,000 (about $160,000 today).

Thanks to Dawson's absence, it would be another five years before Coe erected the gates. He had assumed that they would be located at the current entrance, off Planting Fields Road. The gates, which had large side panels, were more than a hundred feet wide, and Dawson, who had seen them in their original location, judged that the monumental structure would look out of place squeezed into a woodland setting. "I think it would be a great mistake to have to come upon these gates suddenly from the country road," he wrote to Coe from California. "Where they were placed before, they were seen at a considerable distance from the house, and as I remembered these gates they separated the 'house lawns' from the outer fields."[68] Dawson suggested an alternative location on the west side of the estate, where it bordered Chicken Valley Road, an important local thoroughfare. He explained that this location had room for an ample forecourt as well as a generous backdrop. Coe agreed. Dawson laid out a new entry drive that began at the gates, curved as it climbed the steep slope, and offered a variety of views—forest, open fields, flowering shrubs, and specimen trees—before joining the existing allée just south of the house. To create an appropriate forecourt for the gates, additional land was purchased from a neighbor, and the county agreed to

The monumental Carshalton Gates, installed in a landscape setting created by Dawson; Walker & Gillette designed the gatehouse. Harry G. Healy, c. 1927. *Planting Fields Foundation Archives.*

slightly realign Chicken Valley Road (at Coe's expense). Walker & Gillette designed a limestone gate lodge and a long boundary wall. All this took time, and it was the end of 1927 before the project was finished.

A ten-minute film, made in June 1928, shows the completed grounds of Planting Fields. A late model Rolls-Royce Phantom stands in the drive, horses graze placidly in a fenced paddock. What the garden lacks in dramatic features such as fountains and parterres it more than makes up for in horticultural aplomb. The grounds are exquisitely maintained, every square inch has received careful attention: the flowering shrubs lining the road, the specimen trees on the rolling lawn, the espaliered greenery shrouding the house.* The sunken garden brims with flowers. The greenhouses are barely visible behind the heavy planting.

In 1930 Dawson enlarged the palm house, adding a hibiscus house with an elegant pedimented entrance. This effectively marked the end of Olmsted Brothers's major work on the estate, although not the end of the firm's involvement with the Coes. That same year, the couple acquired an 11,000-acre antebellum rice plantation in Yemassee, South Carolina, to use as a winter retreat and hunting preserve.[69] Olmsted Brothers—and Dawson—were in charge of landscaping the extensive grounds, which

---

* The December 1928 Planting Fields payroll lists 62 full-time estate workers, who included gardeners, groundskeepers, nurserymen, farm workers, and grooms, as well as teamsters, chauffeurs, truckers, and assorted handymen. The monthly payroll added up to $7,500 ($137,000 today). About a dozen men lived on the estate, in a wing of the haybarn, and in a nearby boarding house; the rest lived off-site.

Aerial view of Planting Fields during the SUNY period, with geodesic domes and lab buildings (no longer extant) built for the school. Chicago Aerial Survey, c. 1961. *Planting Fields Foundation Archives.*

included turning rice paddies into an artificial lake. The original plantation house had been destroyed during the Civil War, and the Coes engaged the New York architect Philip Alain Cusachs (1887–1931) to design a new house, which resembled a colonial Virginia Tidewater mansion. Work proceeded quickly, and by 1931 the house and garden, now named Cherokee Plantation after the local *rosa laevigata*—the so-called Cherokee rose—were complete.

Four years later, Dawson received an unexpected request from his old client. Alarmed by rising local property taxes, Coe felt he might be obliged to sell some or all of Planting Fields, and he wanted Olmsted Brothers to prepare a subdivision plan.[70] The following year Dawson sent him a detailed topographic plan that showed the estate subdivided into thirty large house lots linked by a network of winding roads; the largest lot—fifty acres—was reserved for the main house. The following year, judging the Depression-era real estate market to be weak, Coe decided not to proceed. Over the next decade, Planting Fields had a series of estate managers who added to and subtracted from the original design as planting became overgrown or diseased. Shrubs and trees were culled following the Great Hurricane of 1938 and a disastrous ice storm in 1940. Coe and Dawson continued to correspond on landscape matters until the latter's death in 1941.

In 1946 Coe suffered a heart attack that led him to resign his chairmanship of Johnson & Higgins. The brush with mortality raised the question: what would happen to his beloved Planting Fields after his death? His children had their own lives; Robert was a foreign service diplomat living abroad, Henry had settled in Wyoming, and Natalie had married an Italian count. His eldest son, William, who had a country house in Oyster Bay, shared his father's horticultural interest, but times had changed, and the cost of running such a large house and maintaining the extensive grounds had become prohibitive. The most likely fate awaiting Planting

Fields was to be dismembered and sold, as many Gold Coast estates had been. That was the uncomfortable truth of the Country Place Era. The descendants of the country place builders were unable—or unwilling—to continue the way of life imposed by these lavishly appointed estates and, as a result, the impressive family seats, which were designed to evoke timeless tradition, generally endured barely a single generation.

In 1949 Coe reached a momentous decision. He deeded the entire property—the buildings and 409 acres—to the State of New York. The understanding was that after his death Planting Fields would become a public arboretum and a horticultural and arboricultural center. Unlike many Gold Coast estates, including Harbor Hill, Oheka, Veraton, and Farnsworth, Planting Fields would remain intact. To provide support and guidance, in 1952 Coe established the Planting Fields Foundation and endowed it with $1.5 million ($17 million today), with the proviso that family members would always serve on the board of trustees.[71] His Will provided amply for his descendants, relatives, and friends, and included a variety of charitable bequests—to the American Museum of Natural History, the Buffalo Bill Museum, the Boys' Club of New York, and several hospitals. Coe, who kept exotic birds at Planting Fields, also endowed a chair in ornithology at Yale.

Coe was a magnanimous philanthropist. When the University of Wyoming ran into difficulties funding a new library, he donated money to build what became the Coe Library. He presented his extensive Western collection—more than ten thousand items—to Yale and endowed chairs at Yale, Stanford, and the University of Wyoming. These professorships were in American studies—"a positive and affirmative method of meeting the threat of Communism, Socialism, Collectivism, Totalitarianism and other ideologies opposed to the preservation of our System of Free Enterprise," as Coe would write in his Will.[72]

The final version of the Will, dated January 7, 1955, was signed in Palm Beach, Florida, where Coe and Caroline had recently acquired a house on Ocean Boulevard designed by Maurice Fatio, having sold Cherokee Plantation the year before. Coe died two months later. He was not entombed in the Laurel Hollow mausoleum with Mai but interred in the Locust Valley Cemetery; there is no direct evidence, but it seems likely that this was Caroline Coe's influence. The Coe children had never warmed to her, and there is something poignant about the two solitary gravestones.* Hers is pointedly inscribed "Wife of William Robertson Coe."

**A PUBLIC COUNTRY PLACE
1955 TO THE PRESENT**

On Coe's death, Planting Fields passed into public hands, specifically the hands of the State University of New York, whose Long Island Agricultural Institute managed the greenhouses and plant collections. SUNY had plans for Planting Fields. The public university system was undergoing rapid growth, and a State University College on Long Island was part of that expansion. While a new college campus was under construction in Stony Brook, Planting Fields became its temporary

---

* Three of the Coe children—William, Robert, and Natalie—are interred in the Laurel Hollow mausoleum with their mother. Henry is buried in Cody, Wyoming.

home, receiving the first 148 students in 1957. From private estate to public campus was a radical transformation. A complex of prefabricated laboratories and a gymnasium were constructed near the Hay Barn, which itself was converted into men's and women's dormitories, and a cafeteria.[73] The silo tower was demolished, the vegetable gardens in front of the barn became athletic grounds, tennis courts were built, and open fields became parking lots. A temporary classroom building for the Agricultural and Technical Institute was built next to the large greenhouse. The main house, now called Coe Hall, was the heart of the college. The Living Room was used for assemblies, the Gallery housed the college library, the dining room served as a study hall, and the bedrooms were converted into seminar rooms and faculty offices. A surviving photograph shows Mai Coe's "delicious" salon furnished with utilitarian office furniture and filing cabinets.

There was one remaining Coe family presence on the Planting Fields campus: five acres in the southern part of the estate had been reserved for a residence for Caroline Coe. Following her husband's death, she engaged the architectural firm of Gugler & Kimball to design the house and grounds, including a formal rose garden. Eric Gugler (1889–1974), who had apprenticed with McKim, Mead & White, had been responsible for modifications to the West Wing of the Franklin Delano Roosevelt White House, including the new Oval Office. The porticoed residence he designed for Caroline Coe was similarly classical in conception, though simplified in execution and detailing, and likewise laid out to accommodate an occupant in a wheelchair.[74] The house remained her home until her death in 1960.

By 1964 the State University College on Long Island had moved to its permanent campus in Stony Brook, and Planting Fields became the home of SUNY's Center for International Studies and World Affairs. In 1968, when the center relocated to Albany, the estate once more became a temporary campus, this time for the newly established College of Old Westbury, which moved to its permanent home in Old Westbury in 1970. That marked the end of an academic presence at Planting Fields. The SUNY system had become financially overextended, and as part of a retrenchment the state shifted ownership and management of the estate to the newly founded New York State Office of Parks and Recreation. In 1971, now designated a State Historic Park, Planting Fields re-opened as a public park and arboretum. After seventeen years, Coe's original intention was fulfilled.

In 1979, on the initative of the Planting Fields Foundation, the house and grounds were placed on the National Register of Historic Places. "Historic" suggests the home of an important person, or the site of a significant event, which does not apply to Planting Fields. *The Secretary of the Interior's Standards for the Treatment of Historic Properties* included the category "Historic Designed Landscape," which was defined as a "landscape that was consciously designed or laid out by a landscape architect, master gardener, architect, engineer, or horticulturist according to design principles."[75] Planting Fields was certainly consciously designed, and architects, landscape architects, and master gardeners were involved. But this complex and multi-layered place is a palimpsest that includes James Greenleaf's Cloister Garden and Vista Path, Guy Lowell and Robeson Sargent's sunken garden and greenhouses, Olmsted Brothers' extensive interventions, the well-preserved Walker & Gillette mansion (not forgetting Grosvenor Atterbury, who was responsible for the house site), and echoes of Helen Byrne, who assembled the property in the first place. Then there are

Mai's contributions, Everett Shinn's charming Teahouse and the remarkable Robert Chanler murals, and not least, Coe's extensive horticultural collections (as well as post-1972 additions such as a synoptic garden, a daylily garden, and a collection of mountain laurels).

As an estate, Planting Fields is a relic of the Country Place Era, and by now it has been a public place much longer than it was a private residence. That public function is part of its history, too. There is scant physical evidence of the seventeen-year interlude when college students inhabited—and enlivened—the old house: movies and student dances in the Living Room, seminars in the dining room, and study sessions in the Gallery beneath the placid gaze of elk and bighorn sheep. The garden was the site of volleyball games, and the flat grassy area opposite the picturesque playhouse cottage was used for graduation ceremonies. An old photograph shows student members of the Astronomical Society posed stiffly in the Cloister Court, the Tudor arches forming a perfect collegiate gothic backdrop.

Planting Fields is well established in its public role. Groups of schoolchildren attend outdoor horticultural talks, audiences enjoy concerts in the Cloister Court, and hikers happily tramp the woodland trails. Visitors tour the restored house, admiring the richly decorated rooms, no doubt put in mind of *The Great Gatsby*. Bridal parties regularly use the house and garden as a romantic setting for photo shoots. For most of the hundreds of thousands who visit Planting Fields annually, this is less a museum-like experience of days gone by than it is simply an occasion to stroll the secluded pathways, admire the flowering shrubs, and stop by the camellia greenhouse. For them, the layered landscapes of Planting Fields are neither historical nor cultural but simply living examples of the gardener's art.

I would like to acknowledge the kind advice and support of Gina J. Wouters, President and CEO of Planting Fields Foundation, and the invaluable assistance of Marie Penny, the Foundation's Michael D. Coe Archivist, as well as the thoughtful editorial counsel of my friend Jerome Singerman.

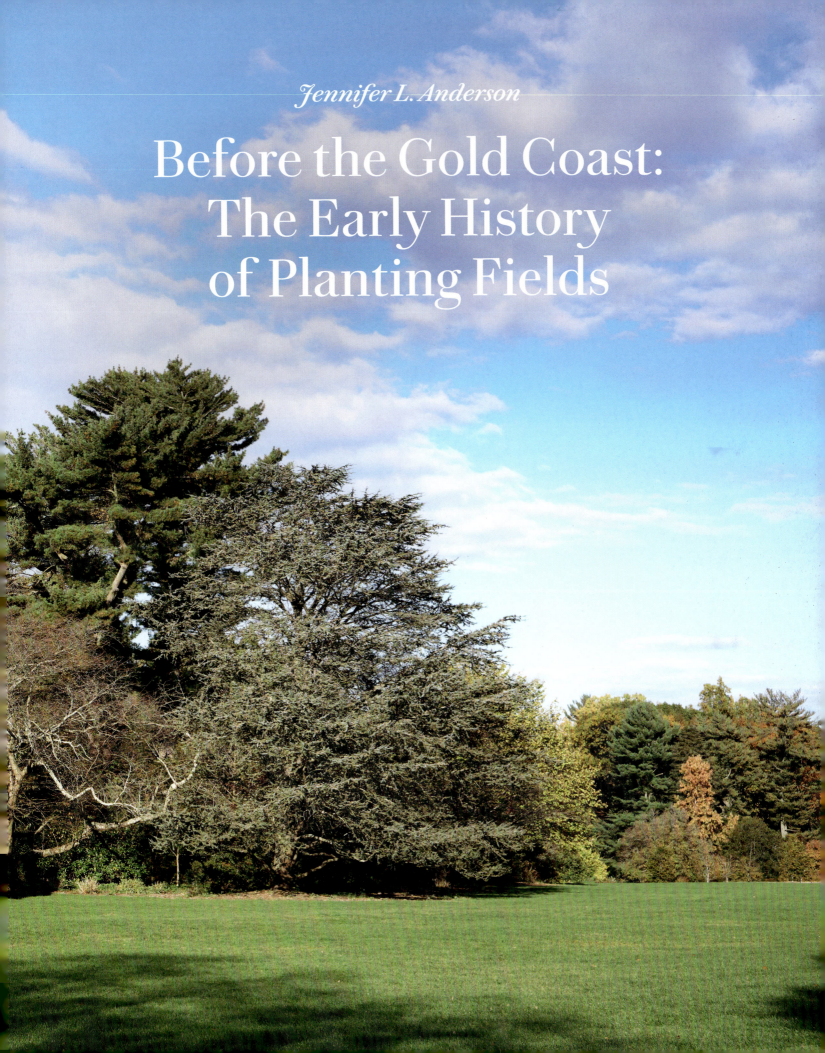

Jennifer L. Anderson

Before the Gold Coast: The Early History of Planting Fields

CARVED IN STONE ABOVE THE FRONT DOOR OF THE MAIN HOUSE AT PLANTING Fields is a relief of heavily laden cornstalks, centered between mounds of pumpkins, sunflowers, and more ears of corn.

This bountiful array—along with a ribbon incised with the name Planting Fields—was presumably intended by W. R. and Mai Coe as an homage to the history of their newly acquired property. Although now famous for its arboretum and ornamental gardens, the estate is situated on land that, as part of the ancestral homeland of the Matinecock people, has a history of cultivation dating back thousands of years. Long before the twentieth century, the land was used for the production of corn and other essential crops. Even as the surroundings underwent dramatic physical and demographic transformations, annual harvests sustained the inhabitants and generated prosperity. The story of Planting Fields is incomplete if we do not place it within broader local and regional contexts from the precolonial era, when generations of Matinecocks cultivated the land, to the colonial period, when Dutch and English settlers converted Native fields into European-style farms, to the late nineteenth and early twentieth centuries, when their descendants, in turn, sold long-established family homesteads to wealthy outsiders for use as pleasure grounds.

Through all these changes, the evocative name of "planting fields" has continued to be associated with this tract of Long Island land. In colonial treaties, early maps, land deeds, and antiquarian histories, local residents carefully differentiated new from old fields, identifying the latter variously as the "Old Planting Fields," "Indian Planting Fields," or "Old Indian Fields." While initially retained as a matter of convenience, these terms still recalled the area's ancient origins. In the early twentieth century, when new owners reconfigured these former farmlands into a grand country estate, they too opted to retain the name. By that time, however, the words had gained a certain mystique and an appealing aura of nostalgia. Still today, the name is inscribed upon the Oyster Bay landscape—quite literally on street signs and historical markers—and upon the popular memory of the larger Oyster Bay community. Then as now, "planting fields" recalls the first cultivators who nurtured this land into fruitfulness.

FIRST PLANTERS: THE MATINECOCKS' HOMELAND IN THE PRECOLONIAL ERA

The Matinecock territory, of which Planting Fields was part, once encompassed much of central Long Island, extending roughly from the shore of Long Island Sound to the

New World iconography is incorporated in the ornament over the entry to the main house at Planting Fields. David Almeida.

Atlantic Ocean. The Matinecocks are one of at least thirteen Indian nations indigenous to Long Island. Their ancestral homeland was located at the convergence of two major Algonquian linguistic and cultural subgroups; to the west were Munsee-speaking Lenapes (including the Canarsies, Rockaways, and Merricks) while to the east were Shinnecocks, Manhansets, Unkechaugs, Setaukets, Setalcotts, and Montauks who were more closely affiliated with Algonquian Indians across Long Island Sound.

While each of these nations had a distinct identity, they shared a common ancestry with the Paleo-Indians, who migrated to the barrier island, newly formed out of vast deposits of glacial moraine, at the end of the Pleistocene epoch. As fields of ice were replaced by fields of green, they were drawn to the region's hospitable environment and rich natural resources.[1] By the mid- to late-Archaic era (3000–1000 BCE), the whole island was settled by small groups of people, with defined territories, who gradually developed into separate socio-political entities (or tribes).[2] At the same time, they remained within the Algonquian language group that also included all the Native

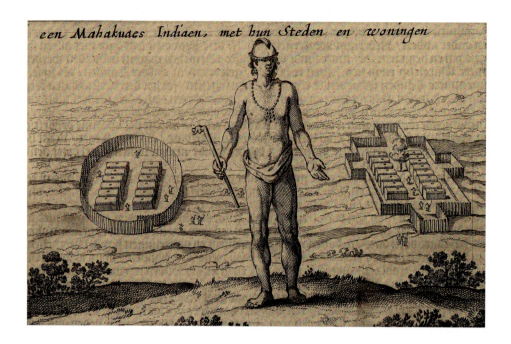

From a seventeenth-century text describing the Mahican (Algonquian) natives of the New Netherland colony. Two fortified villages are in the background. *Beschrijvinghe van Virginia, Nieuw Nederlandt, Niew Engelandt, en d'eylanden Bermudes, Berbados, en S. Christoffel,* Amsterdam, 1651. *Courtesy of the John Carter Brown Library, Providence, Rhode Island.*

peoples in what is now southern New York and southern New England. Thanks to this shared linguistic heritage, their dialects often were mutually intelligible enough to facilitate communication. They also had similar spiritual beliefs, cultural practices, and social relations, and, in many cases, faced similar problems and threats. Native peoples on Long Island and the mainland were thus interconnected through bonds of kinship, trade, and strategic alliances. Throughout the Woodland epoch (1000 BCE–1500 CE), the region experienced an extended period of relative social and political stability.

Like most Algonquian peoples, the Matinecocks migrated seasonally among permanent villages and temporary homesites to hunt, fish, and access natural resources within their traditional territory. To facilitate their annual migrations, they lived in longhouses and wigwams, fabricated from saplings and bark cladding, that could be easily disassembled and relocated as needed.[3] Every spring, year after year, they returned to the same favored locations along the shores of Long Island Sound, which provided ready access to bountiful marine resources. Fish, whales, and shellfish—including seemingly limitless oysters that could be collected by hand at low tide—provided ample sustenance. Relying on agriculture as well, they established numerous planting fields adjacent to their dwelling places, reusing the same areas for many years. To sustain the productivity of these lands, Matinecock farmers rotated their fields, leaving some fallow at times, and enriched the soil by applying ashes, fish, and other organic fertilizers. Long before the arrival of Europeans, these planting fields were foundational to the Matinecocks' world, rooting them, physically and spiritually, in the land of their forebears.

According to their customs, many aspects of the Matinecocks' lifeways were organized based on gender. Typically, men engaged in activities such as hunting, trapping, trading, fishing, and warfare that occurred away from their villages. Women's responsibilities primarily centered around their homesites and adjacent foraging areas, including nearby woods, marshes, salt meadows, clam banks, and tidal pools.[4] Within that realm, women's tasks included gathering nuts, berries, shellfish, and other wild foods, preserving meat and hides, cooking, sewing, basketry, pottery-making, and caregiving.[5] As the primary cultivators, women also devoted much time and effort to maintaining the planting fields. Since corn and other crops were critical to their community's survival, however, every able-bodied person was expected to assist with some aspect of agricultural labor. Each spring, men and women participated in preparing the fields. The men cleared new land using the slash-and-burn method, removing large trees either by girdling or felling them with stone axes and then setting them alight. The women and children then mounded up small hills and planted each one with corn, beans, and squash. As the growing season progressed, they dutifully tended the plants and harvested the crops, storing a major portion for use over the winter.[6] When the colder months set in, the Matinecocks returned inland to village sites in more sheltered areas.

While individuals could not "own" lands in the way that Europeans conceived of private property, Algonquians recognized proprietary rights as hereditary; those who established and maintained specific fields, fishing weirs, and trapping routes could pass them down to relatives.[7] To trade or transfer a planting field outside their kinship circle or tribe, however, required prior approval from family members and from local sachems and sunksquaws (male and female leaders), who served as guardians of all tribal lands.[8] At the same time, the concept of who exactly qualified as kin within Algonquian societies could be quite fluid.[9]

A distinct advantage enjoyed by the Matinecocks over non-coastal Indians was access to an important, but geographically limited, natural resource—namely, the whelks and quahogs that thrived in the tidal zones of Long Island Sound. Their purple and white shells were highly prized for making wampum (small, cylindrical beads, which were strung together into necklaces or woven into patterned bands). The precious beads were worn by prominent individuals, exchanged among Indian nations to facilitate trade and cement alliances, and included as grave goods to honor the dead. Even Native peoples who lived far from the ocean believed wampum held spiritual power and signified social prestige.[10] Archaeologists have unearthed Long Island–sourced wampum as far west as the Great Lakes, revealing that Native peoples engaged in extensive long-distance trade long before the arrival of Europeans.[11]

On Long Island, most Indian nations preferred a form of self-governance that emphasized inclusivity and consensus-building. The whole community, both men

Detail of a small wampum belt woven on hide and made up of eight rows of quahog and whelk beads, c. 1800. *Penn Museum (NA9143).*

and women, was involved, at least to some degree, in decision-making about the allocation, use, and disposition of lands and resources. Rather than defer to one powerful grand sachem, they selected local leaders who, in consultation with others, addressed internal issues and represented the community in external affairs.[12] While Indian peoples on Long Island regularly entered into short-term alliances with various constellations of neighboring tribes based on changing needs, interests, and perceived threats, they eschewed ever forging a single unified confederacy. While beneficial in many ways, their decentralized governance and relative autonomy, at times, made them vulnerable to domination by Native rivals and later exploitation by European colonizers.[13]

EUROPEAN COLONIZATION

Beginning in the early seventeenth century, Dutch and later English settlers landed on Long Island's shores, intent on acquiring Native lands and establishing homes and farms like those they had left behind. The same natural endowments that attracted the first Matinecock planters also captured the attention of Europeans. In 1650 Cornelis Van Tienhoven, Secretary for New Netherland, compiled an assessment of the area, which English settlers later named Oyster Bay after its abundant mollusks. By then the New Netherland colony, founded by the Dutch West India Company in 1623, had grown to include the western end of Long Island, today's Brooklyn and Queens. As its settler population became increasingly land hungry, the company directors and colonial council were determined to annex more of the island, still largely in the possession of its indigenous inhabitants, and to block the advance of English settlements on the eastern end.

With an eye toward its economic potential, Van Tienhoven praised Oyster Bay and its surroundings, highlighting the "beautiful bay and rivers," "valleys of sweet & salt meadows," dense woodlands, and abundant shellfish banks and fishing grounds. He also pronounced the land itself to be of "good quality, well adapted for grain and rearing all sorts of cattle." Most enticing, however, was his enthusiastic account of the "fine maize lands, formerly cultivated by the Indians, some of which they still work, and [which] could be had for a trifle . . . [to convert] into good Farms, fit for the plow."[14]

Van Tienhoven was clearly aware that the Matinecocks still inhabited the area, but he minimized their presence and emphasized that this desirable land was open and available to newcomers. Even after describing an Indian village of thirty families near Matinecock Bay "where they have their plantations," he claimed that the tribe was "not strong" and that "great numbers of Indian plantations . . . now lie waste and vacant."[15] Casting their population as dwindling and their planting fields as abandoned, Van Tienhoven effectively cleared the way for New Netherland to assert dominion over the Matinecocks' ancestral lands.

During the early seventeenth century, many European observers in the Northeast arrived at similarly self-serving conclusions. Whether ignorant or indifferent to Native modes of land use and agriculture, they often derided Indians' unregimented plantings of intermixed crops as haphazard and primitive, misinterpreting their practice of leaving fields fallow as evidence of neglect, decay, or abandonment. In some cases, indigenous cultivators may indeed have died or permanently relocated. More often,

View of Fort Amsterdam at the southern tip of Manhattan. Considered the earliest known depiction of New Amsterdam, it is almost certainly fanciful. *Beschrijvinghe van Virginia, Nieuw Nederlandt, Niew Engelandt...*, Amsterdam, 1651. *Courtesy of the John Carter Brown Library, Providence, Rhode Island.*

however, Native fields that seemed obsolete to European eyes were still in active use, if intermittently. Since Europeans defined ownership and sovereignty as predicated upon demonstrable improvements to the land, such false characterizations of Native stewardship as negligible, deficient, and transitory justified not only usurpation of Indians' planting fields but negation of their deep history on the land.

In the best of circumstances, preparing "virgin" land for agriculture involved a tremendous amount of back-breaking toil, and even more so when following traditional European farming methods that required large expanses of cleared land. To convert a single acre of forest into a tillable field, one had to fell vast numbers of large trees, remove tons of timber, rocks, and other debris, then plow and harrow the unyielding ground—all before any seeds could be planted. Given that harsh reality, it is scant wonder that Indians' planting fields were greatly coveted by Dutch and English settlers, regardless of whether they were still in use or not. From Virginia to New England, newly arrived settlers thus joyfully greeted the providential discovery of Native planting fields, mysteriously emptied and prepared for them, not as evidence of Indian toil but as a sign of Divine approval.

One of the most disastrous consequences of prolonged encounters between Native peoples and Europeans throughout the Americas was the inadvertent transmission of contagious diseases to which indigenous communities had no immunity. Consequently, mortality rates were astronomical. A smallpox outbreak in 1633, for example, is estimated to have decimated a third of the Indian inhabitants around Long Island Sound.[16] After such devastation, Native communities struggled to recover. To meet the needs of daily life, they increasingly sought out European manufactured wares. In the short term, they found it more convenient to buy imported guns and gunpowder, metalwares, and textiles than to make their own bows and arrows, stone tools, pottery, and deerskin clothing. Over the long term, however, their preference for buying such essential items led to dependency on Europeans and a gradual loss of traditional skills and knowledge. They also developed a taste for imported luxuries such as tea, sugar, and rum.[17] Taking advantage of the situation, Dutch and English traders often manipulated their Indian customers into unfavorable deals so they would accept paltry amounts of goods in exchange for furs and tracts of land. Finding that wampum served as a convenient form of currency, traders also pressured the Matinecocks and other coastal tribes to increase production, even providing steel drills to speed the process.[18] By the mid-seventeenth century, millions of the handmade shell beads circulated throughout the Northeast.[19] Seeing an opportunity, powerful New England tribes tried to control wampum manufacturing by Long Island Indians, whom they had long regarded as subordinates, or, failing that, demanded huge wampum payments as tribute, ostensibly in return for protection.

The sheer volume, rapidity, and pervasiveness of these cumulative disruptions profoundly transformed Algonquian societies on Long Island and elsewhere. Increasingly enmeshed within European systems of law, private property, and debt, their only options were either to involuntarily abandon their ancestral homelands or adapt to the new colonial regime. Real estate transactions involving the sale of Indian lands were especially fraught. As period accounts reveal, Dutch and English settlers sometimes acted in good faith toward Indians, though in many cases they clearly did not. Furthermore, as Indians had very different concepts of land tenure, European accounts of the meaning and validity of these transactions must be regarded with skepticism.

Predictably, as Dutch and English settlements came ever closer to Native villages, confrontations between their inhabitants became more frequent and more contentious, sometimes culminating in outright warfare. Colonial officials and local sachems struggled, with limited success, to keep the peace. An important precedent was set in 1639, when Mechowodt, a Massapequa sachem, concluded a treaty with the Dutch, securing their protection in exchange for a large chunk of his people's homeland, including parts of present-day Brooklyn, Queens, and Nassau County. Upon Mechowodt's insistence, the Massapequas approved the agreement because it allowed them "to remain upon the aforesaid land, plant corn, fish, hunt and make a living there as well as they can."[20] Peace proved elusive, however, and, in the spring of 1643, Mechowodt was apparently killed during renewed hostilities between Native peoples and the Dutch across western Long Island and Westchester.

Over the next year, John Underhill, an English mercenary employed by the Dutch, carried out a series of ignominious attacks, reportedly killing hundreds of non-combatant men, women, and children. To quell the brutal violence, a group of allied Indians, including the Matinecocks and Massapequas, initiated peace negotiations with the Dutch, following Mechowodt's example, but in hopes of a better outcome. On April 15, 1644, Gauwarowe, another Massapequa sachem and lead negotiator, appeared before the New Netherland council to request guarantees that the allied Indians be allowed "to have peace and to plant" in specified areas in return for refraining from making any future attacks on Dutch villages.[21] That same year, Indians on Long Island's East End concluded a similar collective agreement with the English. Throughout this period, Wyandanch, the Montauket sachem, played a central role in brokering real estate and political agreements between the Native peoples and Europeans. While some questioned his claims of ultimate authority and power, the Matinecock and Massapequa communities apparently acknowledged that he held a limited hereditary interest in their territories through his Matinecock

Coats of arms of New Amsterdam and New Netherland, 1630. *Courtesy of the Manuscripts and Archives Division, New York Public Library Digital Collections.*

grandmother and his kinsman Tackapousha, the Massapequa sachem.[22] Finding his knowledge and connections useful, the English (and to a lesser degree the Dutch) looked to Wyandanch for advice and assistance with land sales, which at times provoked resentment and distrust within his tribal network.

While tacitly acknowledging Native peoples' prior territorial claims, the Dutch and English jockeyed to assert their own sovereignty over Long Island and squabbled over the precise location of the border between their territorial claims. Having maintained a strong presence for decades, the Dutch considered the island's western half, as far east as the village of Huntington, to be integral to New Netherland. The English, meanwhile, sought to incorporate the remainder of the island into New England. As long as these vying factions were at an impasse, Native peoples retained some leverage. Meanwhile, European settlers in the disputed areas, whatever their ethnicity or national allegiance, faced great uncertainty about their land tenure.

Under pressure to increase the settler population, colonial officials in New Netherland allowed some English people (especially Quakers and other religious dissidents) to relocate to western Long Island, as long as they first requested permission and agreed to become Dutch subjects. Despite this new policy, however, growing numbers of unauthorized English settlers moved into Dutch-claimed areas. In May 1640, for example, the leaders of New Netherland were furious to learn that in Oyster Bay, some English "vagabonds had come on the land that we had purchased from [the local sachem] and there begun to build houses, cut trees, and do other work."[23] Adding insult to injury, these upstarts had reportedly pulled down the Dutch coat-of-arms and mockingly "carved a fool's head on the tree [where] it had been nailed."

In response to this affront, the company director and colonial council dispatched Van Tienhoven to evict the intruders and bring whoever was responsible back to New Amsterdam for punishment. If the English proved "innocent of the matter and willing to depart," however, he was "to let them do so quietly" and arrest the local Indian

"Novi Belgii, quod nunc Novi Jorck vocatur...," 1671. On this map, published after the English takeover of New Amsterdam, Long Island looks like an extension of Connecticut to the north. The Native Americans pictured at right seem to be hunters rather than farmers. *Courtesy of the Lionel Pincus and Princess Firyal Map Division, New York Public Library Digital Collections.*

sachems instead.[24] Accordingly, Van Tienhoven and twenty-five soldiers carried out a dawn raid on the English settlement. To their surprise, they found only a scruffy group of eight men, one woman, and a child, along with "a small house built by them and another not yet finished." Ascertaining that they had no patent for the land, Van Tienhoven expelled these "English strollers," who reportedly sought refuge in one of the established English settlements on Long Island's East End.[25]

In 1650 English and Dutch representatives concluded the Hartford Treaty, which designated a new official border dividing Long Island—from Oyster Bay south to the Atlantic coast—with Dutch territory to the west from English territory to the east.[26] While local land disputes continued, the larger geopolitical conflict was now resolved, leaving the Matinecocks increasingly marginalized. Whatever hopes they and other Long Island Indians still harbored of playing one imperial power off another evaporated less than a decade later when, in 1664, the English took over New Netherland from the Dutch and renamed the colony New York.

ENGLISH PLANTERS: CULTIVATING THE FIELDS IN THE COLONIAL ERA

The first permanent English community was established at Oyster Bay in 1653, after a small group of New England men scouted out the area. Finding the land appealing and the bay suitable for a harbor, their emissaries—Reverend William Leverich, Peter Wright, and Samuel Mayo—approached Assiapum, sachem of the local Matinecocks, about buying the land. The minister's primary objective was to establish a mission in central Long Island, in hopes of converting the Indians to Christianity. The other men, however, sought to improve their families' economic prospects by starting afresh on what, in their eyes, seemed like under-utilized land across Long Island Sound from New England. After some negotiations, both parties agreed to the sale of the lands surrounding Oyster Bay, including woods, rivers, marshes, uplands, ponds, and adjacent islands. The deed of sale included one important exception, which specified that the "Island commonly called Hog Island" (modern-day Centre Island) was to remain for the exclusive use of Assiapum and his people. Such legal caveats to preserve Indians' customary rights of access and usufruct (such as the right to hunt, maintain a fishing weir, or claim any beached whales for their own use) were not unusual during the colonial era, but were often disregarded by the English.[27]

In exchange for this large, valuable territory, the settlers promised to pay the Matinecocks with "6 Indian coates, 6 ketles, 6 fathom of wampum, 6 hoes, 6 hatchetts, 3 pair of stockings, 30 aule blades [for eel spears] or minxes [i.e. muxes, iron drills used to make wampum], 20 knives, 3 shirts, and as much Peage [black wampum] as will amount to four pounds, Sterling."[28] Rather curiously, ten English representatives, including the minister, signed the deed, but Assiapum was the only Matinecock to affix his mark; on the reverse side, however, an addendum stated that the sachem acted "with the consent of other Indians respectively interested, and in the names of such as were absent." Whether or not this was true, Assiapum could not legitimately have concluded any agreement without the Matinecocks' consent, since such important matters had to be decided collectively within their community. Judging by later challenges levied against the 1653 deed, many Matinecocks would come to reject Assiapum's authority and the transaction's terms. At the time, however, they seem not to have fully comprehended its ultimate consequence—that the heart of their ancestral homeland was conveyed to the English, outright and in perpetuity.

Friction developed between the Matinecocks and their new English neighbors from the outset. Even before delivering the promised goods, the settlers started surveying for new highways and laying out house lots. Aggravated by such temerity, the Matinecocks understandably became "very unruly and dissatisfied." To smooth over the situation, the settlers hastened to sell an ox and a cow to pay off the outstanding balance.[29] But new problems soon arose. Apart from the specific clause regarding Hog Island, the exact boundaries of the 1653 land sale were unclear. Whereas the Matinecocks insisted Oyster Bay's west side, including the area around present-day Planting Fields, remained in their possession, the English settlers just as adamantly disagreed. Like generations before them, the Matinecocks nevertheless continued to traverse their customary hunting, fishing, and fowling grounds on lands from which the colonizers now sought to exclude them. For their part, the English regularly intruded on the Matinecocks' hunting grounds and allowed their free-ranging livestock to trample the shellfish banks and unfenced Indian planting fields.[30] Making no pretense of honoring their agreement with Assiapum, the English inhabitants even began using Hog Island for grazing their livestock.

Meanwhile, upon receiving word of this new English venture, New Netherland's Director General and Council expressed outrage that, once again, unauthorized settlers were infringing upon their territorial claims. In October 1654, they sent a formal complaint to the governor of Connecticut, the closest English colonial official, demanding that he recall his countrymen.[31] By early January 1655, having received no response, they grew even more alarmed over rumors that the Oyster Bay settlement was just the opening salvo in an English plot to take over all of Long Island. Since "the rivers are frozen, the ground and roads are full of snow . . . [making it impossible] to gather intelligence about English designs," they vowed to investigate the situation during the first spring thaw.[32] Hence, in early March, the council once again dispatched Van Tienhoven "to protest against the usurpers of the honorable patroons' territories, and to summon them to depart."[33] As before, he informed the squatters of their illegal presence "upon lands purchased by the Dutch nation from the native owners" and commanded them to depart, along "with all your people, servants, slaves, furniture, livestock, implements, and everything that you and your nation have brought here." Otherwise, he warned, they would be forcibly evicted and any "damages, misfortune, mishaps, and tragedies" would be upon their heads.[34] But this time, the settlers were more confident—especially since many other English outposts were also encroaching on Dutch-claimed territory—and, in spite of Van Tienhoven's sword rattling, they could not be dislodged. Thereafter, Oyster Bay's early English settlers had high hopes of establishing a flourishing community.

PLANTING FIELDS AND THE DEVELOPMENT OF OYSTER BAY

Like their indigenous predecessors, English planters soon realized that long-cultivated areas—such as those that would become Planting Fields—required ongoing effort to sustain their agricultural productivity. Every tilled field needed regular and labor-intensive applications of manure and other organic fertilizers to prevent soil exhaustion. Although the natural grasslands and salt meadows provided ample forage for livestock, these resources also required careful management to avoid overuse.

Meanwhile, conflicts proliferated between the English and Native populations over contested land claims, exacerbated by local sachems' common practice of reselling the same land to different parties.[35] In the 1650s, tensions flared when the Matinecocks questioned the borders and demanded additional compensation for a tract of valuable land that Oyster Bay acquired for a pittance but subsequently transferred to neighboring Huntington. Since neither community wanted to accept responsibility, the Montauket sachem Wyandanch sought to mediate by convincing the feuding parties to undertake a new perambulation survey, which involved literally walking around the tract together and marking trees to indicate its exact border. A similar controversy arose after the sachem Asahroken sold Caumsett (Horse Neck), part of his people's traditional hunting grounds, to an English settler, but then claimed to have "orally reserved" the area for their continued use. In exchange for clear title, Peter Wright, Samuel Mayo, and Daniel Whitehead of Oyster Bay offered to take over the land and pay an additional sum to the Matinecocks. The revised deed was signed by twelve Matinecocks, in addition to Asahroken and Assiapum; the large number of signatories underscored the Matinecocks' preference that major issues be decided by consensus within the community, rather than by wayward individuals, even respected sachems.[36]

A decade later, the Matinecocks again challenged the validity of the 1653 land sale on account of its imprecise boundaries and the paltry sum paid. While they sought an equitable resolution, colonial officials refused to address the matter; ultimately, the case was dismissed after Reverend Leverich (who had helped negotiate the original transaction) vouched for the validity of the deed. His statement reads:

> Whereas, I understand that there is some controversy about a sale of lands, made by Assiapum . . . to Samuel Mayo, Peter Wright, and William Leverich, for want of sound formalities usual in English deeds . . . I do therefore testify that the intention of the said Assiapum was to convey, not only his right, but the right of his heirs . . . which, though not expressed, is easily understood . . . The Indians, so far as I can understand, have never made any sales for lives, but of custom—which is their law—passed the right of their heirs . . . unless they made any express exceptions.

Despite his earlier desire to proselytize to Long Island Indians, Reverend Leverich's interpretation of Assiapum's unexpressed intentions clearly favored the settlers' desired outcome. Lest "better intelligence" prove him wrong, the minister hastened to add, "I shall be sorry that such as profess themselves Christians shall teach heathens less honesty, under pretense of teaching them law." As that hedging statement suggests, this man of the cloth was acutely aware of his countrymen's manipulative and deceptive tactics to acquire Indian lands.

Within a year of assuming control over New York in 1664, English colonial authorities began making legal and political changes that impacted Long Islanders. Most significantly, they passed the Duke's Law, which among other provisions, regulated relations between masters and indentured servants. Over time, they enacted numerous laws specifically to control "Indian, negro, or mulatto servants and slaves," with stiff punishments or fines for vagrancy, drunkenness, insolence, and more serious offenses such as thefts. Even if free, people of color could face heavy fines or be forced into terms of involuntary servitude for minor offenses or unpaid debts. This punitive system often condemned families and whole communities to an unending cycle of poverty, incarceration, debt peonage, violence, and degradation.[37] For white settlers, on the other hand, the same legal mechanisms redounded to their economic benefit by putting additional Indian lands and labor at their disposal. By the late eighteenth century, local sachems, including Tackapousha's son, had reluctantly sold the remainder of Matinecock land around Oyster Bay to provide for their people.

From the late seventeenth to the early nineteenth century, the land that now comprises Planting Fields was largely divided among a cohort of Oyster Bay's founding families—including Wrights, Townsends, Crabbes, Frosts, Coles, and Sammises—along with their close affiliates and later descendants. All who arrived in the first wave of English colonization were allocated tracts of land out of the town's initial 1653 land purchase from the Matinecocks. To ensure an equitable division of land, settlers initially agreed to limit private landholdings to six-acre home lots (which could later be enlarged in increments of up to five acres at a time). The remainder of the land was retained by the town to be held in common, with each home lot entitled to use specified shares of meadow, pasture, and woodlands. At regular Town meetings, Oyster Bay's freeholders—propertied free white men (and some women), who were entitled to vote—gathered to make decisions about the town's management and future development.

After the early restrictions were lifted in Oyster Bay, some of the early settlers and their descendants were able to acquire substantial landholdings through additional grants, sales, trades, and, most importantly, inheritance. In the process, they also gained social status and political influence within the community. As they intermarried and developed close kinship ties, they further consolidated and transferred their accumulated wealth across generations. Gradually, they also gained control over almost half of the town's remaining common shares and increasingly claimed ownership over lands previously held in common. Even Hog Island, long an important grazing area, was gradually divided up and privatized. In the 1660s members of the Townsend family claimed portions of Hog Island as their own. Nicholas Wright likewise specified in his 1674 will that "my Lands upon Hog Island . . . be equally divided among my three sons."[38] This trend raised the hackles of their less affluent neighbors who relied on shared access to this valuable resource; compared to established families like the Wrights and Townsends they had little influence or leverage to challenge or rectify such inequities. Indeed, the Wright family offers an illuminating example of this pattern of property accumulation, inheritance, and social advancement.

Among Oyster Bay's first English settlers, the Wright brothers—Peter, Nicholas, and Anthony—had emigrated from England to Massachusetts in 1635. Although soon established as freemen there, they joined Reverend Leverich's 1653 expedition to Long Island. Whether or not they shared his religious zeal, they were likely determined to acquire more land than was possible in heavily settled New England. Having helped to negotiate the initial land purchase from Assiapum, Peter Wright, the eldest brother, was entrusted with many important responsibilites during Oyster Bay's formative years, including allocating home lots and commons privileges to newly arrived male settlers. Whenever the town acquired additional lands from the Matinecocks, he was thus perfectly positioned both to ensure his family's access to the choicest tracts and to participate in widespread land speculation, reselling lands to newcomers at inflated prices. In the 1670s, Suscaneman, a Matinecock sachem, expressed astonishment when 60 prime acres in Oyster Bay, which he sold under duress for only twelve pounds, were resold only two years later for well over twice that sum.[39] As the minutes of Oyster Bay's town meetings attest, all three of the Wright brothers became prominent community members, holding public offices and engaging in a wide range of legal and political affairs.

Following the pattern of property accumulation described above, Peter, Nicholas, and Anthony were each issued a home lot upon arrival, situated in prime locations in the village and close to the harbor. Building upon that initial foothold, they and their progeny snapped up additional acres throughout the Oyster Bay area. Nicholas acquired a large tract, lying between present-day Mill River Road and Beaver Creek, that now is a part of Planting Fields. In 1672 the Town granted a 20-acre lot to each of his adult sons, Edmund, Caleb, and John Wright, located "on the South Side of the old planting fields."[40] During the 1680s, Peter's sons, Job and Adam Wright, sought to improve and rationalize their respective landholdings through a series of strategic transactions; first, Job sold his kinsman Robert Townsend Jr. three acres "lying at the planting field so called, bounded on the north by John Townsend's field, formerly Adam Wright's, on the west by Job Wright's Land." Then he sold John Townsend another plot at "the old planting fields" (which had woodlands on one side and planting fields owned by Wrights and Townsends

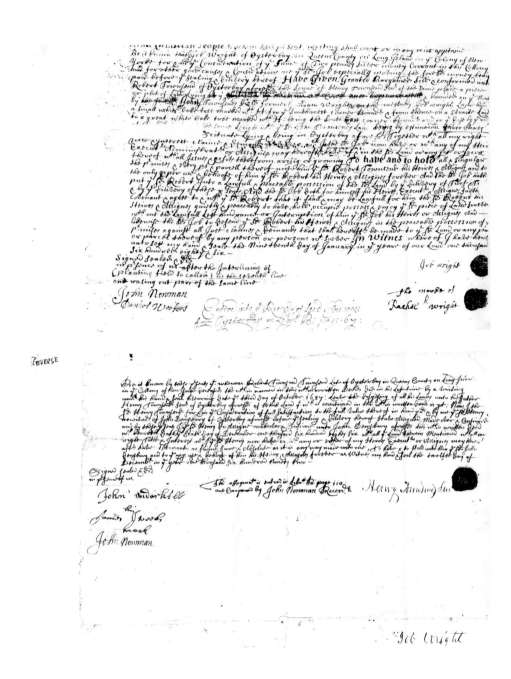

Deed dated January 19, 1686, recording Job Wright's sale to Robert Townsend of three acres "lying at the planting fields so called" (facsimile). *Planting Fields Foundation Archives.*

on the other sides). Adam, meanwhile, sold another 11 acres in the area "called the old planting field," to John Townsend.[41]

During this period, propertied white men on Long Island typically left their lands to their sons, often prioritizing the eldest, and provided for their wives and daughters with smaller bequests, consisting primarily of housewares, textiles, livestock, and enslaved persons. Accordingly, when Peter and Nicholas died, their ample landholdings were distributed among their sons and grandsons, while their female kin shared the remainder of their worldly posessions.[42] Over time, this inheritance pattern ensured that the intergenerational transfer of wealth remained concentrated within a closed circle. Consequently, the surnames of the Wrights, the Townsends, and the other founding families recur with great frequency as deed holders in what would become Planting Fields.

While land and livestock were both essential to prosperity in a rural community, the other key ingredient was labor. Throughout the colonial period, Long Island's labor force—whether on farms, workshops, mills, shipyards, or other enterprises—usually included a mix of enslaved Africans, European and Indian wage workers, and indentured servants (voluntary and involuntary). The first enslaved Africans in the region were imported by the Dutch West India Company to address New Netherland's chronic labor shortages. Although small in numbers, they played an outsized role in building, provisioning, and defending the colony. Over four decades, some managed to secure their freedom, acquire land, and negotiate basic legal rights, even while still relegated by the Dutch to a racially defined underclass.[43] Following the English takeover in 1664, however, conditions for the Black population significantly deteriorated, even as their numbers were increased through the slave trade from West Africa and the Caribbean. Determined to control and dominate them, the English imposed harsh slave codes, emulating those developed in the sugar islands.

As was typical elsewhere in colonial New York (with the exception of the largest plantations of Long Island and the Hudson Valley), families who settled in the vicinity of modern Planting Fields owned small numbers of bondspeople. Oyster Bay's town records offer clues about their identities and living conditions. In 1673 for instance, a young boy named Owah was sold to Richard Crabbe by a Glen Cove resident.[44] Renamed Tom by his new owner, Owah grew up in bondage, working within the Crabbe household. In an unusual twist of fate, however, he was manumitted in 1685 by his owner's widow, Alice Crabbe, a Quaker who believed in spiritual equality and rejected the institution of slavery. Even so, she still required him to pay four pounds toward the support of her young grandson. In his early twenties, Tom (né Owah) adopted the surname Gall and settled in Oyster Bay, where he eventually acquired a small homestead and started a family.[45]

As a free Black man, Tom Gall's success in acquiring property and, even more remarkable, in passing it on to his children was an extraordinary achievement at the time. Prior to the American Revolution, the majority of enslaved Africans in the North remained in bondage for their entire lives. At any time, their owners could decide to sell, lease out, or relocate them, leaving them with no means of protecting their families or providing for their futures. In short, Long Island slaveowners typically regarded these human beings as property, along with the rest of their worldly estates. In 1705, for example, Nathaniel Coles Jr.'s Will transferred ownership of his farm to his sons and his "negro slaves" to his daughters.[46] In 1731 Edmund Wright's bequest to his wife included a "negro man called Raff."[47] In 1738 Wright Frost's Will likewise left "my negro boy, Natt," "my negro boy, Robin," "my negro, James" to his sons and Nanny, Charity, and Dick to his wife (until she died or remarried). In his role as master and patriarch, Frost sought to control his bondspeople even after his death, specifying if "any of the young negroes" were to be sold, his other sons were to have first refusal to buy them.[48]

Given Oyster Bay's proximity to New York City and other seaports, some enslaved persons managed to secure their freedom by fleeing to more densely populated urban areas. In 1761, for instance, "William Negro slave with gray Beard and Hair" was sought by his owner, "George Townsend in Oyster Bay."[49] In 1766 a Boston newspaper advertised a five-dollar reward, offered by Doris Van Wyck of Oyster Bay, for the return of "a Negro Man, named Dick" who reportedly crossed Long Island

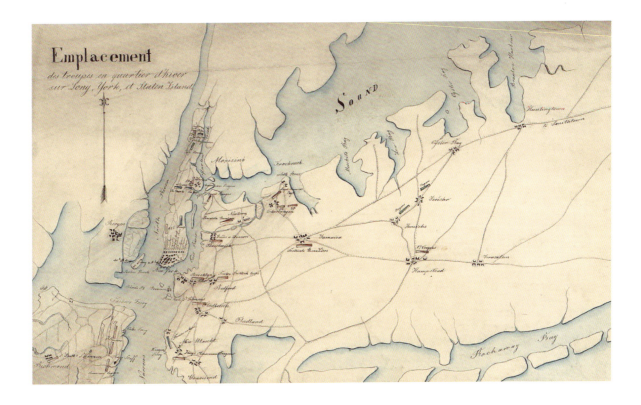

"Emplacement des troupes en quartier d'hiver sur Long, York, et Staten Island," 1776. The map shows the location of winter quarters for Hessian troops (in blue) and Loyalist and British troops (in red). Oyster Bay is spared for the moment. *Courtesy of the Lionel Pincus and Princess Firyal Map Division, The New York Public Library Digital Collections.*

Sound, "with a false dirty Pass all written by one Hand . . . [and] enquired the Road to Boston."[50] In other cases, enslaved individuals fled to Long Island, usually because they had been sold away or leased out, to reunite, if briefly, with family and friends. Such may have been the case in 1760 with "Wall, Negro slave, born at Oysterbay, L.I., age c 40," who returned home from New York City on the day after Christmas.[51]

With the outbreak of the American Revolution, almost every aspect of life was disrupted for Long Islanders, free and enslaved. The island suffered through seven brutal years under British occupation, and the populace was deeply divided between Patriots and Loyalists. After the Battle of Long Island on August 27–29, 1776, when General Washington's Continental forces suffered an ignominious defeat, the British Army established its headquarters in Lower Manhattan and looked to the surrounding countryside to supply its forces with food, fodder, and civilian labor. Although several thousand Long Islanders immediately sought refuge in Connecticut, others chose to stay, either because they had Loyalist sympathies or because they were reluctant to abandon their homes and farms.

Everyone remaining in Oyster Bay was impacted by the presence there of a British garrison. Any free white man not already under arms, along with his servants, enslaved workers, and draft animals, could be impressed into service by the military to cut firewood, transport arms and provisions, or assist in building fortifications. The King's army also requisitioned vast quantities of food and fodder that local families needed to sustain themselves. In 1776, for example, John Sammis sought payment from the British for a cow, five hogs, nine bushels of wheat and oats, a ton of hay, and 400 chestnut fence rails. In December 1777, Silas Sammis and Jeremiah Wood of Huntington sought reimbursement for livestock, money, goods, and timber valued at over £150. After the war, John Silas submitted yet another claim for compensation for "being turned out of my House for three months and six days," as well as for 10 apple trees, 1,566 feet of boards, and 2,510 chestnut rails "some of which was put in the Fort and some burnt."[52] Even those with Loyalist sympathies were soon alienated by the intrusive British presence in Oyster Bay, especially as the military presence became more oppressive but afforded little protection against Patriots' midnight raids across Long Island Sound. For some enslaved Africans, however, the wartime upheavals allowed opportunities to pursue liberty behind British lines.

AMERICAN PLANTERS IN THE NINETEENTH CENTURY

After the Revolution, Long Islanders struggled to restore their shattered economy. At the time, small and mid-sized farms still predominated in the area around Oyster Bay, and most of these properties, including the acreage now comprising Planting Fields, remained in the hands of families whose roots in the area dated back to the early settlement era. As they tried to resume their traditional agricultural and maritime activities, however, they faced an array of new challenges, such as soil exhaustion and overfishing. At the same time, they faced growing competition from farmers in upstate New York and the West, where fertile land was still cheap and abundant.

Another important development was the slow but steady transformation of the labor system. In 1799 New York passed a Gradual Manumission Law that phased slavery out of existence over the next two decades. Some slaveowners were prompted to manumit their bondspeople early. In 1804 Epenetus Sammis registered the birth of "a female child named Rachel" to Hannah, one of his bondswomen, but opted to abandon the child—that is, not to claim her as his property.[53] He did not free Hannah, however, until 1823. In many cases, African Americans on Long Island continued to work on or near the places where they had been formerly enslaved. Nevertheless, many local farms still struggled to secure sufficient labor.

Given the myriad difficulties associated with farming, some affluent landowners began to diversify into non-agricultural businesses as well. As these other ventures began to prosper, they had less need or desire to cultivate all of the acreage in their possession. Some leased unused fields to smaller farmers or made tenancy agreements with unpropertied men to till the land in exchange for rent or a share of their produce. In 1827, for example, T. W. Burtis placed a newspaper advertisement that stated: "A Farmer Wanted—A man and his wife, or small family, who understand their business, can obtain a good situation on a Farm upon shares or otherwise, in the pleasant village of Oyster Bay."[54] As that description suggests, the area remained largely rural in character.

From the 1860s on, new modes of public transportation made Long Island's North Shore increasingly accessible to people living in New York City. With the advent first of regular stagecoach and steamboat service and then, in 1869, extension of the railroad as far as Locust Valley, Oyster Bay became a vital transit hub and attracted a diverse array of new businesses and light industry. The combination of its new accessibility, attractive amenities, and beautiful natural surroundings—with shady woodlands, undulating meadows, sparkling ponds, sandy beaches, and appealing vistas of the Sound—also made the area an attractive summer destination. Consequently, summer hotels began to be built in the area, catering to urban visitors. By the 1890s, elite members of New York society began building great estates along the North Shore, bringing an influx of wealth and luxury that gave rise to its reputation as the "Gold Coast." The proliferation of mansions, country clubs, and other amenities catering to affluent New Yorkers created new employment opportunities for many immigrant builders, craftsmen, and service workers.

Meanwhile, farming was becoming ever more expensive and labor intensive, especially with the introduction of costly commercial fertilizers (such as bird guano imported from South America). In the 1880s, a local antiquarian stated that the "regular farm routine has varied but little since the first settlement," with a reassuringly predictable cycle of plowing, planting, cultivating, and harvesting; but even he had to concede that conditions had fundamentally altered, because now the "cost of fertilizers would buy the land at a hundred dollars an acre every seven years."[55] Land was quickly becoming more valuable for building high-end residential housing and great estates than for growing crops or raising livestock. Consequently, some long-term landowners began to sell off surplus acreage to newcomers.

The career of John Merritt Sammis (1820–1908), whose land would be purchased to create Planting Fields, exemplifies the way changing economic and social conditions affected the descendants of Oyster Bay's early settlers. As a member of the sprawling Sammis clan, his heritage was grounded in farming and milling interests dating back to the 1650s. Moreover, he was also tied to another important founding family through his 1846 marriage to Rebecca Townsend (1827–1919). Through inheritance and purchase, he accumulated more than 400 acres of land, which contemporaries described as the "most desireable" in Oyster Bay; among his holdings were 164 acres in the old upper planting fields, which were once cultivated by the Native inhabitants.[56]

Although the son of a farmer, Sammis did not aspire to become a steward of the land. Instead, he acquired a successful lumberyard and built a steam-powered sawmill in Oyster Bay. These profitable ventures, in turn, allowed him to expand into real estate and other businesses. Given his numerous enterprises, Sammis did not attempt to cultivate all the land that he owned. Around 1890, he took on a tenant named William E. Cheshire, a young man in his thirties and a lifelong resident of Oyster Bay. Along with his wife and two children, Cheshire took up residence on Sammis's farm. Soon he was making regular "trips to the city on the farmers' train" to bring his produce to market. In addition, he ran a dairying operation with a milk delivery route in Oyster Bay.[57] When the men's partnership foundered, however, Sammis seems to have decided that farming was no longer worth the trouble.

After that negative experience, Sammis focused more on real estate development, hoping to capitalize on Oyster Bay's rapid expansion. When the railroad was extended in the 1890s, for example, the village offered him $1,000 for a tract of his land needed for an access road between the new railroad depot and the village center. Convinced that its value would soon be more than $10,000, he saw no point in "opening up building lots and improving the private property of others, without receiving any benefit himself." For three years, a "bitter fight raged in the otherwise quiet village," until Sammis finally relented and sold the land for less—but then successfully sued the village for damages.[58]

Despite his battles, John Sammis commanded respect in Oyster Bay as a prominent landowner and businessman. He also took considerable pride in his status as a scion of one of Long Island's founding families. And although no longer a full-time farmer himself, he seemed quite resentful of the wealthy newcomers who were reshaping the rural surroundings and the formerly sleepy village of Oyster Bay, with major economic impacts on the community, for good and for ill.

Sammis and other local residents were particularly annoyed by the proliferation of private clubs in the area, which usurped large tracts of land and actively recruited outsiders to buy memberships. At times, these new institutions seemed, quite literally, to ride roughshod over local farms. The Meadow Brook Club, a popular equestrian club located a few miles south of Oyster Bay, received constant complaints about its members trespassing on private lands during steeple chases and foxhunts. Given his money-making acumen, Sammis reportedly found a way to subsidize his yearly farm taxes by extracting compensation from the club "for fences thrown down or crops destroyed by riders following the hounds." When his bill went from $10 one year to $50 the next, club officials thereafter carefully avoided his fields when planning equestrian events. Many of his neighbors, however, opted to sell land "at fancy prices" or rent their farms to new club members, garnering twice what could be taken "out of them in crops." Others turned "an honest penny by boarding . . . puppies, born at the club kennels, until the young dogs are old enough to train for hunting." In short order, the Meadow Brook Club had become "too handy a source of income for the farmer to kick about cross-country riding." Club officials were harder pressed to placate charges that their elitism undermined American culture by "aping the blasted British aristocracy."[59]

Whatever ill feelings John M. Sammis engendered among his neighbors, new or old, apparently dissipated over time. A biographical profile published in 1901, when he was 81 years old, fondly described him as one of "the rugged, honest, and successful residents of Oyster Bay." Compared with the "kid-glove people" who brought "into many country places much glamor and pretense with nothing back of it," its author described Sammis's blunt style as refreshingly honest and unaffected.[60] That same year, the octogenarian began to wind down some of his business ventures. Probaby realizing that his grown children would appreciate the proceeds of a sale more than the responsibility of managing tenant farmers, he sold the 164-acre Upper Planting Fields Farm in 1904 (along with an adjacent lot of 14 acres) to James Byrne, a prominent attorney, and his wife, Helen Macgregor Byrne. Although their primary residence was in New York City, the couple desired a more healthful location to raise their children.[61] Having accrued considerable status and affluence as legal counsel to James G. Blair, "the millionaire coal operator," James Byrne was also eager to gain a foothold on the fashionable North Shore, where his law partner and other associates had already established summer homes.

Over the next several years, the Byrnes began buying up and consolidating adjacent properties, eventually totalling almost 400 acres. In June 1905 they purchased Sidney McCoun's 90-acre farm and orchard for $40,000. In operation since 1838, the property had been "one of the largest peach orchards in the country . . . [with] over 8,000 trees until the San Jose scale and other insects destroyed them." After that disheartening experience, the McCoun family was probably relieved to find a buyer for their ravaged orchard. In an article entitled, "Big Deal near Oyster Bay," the *New York Times* reported that local inhabitants surmised, correctly as it proved, that the Byrnes' objective in buying it—on top of "the old John M. Sammis farm"—was the "accumulation of land for another large country estate in that neighborhood."[62]

Postcard of a horse-drawn carriage on the unpaved Shore Road, Oyster Bay, c. 1906. Henry Otto Korten. *Nassau County Department of Parks, Recreation, and Museums Photo Archive Center.*

The Byrnes, of course, had no aspirations to become farmers. Nevertheless, in honor of the ancient agricultural heritage of the land and its former inhabitants, they named their new estate "Planting Fields." They also built an impressive mansion, designed by noted architect Grosvenor Atterbury, and developed a large garden. Before long, Helen was exhibiting flowers at the Nassau County Horticultural Show, alongside beautiful specimens from the gardens of Theodore Roosevelt and Louis Comfort Tiffany.[63] To attend to the more utilitarian aspects of daily life, the Byrnes relied on the labor of servants. According to the 1910 federal census, their household staff included nine live-in servants (seven Irish and two French), plus a Scottish butler.[64]

Within a few years, James Byrne and some of his fellow clubmen—who longtime inhabitants still regarded with great suspicion—became alarmed that Oyster Bay was losing its bucolic character. They worried in particular that the "country lanes and roads, upon which one may ride [horses] unmolested by motorcars and other vehicles," were being "rapidly reduced by the extension of farms into country estates."

"Unless something were done, and done immediately," they insisted, "one of the greatest charms of the neighborhood would soon be lost." They organized a committee to oversee efforts to systematically preserve a network of unpaved roads. Ironically, in setting "their mark of approval on the country lanes movement," they hindered the development of vital infrastructure necessary for the advancement of agriculture, which had been the region's economic foundation since the seventeenth century.[65]

When a luxurious new club was founded at nearby Piping Rock in 1906, James and Helen Byrne were among its early members. According to the *Brooklyn Daily Eagle*, "No more enthusiastic hunting people are there to be found than this contingent of the North Shore." Encompassing more than 1,200 acres of woodlands and old farms—all acquired from "well remembered Long Island owners"—the club featured horse shows, polo competitions, and fox hunts with more than eighty riders. A former British officer and keen sportsman was hired to oversee the "scientific" reintroduction of fifty-three red foxes, relocated from Connecticut, Vermont, and Canada, and to "build up an American pack of foxhounds," bred from a famous line of Kentucky hunting dogs. Since foxes and other troublesome predators had long since been eliminated, he expected some resistance from local farmers. After he

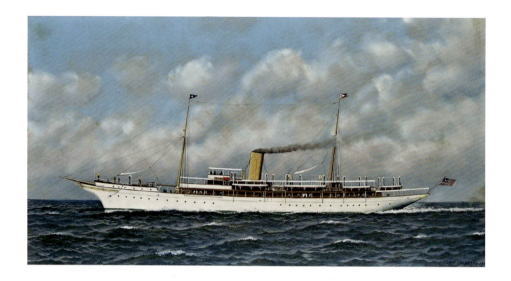

Cornelius Billings's steam yacht *Vanadis*. Antonio Nicolo Gasparo Jacobsen, 1911. *Wikimedia Commons.*

promised that—if only they "would not molest the new foxes"—the club would pay for any poultry killed, the farmers readily accepted his terms.[66]

With luxury properties in high demand and short supply, many prominent people were eager to find appropriate accommodations on the North Shore. In 1913 the Byrnes rented Planting Fields to Robert Livingston for the months of May and June, and to Cornelius Billings and his wife for the rest of the summer; their steam yacht, the *Vanadis*, became a common sight on Long Island Sound.[67] And despite their evident fondness for Planting Fields, the Byrnes permanently parted with the estate in October 1913, after William Robertson Coe and Mai Coe apparently made an offer too generous to refuse. Upon its conclusion, the sale was described as "one of the most important which has taken place in this section for some time."[68]

By then, Oyster Bay had solidified its reputation as the home of the rich and famous. According to one observer, the village had "never before enjoyed such prosperity as at the present time and the real estate dealers are making many cheerful predictions as to the future . . . Many important sales have been reported and several farms adjoining the town have been purchased" and were soon to be replaced by new mansions. At least from his perspective, these well-heeled newcomers were a boon to the community, contributing to "making Oyster Bay as beautiful as art and nature can make it."[69]

Another contemporary article, entitled "World's Greatest Nesting Place of the Multi-Millionaires," declared that the North Shore had not only the "greatest, most luxurious, and complete development of country life that is to be found in America" but also a higher concentration of wealth "than any portion of the earth's surface outside of a town or city." While the latter claim was largely hyperbole, the author proceeded to relate, quite accurately, how better transportation (especially automobiles), the popularity of early housing developments, and the proliferation of private clubs and grand estates contributed to Long Island's real estate boom. "Slowly at first, but subsequently with vertiginous rapidity," land prices soared from $40 to $60 per acre in the 1860s to $10,000 per acre in the 1910s. Although the original settlers initially were slow to sell, he explained, "little by little they parted with their homestead farms which were combined and laid out in vast estates for those who built the palaces that replace the low-roofed rambling houses."[70]

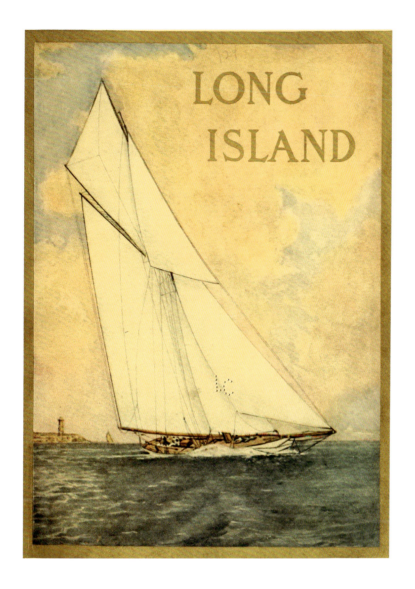

"Long Island, 'where cooling breezes blow.'" Cover of a promotional book published by the Long Island Rail Road, 1913. Isaac H. Blanchard Co. *Library of Congress.*

Lauding the verdant countryside and turreted mansions as reminiscent of the baronial estates of rural England, the writer stated that the only substantive difference between the two was that so many millionaires were concentrated on the North Shore that their "clustered estates practically touch elbows and cover less territory than an ordinary Texas range." Reflecting on this trajectory, he concluded: "It is no wonder, therefore, that not only the very rich have selected this region for their country homes or that those who are only fairly well-to-do have been quick to see its advantages and build their houses there. The developers of suburban real estate also have found this one of their most attractive fields."[71] Hearing that summation, the early cultivators of the planting fields would likely have been astonished, John M. Sammis would doubtless have grumbled, and James and Helen Byrne of Planting Fields would have nodded approvingly at the remarkable transformations that time had wrought.

PORTFOLIO

Planting Fields: The House and the Landscape

David Almeida

Previous spread
Carshalton Gates and the Olmsted Brothers–designed landscape.

Blue Pool Garden. Hewitt and Healy, c. 1926. *Planting Fields Foundation Archives.*

West Portico. Mattie Edwards Hewitt, c. 1926. *Planting Fields Foundation Archives.*

Overleaf
Aerial view of the Main House with Manhattan visible at the horizon line.

Front entrance to the Main House.

View to the Main House from the East Lawn.

Overleaf
Mai Coe's Bedroom.

Dining Room. Mattie Edwards Hewitt, c. 1927. *Planting Fields Foundation Archives.*

The Gallery. Mattie
Edwards Hewitt, 1927.
*Planting Fields
Foundation Archives.*

W. R. Coe's Den.

Reception Room.

Detail of the Buffalo mural by Robert Winthrop Chanler.

Detail of a stained-glass window in the Dining Room.

Detail of a wrought-iron handrail by Samuel Yellin.

Carved wooden rooster on the second floor.

Overleaf
Cloister Garden.

View to the Main House from the Azalea Path.

Vista Path.

Front entrance
and interior of the
Camellia House.

Camellias in full bloom.

Camellia House pool.

Overleaf
West Lawn.

Gate to the Blue Pool Garden.

Teahouse.

Overleaf
Interior of the Teahouse with furnishings and murals by Everett Shinn.

Surprise Pool
with weeping cherry
in bloom.

Playhouse in spring.

Rose Arbor. Mattie
Edwards Hewitt,
c. 1926. *Planting Fields
Foundation Archives.*

Hedge-lined herbaceous garden. Mattie Edwards Hewitt, c. 1926. *Planting Fields Foundation Archives.*

Overleaf
View of the Main House from the Circular Pool Garden.

Entrance to the Main Greenhouse.

Hibiscus House.

Synoptic Garden.

Aerial view of the Heather Garden.

Blossoming magnolia on the West Lawn.

Follies performance by Processional Arts, Catalyst 2024.

Posh Blind by Mark Dion, Catalyst 2020.

Overleaf
The Outside In by Diana Al Hadid, Catalyst 2022.

In the Taxus Field: columnar hornbeam (left) and weeping beech (above).

John Dixon Hunt

On Planting Fields and the Making of Place

"THE MAKING OF PLACE" WAS A COINAGE OF THE FAMOUS EIGHTEENTH-CENTURY gardenist Lancelot "Capability" Brown, from whom I have taken this essay's title and its focus on Planting Fields. Brown was nicknamed for his delight in gleefully rubbing his hands and explaining to a client how a site offered "capabilities" for its improvement, and how he was himself quite capable of making a place better. He would come to be ridiculed by some, yet nonetheless the phrase he invented was ideally suited to work that evolved in later years.[1] Indeed, place-making seems to be a better description of what later came to be termed landscape architecture, a term invented and formalized by the late nineteenth century and adopted by professional bodies in the United States and the United Kingdom around 1900.

Brown made places, and he was good at it. Though it is often forgotten, he was an architect as well as a landscaper, so he is suspected to have designed the Grecian Temple at Stowe, as well as the wonderful meadow down the valley below. This landscape moment is often used to characterize Brown's work, and an early engraving from c. 1800 makes clear how much that element of his work was admired. Yet his contributions to place-making were various; even at Stowe, this addition to the large garden contributed to a conspectus of forms in landscape design.

Today he is thought to be the man to have invented "natural gardening." But that, if you think about it, is frankly ridiculous: if you garden, you invest in, and shape, natural materials; the word "naturalism" is a plausible, but still for me a confusing term.

"Nature" itself is a word that is abused in landscape discussions, where it is assumed we can make our own uses of the term, which we generally fail to do—a thought to which I will return in considering what kind of a place, and what kind of "nature" we encounter at Planting Fields.

The moment of the Grecian Valley at Stowe is but one of Brown's contributions to the way garden history was conceived and promoted in England and in the United States. Above all, what he did and what he passed along to later designers was to register different modes of layout in relation to other, often very different, ones around them. And landscape, perhaps more so than architecture, may conceal or contrast its different layers. What has been described as the park or lawns at Planting Fields may be truly in the lineage of Brown's characteristic modes of designing with nature, but they are heir to a remarkable awareness of garden history and its various design forms. This includes the strong sense, as noted by David Leatherbarrow, that "good gardening meant observing the identities and differences in nature's products."[2] It attends both to local topography, and to what a given client and his or her culture

expects. It is indeed a well-explored topic and not a new perception, for Thomas Whately in the eighteenth century argued the same: different forms can be present in the same landscape, and "may to a degree be intermixed; but each is still a character of such force, that whichever prevails, the propriety of all other characters, and of every species of beauty, must be tried by their conformity to this."³

Even earlier, the third Earl of Shaftesbury, sometimes hailed today as a proponent of "natural gardening" before Brown, saw it as but one of the usual design forms. In a dialogue of 1707 he espoused "a passion in me for things of a natural kind" and regretted the "conceit or caprice of man . . . [to spoil] by breaking in upon the natural order."⁴ But this was in a dialogue, and the other invented speaker, of whom Shaftesbury was equally the author, argued the contrary point. The 1714 frontispiece to his book *Characteristics of Men, Manners, Opinions, Times* depicts the author in his own garden at Wimborne St Giles. It shows the "conceits" of the garden nearest the house, which gave way increasingly to a grove or wilderness, and then to woodlands.

Another early gardenist kind of advice comes from an appeal to the idea of "genius loci," a Latin phrase, which we have assimilated. As Alexander Pope wrote in 1731, "Consult the genius of the place in all." The lines that follow range over a repertoire of landscape features, each of which (he argues) must observe the identity of that segment of topography:

Grecian Temple and meadow at Stowe. John Dixon Hunt.

An early engraving of the meadow at Stowe, c. 1800.

> Consult the genius of the place in all;
> That tells the waters or to rise, or fall;
> Or helps th' ambitious hill the heav'ns to scale,
> Or scoops in circling theatres the vale;
> Calls in the country, catches opening glades,
> Joins willing woods, and varies shades from shades,
> Now breaks, or now directs, th' intending lines;
> Paints as you plant, and, as you work, designs.
> —ll. 57–64, Epistle IV. To Richard Boyle, Earl of Burlington

Pope advises that each element of a site should be encouraged to behave in appropriate ways, and be allowed to articulate its proper forms. The "genius" was originally a Roman divinity who presided over and shaped the space or its meanings. But in later days that can be either the genius of its designer or the guiding genius of its owner and the designers together.

Besides "nature," the concept of "formality" has to be carefully used, or even avoided, in landscape discussions: "regularity" or "geometricality" is better. Everything has its own forms, and the variety of them in a landscape is part of its success. Versailles, so generally dubbed "formal," has within its design its own cultural variety of forms that are dedicated by contemporary notions. Admittedly, new modes of appreciating variety and forms emerged during the eighteenth century, and Planting Fields in the early twentieth century is heir to many of them. Yet its landscape also allows and accepts the rigor of the Italian garden, and the ways in which the buildings mediate between each other the different "formalities" in the lawns, trees, and flowers.

Any garden building acts, at its best, as a link between itself and what surrounds it. The Italian Garden at Planting Fields (as it was called in an Olmsted Brothers drawing of March 7, 1921,[5] simply I assume because it did need a specific designation) uses both the tea house at its rear and the levels of terracing and planting around it to give the ensemble a coherent feel for this section of the ground. It is, after all, the most gardenist moment within the landscape and deserves such treatment.

In 2022, as we celebrated the creativity and invention of Frederick Law Olmsted on the bicentenary of his birth, it was useful to situate these features in the *longue durée* of landscape architecture. The name "Planting Fields" was used to describe this area long before it was taken up and used in connection to the house, gardens, and landscape that we see today. From 1906, when the Byrne family completed their house and established gardens around it, to its acquisition in 1913 by Mai and William Robertson Coe, to the destruction of the house by fire in 1918 and its subsequent redesign and reconstruction, to its mid-twentieth-century uses as a learning institution, to the present day New York State Park, Planting Fields has changed. Sometimes we do not see, or even want to see, any change. Yet over the years, designs are altered for practical and/or cultural reasons when new designers are invited to work and develop

Frontispiece detail from Anthony Ashley Cooper, Earl of Shaftesbury, *Characteristics of Men, Manners, Opinions, Times in Three Volumes*, second edition corrected (London, 1714).

its gardens, as happened with the Italian Garden of 1916, and as new interests and needs are emphasized—not least in the opening of house and gardens to the public. The layout and design of Planting Fields draws on a variety of landscape traditions—unsurprising, as by the early twentieth century in the northeast United States, there were several modes of landscape layout to draw on. The principal ones are the English, the French, the Dutch, and at the start of it all, the Italian. The importance of the last is clear from the publication of Edith Wharton's *Italian Villas and Their Gardens*, which the early landscape designers working at Planting Fields would have undoubtedly known.

Change comes in various forms: over time, for good or bad; in weather and climate; with plant growth; in cultural ideas both generally available or specific to a

Blue Pool, or Italian Garden, at Planting Fields. Emily T. Cooperman.

Heather Garden under reconstruction and the insertion of drains. John Dixon Hunt.

The Great Bird Blind Debate featured two installations, *The Budding Blind* by David Brooks and *The Posh Blind* by Mark Dion, celebrating W. R. Coe's ornithological interests.

client and his or her designer; in how inhabitants use or want to use the house and its grounds for sport or entertainment. Changes happen. The restoration of the Heather Garden that Olmsted Brothers established on the northern edge of the property required the insertion of new French drains, an installation that will not, eventually, be visible (they have just recently been buried), so that is a change we do not see. Some of the original heathers did not tolerate the site and have been replaced by non-heathers, a change we may recognize. Other changes matured when Coe interests or pastimes were recognized and acted upon: W. R. Coe loved birds, and that interest in ornithology is visible with the establishment by the Coes of a chair of ornithology at Yale and the more recent installation of the *Great Bird Blind Debate* on the grounds of Planting Fields.

Olmsted Brothers worked at Planting Fields in many different ways—some still visible, others absorbed into the complex and changing aspects of place, like the surroundings of the Italian garden. The firm installed the Carshalton Gates, which Coe purchased in the United Kingdom and imported, and they then proposed to augment the treescape behind it.[6] They grew plants against the stone facades of the

Carshalton Gates, photograph with sketched landscape proposal by Olmsted Brothers, c. 1927. *Courtesy of the National Parks Service, Frederick Law Olmsted National Historic Site.*

house and augmented the woodlands, though these changes may be hard to discern. They added the Vista Path and plantings around the Azalea Path. We have drawings of proposals they made, sometimes with scribbled sketches of alterations about which they were thinking.

In short, Olmsted Brothers worked to change the genius of place, as they and Coe wanted. He had wanted a mansion in the fashion of an English country house, of which there were many to choose from, for country houses come in all sizes. There are those that are attached to dukedoms, such as at Blenheim (with its landscape by Brown), or to baronets, such as at Hovingham in Yorkshire, or to untitled owners who had probably existed on their estates for centuries.

Styles of architecture, interior furnishing, and gardens could be readily copied from England for the Gold Coast of Long Island, where Planting Fields is situated. British habits of hunting, shooting, and fishing also arrived, and the Gallery at Planting Fields recalls that. W. R. Coe was himself an accomplished sportsman; photographs show him in riding clothes that were imported from London, as were many of the furnishings of the house, purchased from Charles Duveen, also known as Charles of London. By contrast, Mai Coe, who had been schooled in France and was enamored of French design, found French material and interior styles apt for her reception room. No country house in England escaped the chances for and obligations of socializing, and over the years that tradition, too, was well maintained at Planting Fields, from the lavish ceremony for the marriage of the Coes' only daughter to an Italian aristocrat in 1934 (did that cause the name of the Italian Garden to be confirmed, or was it that an Italian Garden was the obvious site there?), to today's galas, weddings, garden parties, and Christmas tree lightings.

While architectural forms could be copied—the outlines and chimneys of the exterior, its half-timbering, its medieval-type gallery within—other customs could not be imitated in America. In one case, the enthusiasm for England led to a misreading. Coe's English taste clearly encouraged the Olmsted firm to look for landscape models there. When they visited Stowe for inspiration, they apparently thought its design was not by Capability Brown, but by William Kent. I have not yet identified the precise source of this Olmstedian supposition, but it is invoked by Henry B. Joyce, former director of Planting Fields, in the discussion of the "Park" in his *Guidebook*

Natalie Coe and Leonardo Vitetti on their wedding day at Planting Fields, May 19, 1934. Pach Brothers Photographers. *Planting Fields Foundation Archives.*

to Coe Hall, and it is also picked up on the same page, where it is asserted that the "Park" at Planting Fields is "Kentian": "the grounds . . . designed as an English landscape garden, a style of naturalistic landscaping invented in the 1720s by William Kent."[7] In reality, the park here is a wonderful recollection of that English tradition in its many versions, and had its inspiration long before William Kent. The importance of Kent lies principally in his nine years in Italy and on the many drawings he made of places in the United Kingdom, which reveal some Italianate allusions. These have been catalogued and discussed, along with the influence of Italy upon his work, and they show a considerable interest in what he had observed there. The issue with Kent's role at Stowe is that little of his life, drawings, and contacts was apparent at the time the Olmsteds visited. He wrote little, and nothing was known about his life and work until Margaret Jourdain's and Michael Wilson's books of 1948 and 1984.[8]

This is an error worth clearing up, especially as it can make more sense of the layout of Planting Fields as we see it today. The Olmsteds might have assumed that Kent designed Stowe on the basis of his designing several buildings in the extensive grounds there—a hermitage, the Temple of Ancient Virtue, and the Temple of British Worthies. But Kent did not design the landscape in which they were situated. In addition to being an architect, he was a painter, which is the reason he is given space in Horace Walpole's last volume of his *Anecdotes of Painting in England,* entitled the *History of the Modern Taste in Gardening,* first published in 1771.[9] The Olmsteds would undoubtedly have consulted this. But Kent was also a theater designer, and his Stowe hermitage was either the basis of this theater design or was borrowed from his theater work.

What he did at Stowe was to propose buildings, like sets on a stage, or backgrounds in painting, that helped visitors to grasp the significance of a particular moment in the theater or garden. But in none of his designs for buildings at Stowe did he lay out their surroundings (though he might have been consulted). I think part of the experience at Planting Fields is that buildings and events in the gardens, such as statues, are likewise stage sets for performance, changing over the years for residents and visitors. The alliance between stage settings and design plans has a long history, dating back to Vitruvius.

Horace Walpole promoted William Kent in his *History of the Modern Taste in Gardening* publications, and it is not therefore surprising that Kent was invoked as the inspirer of the Coe parkland. He has become a ubiquitous yet mysterious figure in the narratives of English landscaping. But he took his place in a sequence of known designers: Charles Bridgemen and Stephen Switzer before him, and after

him, Brown and Humphry Repton, only the last of whom published plans of his designs. Repton, once he decided to take up the mantle of Brown, was given a selection of Capability's drawings by his son. All of these designers invoked parkland as part of their repertoire. Walpole, for example, noted that parks dated to medieval times and still existed in later centuries to maintain deer, and that their function was to connect these with gardens.

Walpole also said that Kent was the painter who "realized the compositions of the greatest masters in painting" that would have included landscapes by Claude and Poussin. And that was why he was included in the last volume of Walpole's *Anecdotes of Painting*, though the word "realized" could mean landscaping as well as in paintings.

The *Cultural Landscape Report*, commissioned by Planting Fields Foundation and submitted in 2019, discussed the "layered past" of the site.[10] It is that palimpsest

William Kent, Stowe Hermitage as a stage design, 1730. Pencil, pen, brown and gray washes. *Sir John Soane's Museum, London.*

Humphry Repton, Red Book for Armley House, Yorkshire, 1800. *Oak Spring Garden Library, Upperville, Virginia.*

that we learn to appreciate today as individual visitors and as more research reveals those layers. Olmsted Brothers worked there between 1918, five years after Mai and William Coe purchased the site, until the late 1930s, but the gardens as we know them were first shaped by the Boston landscape architects Guy Lowell and A. Robeson Sargent, the son of Charles Sprague Sargent, who supervised Harvard University's Arnold Arboretum. The Olmsted work is attested by some aerial photographs from that period. But landscape architecture, as it is now termed, draws its ideas from an often eclectic narrative of this design art, even as it seeks to revive and remake past models in the present day. A genius of place will take many forms, both historically determined and, furthermore, offering different modes of character or "genius" within larger sites.

The term or idea of "genius of place" has several modern formulations, such as spirit of place and nature of place. The English word *spirit* certainly acknowledges that the Roman genius —maybe a divinity or fabled hero—was linked to the place and somehow expressed himself or herself there. But today we lack that full repertoire of presiding presences: thus in Susan Owens's *Spirit of Place: Artist, Writers & the British Landscape* (2020), the word proves too elusive for me, even ultimately somewhat vague.[11] By contrast, Avi Friedman's *The Nature of Place: A Search for Authenticity* (2011) is much involved with the tangible, even factual, the raw materials of built places, elements that for him determine how we respond. And then there is *Representing Place* (2002) by Edward S. Casey, who has written several studies of place and looks to how paintings and maps have sought to understand and explain it. His first chapter asks precisely "What Does it Mean to Represent Landscape," a question that all the images of Planting Fields—from old images to those taken this year—invite us to answer.[12]

Planting Fields is, as its *Strategic Plan of 2020-2023* states, a "Place of History." And history, as the authors also aver, is where "the Olmsted values of landscape design remain relevant . . . and are reflected in our experiences of greenspaces today."[13] I am by training a historian, yet for nearly thirty years, I have sought out the exciting and sometimes precarious role of adjudicating between history and its current landscape designers! Planting Fields is today an assemblage of memories, of other places, other styles of building, and decoration, and ways of bringing into this place images of places that are not here, yet implied. And I think that an approach via reminiscence, association, and even imagined recollections may prove useful here.

One of the associations latent here is derived from a military activity. In the early eighteenth century, Sir Richard Temple, later Baron and finally Viscount Cobham, raised a small detachment of soldiers from the men who worked on the Stowe estate to take them to fight in France. When they returned, the one task they could still exercise was making military fortifications so Sir Richard got them to build a ha-ha around the garden space.

That became for Stowe one of the earliest designs that would shape garden spaces within a huge landscape. The ha-ha became a crucial element in protecting land not from foreign soldiers, but from beasts and wild animals and so was able to maintain and protect a greater range of plants. Planting Fields does not have a ha-ha, but its acres, as at Stowe, engage us to focus on specific garden moments, surrounded by woodlands and open land, referred to variously as lawns, meadows, fields—terms that suggest different characters for each and for views outside. Yet the ha-ha had

Jacques Rigaud, *View of the Queen's Theatre from the Rotunda at Stowe, Buckinghamshire*, 1733–34. The ha-ha is on the right. Pen and ink, brush, and wash. Metropolitan Museum of Art, New York, Harris Brisbane Dick Fund, 1942.

an additional value, in allowing people within the safety and order of the garden to glimpse a wilder world beyond. And at Planting Fields, there was once, alas now lost, a view to the waters of Long Island Sound.

Jacopo Bonfadio and Bartolomeo Taegio, two Renaissance commentators, wrote that gardens were a "third nature," based on the second nature of human settlements, and the first, or primary world of the gods. Their purpose was to compare and dialogue with the different natures in the making of a garden.[14] We can see the distinctions clearly conceptualized in engravings of seventeenth- and eighteenth-century gardens like Stowe, and that dialogue is still around, though as at Planting Fields, these modes and juxtapositions are less visibly announced and the primary view of the Sound has been lost.

It was Cicero who explained that the world humans have devised for their own lives—houses, roads, bridges, and other infrastructures—was a second nature (*alter natura*) because the first was that of the gods. This first nature, with its terrifying aspects of volcanos and oceans, was not always understood by humans. But the two Renaissance writers saw that the rise of contemporary garden-making needed a new explanation, so they drew upon both the second and first natures to make what they decided to call a third. Now it is important to realize that this is a not a numerical absolute, but their natures were to designate different modes of *genii loci*, modes in which there was variety in all three—so by no means a univocal format. Planting Fields itself explores, often with Olmstedian ideas, different versions of wildness, domesticity, and utility.

The Renaissance gardens that Bonfadio and Taegio knew bear only a remote relationship to what Edith Wharton described in *Italian Villas and Their Gardens* (1904), but Wharton's is a study of some importance still, among the (now many) other books on this topic.

It must have been a text consulted by Lowell and Sargent in designing aspects of the Planting Fields gardens, especially the pool and terracing in the Italian garden for Mai Coe. It is apt that the 2018 guidebook features an illustration of its cover.[15]

Several emphases in Wharton's work are relevant here. Wharton is clear that the Italian house, its gardens, and the larger landscape are linked, and that this involved the "subtle transition from the fixed and formal line of art to the shifting and irregularities of nature." Among earlier writings that she quotes is Herman Tuckermann on "the relation between art and landscape [that] is reversed [today]." The "artistic progression" that she also quoted from the French Empire architects Charles Percier and Pierre Fontaine is something that was established and emerged through the landscapes of Planting Fields. In particular, Wharton approved of the Villa Lante at Bagnaia, where "the terraces and garden-architecture are skillfully blent with it, and its recesses are pierced by grass alleys leading to clearings where pools surrounded by stone seats slumber under the spreading branches."[16]

I have always thought that successful places were essentially singular; there may be others like any one, but not identical. Planting Fields is a place where many things speak of its owner, through the rich collections of architectural styles, interiors, and above all gardens. If you have ever been invited by a new acquaintance to "come over to my place," you will recognize how he or she declares themselves by what they have around them. It does not take an amateur detective or a personal obsession to be curious to read into a place or to interrogate its "stuff." Planting Fields is huge, and it is exemplary of a place that speaks of its owners and to its pasts and present. It is a rich and absorbing encounter, and it takes both an instinct to respond quickly as well as a thoughtful grasp of what such or such item may mean in the Coe family's history and our own. It requires imagination, which John Ruskin always assumed was an essential requirement for comprehending the full meaning of, say, the French Alps or Venice. Imagination is not, though, a question of fantasizing, but of an intelligent understanding of what a place signifies through its richnesses, the changes that have altered it, and how other visitors have recorded it.

In her autobiography, *A Backward Glance*, Edith Wharton commented that a critic needs to "penetrate to the very 'soul of the work contemplated' . . . to plumb the 'imponderable something' that contributed to its fullest." This is what I have tried for Planting Fields.

There are several approaches to seeing a site like Planting Fields, all 400-plus acres of it. There are at least three ways to appreciate such a place: through a map; in a drawing, painting, or still photography; and, of course, by walking through it (an experience that I suppose a movie might approximate).

Now, a map is essentially flat to the eye, though it may show contour lines that will indicate the differences in surface that would be encountered. The map of Planting Fields that was inserted in the 2018 guidebook notes where a path is steep, and that a zig-zag path negotiates the steep topography. The virtue of the map is that it shows a large extent, and within it, the connections between sections, especially for those who do not yet know the lay of the land.

But these connections are understood differently when drawn or photographed, for photographs and drawings select or even privilege one particular moment—and in the case of Planting Fields, there are many to choose from. They may hint at connections still to be encountered, as they offer glimpses of places still ahead, or they may draw out specific items and experiences within the section where one finds oneself. They are essentially picturesque, and the vogue for that aesthetic mode is huge and still rife among us, if too vague and unthoughtfully invoked. The picturesque

Looking ahead and looking back: The Surprise Pool and the walk to the Blue Pool Garden. John Dixon Hunt.

tends to eliminate how we move through scenery, yet movement is always essential in responding to and appreciating a landscape as large as Planting Fields.

Walking, on the other hand, allows us to turn around and grasp how we have gotten to that point; or it allows us to retrace our steps. But often forgotten is that from the eighteenth century onward, the picturesque entailed verbal as well as visual responses, sometimes equally skilled and effective, sometimes playing words off against the visual, or vice versa, and words might explain what the looking did not fully grasp or apprehend.

An immediate sense from the map of Planting Fields, or from any walk through its grounds, is the degree to which variety is the key characteristic. Now "variety" has always been an aesthetic term to mark landscape. Even in gardens like Versailles there is variety, though that notion would be complicated by the eighteenth century to mark individual moments of that variety rather than how variety marks the whole.

The sheer profusion of what I would call the immediate garden at Planting Fields, when encountered close to the main house, is clear enough. And we should recall that when the family lived in the house at Planting Fields, it gave them very different impressions from those offered to visitors from outside, as we all now are.

The immediate garden of azalea walks, rose gardens, greenhouses, daylily and dahlia gardens are dissolved first into open spaces, and these in their turn are drawn, by a variety of paths, into an extensive woodland that surrounds all but a fraction of the landscape. This seems to me an acknowledgment both of Wharton's sense of the formats of many Italian gardens and of how English gardens developed by design, including inheritance or circumstance, into a juxtaposition of regular and irregular topography and treatments. The Olmsteds were good at creating similar movements in their designs.

But the most striking aspect here is the plenitude of different plants, which signals this place as both arboretum and botanical garden. These are clustered to emphasize parts of what is essentially a collection of hydrangeas, hollies, heathers, magnolias, native plants, rhododendrons, camelias, cherries, taxus or yews, each of which has its own forms.

Throughout the garden, signage orients visitors, sometimes accompanied by quotations, whether from the Olmsted firm or from Frederick Law Olmsted himself, that suggest how to read what is there. Some are apt, but some leave one a touch puzzled as to the connection of the remark to what we see. I noted earlier that the picturesque was always, at its best, a moment where words and sights contributed their rival perspectives. I have spent many years working from words to images, from seen to saying, and that is a fundamental issue with responding to something as large and resonant as Planting Fields. This book "says" what it sees of the place, so it is a form of the picturesque. But as Le Corbusier said, while "we must always say what we see[, a]bove all, and more difficult, we must always see what we see," and a book such as this one, I hope, can help us to achieve that as well.[17]

View from the West Portico. Mattie Edwards Hewitt, c. 1921. *Planting Fields Foundation Archives.*

View to the West Portico. Emily T. Cooperman.

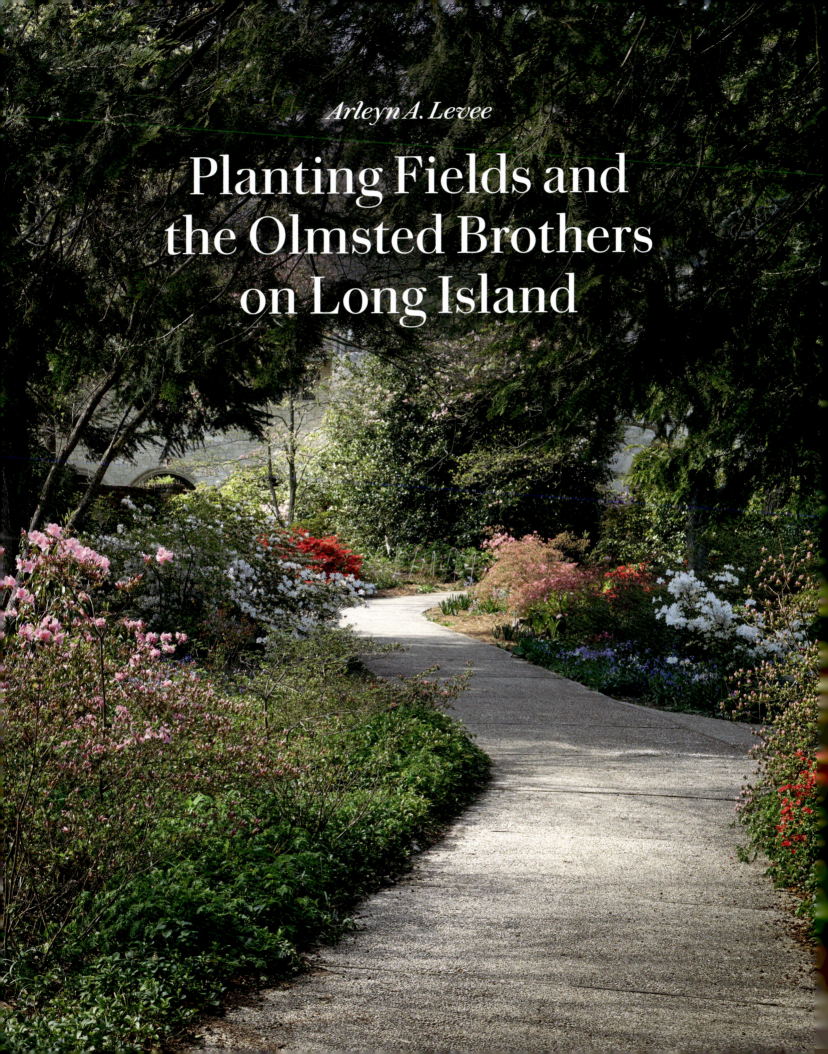

Arleyn A. Levee

Planting Fields and the Olmsted Brothers on Long Island

CHISELED BY GLACIERS AND THEN THE SEA, LONG ISLAND'S UNIQUE GEOMORPHIC character was heralded first for its agricultural and fishing advantages rather than for its extraordinary scenery. Encircled by waters, the 118-mile land mass was sculpted into alluvial moraines and outwash plains, punctuated by picturesque kettle-hole lakes, densely wooded valleys, and rolling meadows. Its northern coast of rocky escarpments with protected coves and deep harbors contrasted with the windswept dunes, sandy beaches, and narrow barrier islands along its southern edge. Numerous indigenous peoples, associated with the Algonquian confederacy who originally occupied these lands, subsisted by hunting, fishing, and some farming. Displaced by Dutch and English colonists starting in the seventeenth century, they have left their echoes in many of the place names of Long Island—Manhasset, Massapequa, Setauket, Montauk, Shinnecock.[1]

In the decades after the Civil War, the Long Island landscape increasingly drew visitors seeking leisure destinations, an allure that continues to this day. The beneficial climate in these coastal fishing communities with their horizon views and water access, or in the agrarian landscapes with their superior tilth, all beckoned the casual visitor, the real estate speculator, and the wealthy, who established country seats, many of vast acreage, dominated by grand houses with multiple outbuildings. As in other fashionable vacation destinations of the period, these new Long Island residents sought to demonstrate their wealth and taste by building ever more monumental residences, enhanced by elaborate gardens and picturesque farmsteads.

This transformation of land usage, particularly from the 1880s to the early twentieth century, forever altered the economic, political, and social realities of Long Island, changes made more profound with the consolidation of New York City in 1898. At that time, Kings County (Brooklyn) and the eastern section of Queens County, often considered part of Long Island, were annexed as boroughs of New York. The western section of Queens, now known as Nassau County, and Suffolk County became what we now know as Long Island.

FROM FREDERICK LAW OLMSTED TO OLMSTED BROTHERS

The multi-dimensional firm of Olmsted Brothers was in the vanguard of architectural advisors required to effect this metamorphosis. In the decades around the turn of the century, as its leadership passed from Frederick Law Olmsted to his sons, John Charles and Frederick Law Jr. (Rick), the firm was at the pinnacle of the embryonic profession of landscape architecture.

This was a growing firm of talented men undertaking projects of all types across the United States, in Canada, and elsewhere—and they were all men, with women in the back office, keeping the accounts, typing the letters, and managing a widespread staff.[2] The Olmsted partners and their chief associates crisscrossed the country, attending to distant clients, with the principals also involved with meetings of newly formed professional organizations such as the American Society of Landscape Architects (ASLA), which they had helped to found in 1899. Additionally, Rick Olmsted, having initiated the nation's first comprehensive degree-granting program in landscape architecture in 1900 at Harvard, was expanding this discipline into a corollary professional track of urban planning, with its own emerging associations. While John Charles Olmsted advised communities on developing park and parkway armature with associated neighborhoods, Rick worked with cities at a larger scale to meet growth demands with visionary planning.[3] Such nationwide endeavors involved business, civic, and philanthropic leaders throughout the country, many of whom became the firm's clients. There was a notable concentration of them on Long Island.

As the nationwide demands grew with calls for the brothers themselves to travel more, other professionals in the firm assumed greater responsibility for the New York clientele. In particular, James Frederick (Fred) Dawson, Percival Gallagher, Edward Clark (Ted) Whiting, Carl Rust Parker, Henry V. Hubbard, and Leon Zach, all eventually Olmsted partners, took on major design and management of projects, while Harold Hill Blossom, Hans J. Koehler, Jacob Sloet, and Hammond Sadler, among others, handled the planting requirements. Charles R. (Chick) Wait, a Harvard-trained architect with sensitivity to landscape values, designed arbors, fences, shelters, and other decorative elements. To celebrate and preserve the unique natural features of Long Island, the firm faced an ongoing struggle to persuade clients to modulate their grandiose architectural expressions.

From the 1880s, and continuing for nearly seventy years, the firm tackled more than 200 projects on Long Island alone, most of them between 1900 and 1930. The preponderance of these (162), like Planting Fields, were listed in the firm's records as "private estates or homesteads."[4] Some were simply consultations, but at least 125 properties of different sizes for clients of varied incomes advanced to design work, with some generating detailed plans numbering into the hundreds. Planting Fields was among the larger of these.[5]

Although Olmsted Brothers had designed several neighboring properties, the firm's relationship with Planting Fields did not begin until spring 1918, when W. R. Coe enlisted Fred Dawson to accommodate and develop the extant landscape surrounding a new mansion to be built after a fire had destroyed the original house on the site. This design and advisory relationship was to continue well into the 1930s.

Coe was a demanding client who often had difficulty deferring to others, but he developed respect for and dependence upon Dawson's judgment and skill and was perturbed when Dawson was not readily available to consult.[6] What emerged from their collaboration at Planting Fields was a multilayered interweaving of artful landscape and architectural design, respectful of the natural environment, which also met the challenges of owner expectations and the taste of the times. That this artistry has survived for nearly a century to educate and captivate contemporary visitors is a tribute to the alliances forged in the original relationship of client and professionals (a group that included Walker & Gillette, architects of the new house, with whom the Olmsted firm frequently collaborated). Their design skill and artistry of these professionals, together with the estate's stewards in the post-Coe eras and the present visionary planners, have made Planting Fields a model of exemplary preservation practices.

FREDERICK LAW OLMSTED'S LONG ISLAND ESTATES AND COMMUNITIES

To fully understand Planting Fields, it is important to situate the place and its patrons within the wider context of the Olmsted firm's Long Island projects. Only a few of these projects were from the hand of Frederick Law Olmsted himself, but his social concerns, design credo, and landscape values, his profound respect for natural conditions and the power of scenery, and his faith in the restorative effects of nature were fundamental to the work of Olmsted Brothers.

Beginning in 1887, the senior Olmsted was called to advise entrepreneur Bayard Cutting on his acquisition of hundreds of acres from the former Lorillard hunting grounds in Westbrook (now Great River). Seeking to preserve the natural conditions around a newly built Tudor mansion and its farmstead, Olmsted proposed a simple setting, keeping decorative garden constructions to a minimum. Instead, he emphasized the rolling meadows and densely wooded dells interspersed with marshy lowlands along the Connetquot River and recommended supplementing the native tree palette with a rich variety of native understory shrubs—rhododendron, leucothoe, holly. Respected by generations of Cuttings for the restorative pleasures of its informal landscape, the property was donated by the family to the Long Island State Park Commission in 1936. After the 1949 death of Mrs. Cutting, who had set up an endowment fund, the State of New York took full control in 1952. The Bayard Cutting Arboretum State Park opened to the public in 1954. The extraordinary woodland and riverine scenery, protected and enhanced by the Olmsted plan, thus became a oasis for all to enjoy.[7]

Even earlier, beginning in 1881, a consortium of prominent New York businessmen planning a select enclave for their families amid the windswept wildness of southern coastal scrub had requested Olmsted's advice regarding house placement

and landscape treatment. The Montauk Association was spearheaded by Arthur W. Benson, president of Brooklyn Gas Light and developer of Bensonhurst, who in 1879 had purchased 10,000 acres of wild moors from the Montauket tribe; among the Association's members were lawyers Robert and Henry de Forest, who would become significant clients of the Olmsted firm. Emphasizing the "powerful impression of the scenery . . . to be had from the higher ground," Olmsted recommended a simple but compact composition around a central clubhouse, siting seven picturesque shingle-style houses by McKim, Mead & White, all connected by paths, to take advantage of the ocean views and breezes. Although Olmsted's advice was only partially followed and today Montauk is no longer a remote outpost, the subtlety of his intention for this residential community is now recognized by its protection as a National Historic District.[8]

Westbrook, the property of W. Bayard Cutting, Great River, Long Island. The house was designed by Charles Coolidge Haight with landscape by Frederick Law Olmsted.

Montauk Association Houses sited by Frederick Law Olmsted and designed by McKim, Mead & White, mid-1880s. *Courtesy of Carlton Kelsey.*

PLANTING FIELDS AMONG OLMSTED BROTHERS ESTATE PROJECTS

Planting Fields is at once a representative example of many Olmsted Brothers estate landscapes now lost, and a distinct place shaped by and for the tastes and talents of its patrons. In the decades before the Depression, the firm had numerous residential commissions, some of great size and complexity, all being handled simultaneously, with all the challenges that accompany long-distance management. More problematic still were issues of design individuality within what were very entangled social circles. These landscapes all had their *de rigueur* elements, many also in evidence at Planting Fields: the sunken garden, ebullient with color, textures, and scents; the spacious sunny greenswards, encircled by shadowy woods and punctuated by specimen trees providing verdant foregrounds for shore views; the various water features, pools, and

Sunken garden ("Turf Court") at Black Point, Southampton, New York, the estate of H. H. Rogers, Mai Coe's brother. Samuel Gottscho, c. 1920s. *Courtesy of the National Park Service, Frederick Law Olmsted National Historic Site.*

Greensward with a view toward Long Island Sound at Ormston, Lattingtown, New York. Samuel Gottscho, c. 1920s. *Courtesy of the National Park Service, Frederick Law Olmsted National Historic Site.*

fountains introducing reflections and sparkle; the curvilinear approach road, manipulated to provide visual surprises; gazebos and teahouses for sheltered repose; vine-laden trellises and arbors separating garden rooms; the endlessly inventive sculptural adornments to terminate the axes and allées; the vegetable and cutting gardens shaped to be decoratively utilitarian; and, of course, the picturesque farmstead/cottage/greenhouse complexes, where the staff who managed all this splendor lived. Added to this would be items from a menu of tennis courts, swimming pools, bridle paths, and beach pavilions—an inventory of conventionalized features that needed to be treated with individuality and originality. The North Shore's often dramatic terrain made it challenging for designers to respect Olmsted's credo of "suitability" to preserve and enhance the quintessential natural landscape while accommodating client requests for accoutrements. Perhaps equally challenging was the need to provide the frequently neighboring properties with landscapes of unique distinction without repetition of design modalities. With their consummate design skills and discretion, the firm succeeded on both fronts more often than not. A selection of some of the significant Olmsted Long Island projects reveals the firm's many modes of design for these varied site conditions and client demands.

Garden structure at Nethermuir, Cold Spring Harbor, New York. Frederick Law Olmsted Jr., May 1914. *Courtesy of the National Park Service, Frederick Law Olmsted National Historic Site.*

Rosemary Farm, the 200-acre Lloyd Harbor property of entrepreneur Roland Ray Conklin and his wife, a former opera singer known as Mary MacFadden, presented the topographic challenges of coastal bluffs. In 1907 Philadelphia architect Wilson Eyre had sited a shingle-style house atop a hill overlooking a steep west-facing declivity with views to Long Island Sound. Beginning in 1912, Rick Olmsted was asked to transform this unstable sandy slope into a terraced garden asset. Taking the clients' interests into account, Olmsted, together with the firm's chief architect Charles Wait and a consulting engineer, developed an inspired plan. He designed a multi-tiered grass-covered amphitheater to provide a performance stage surrounded by a moat for Mrs. Conklin and her theatrical colleagues.

Conklin decided to construct it himself. Instead of the recommended rectilinear quarried stones, he used raw rounded boulders, dug from his fields, to build the walls, interspersing stones with created plant pockets. The final effect, while theatrical, contained none of the intended design refinements, though this doubtless went unnoticed when the amphitheater was used as the setting for notable performances and fundraisers for World War I causes.

With his wife's death in 1919, Conklin lost interest and sold the property to the Brooklyn Diocese for use as a seminary. Although the house burned in the 1990s, the dramatic landform of bluff and amphitheater remains, along with some other artifacts, sparking renewed appreciation for the artistry of the landscape.[9]

For Walter Jennings, a Rockefeller cousin, Rick Olmsted again took advantage of the challenging landforms of a steep Cold Spring Harbor bluff on which the estate

Rosemary Farm, Huntington, New York. Aiglon Aerial Photo Company, c. 1924. *Courtesy of the National Park Service, Frederick Law Olmsted National Historic Site.*

Performance at the amphitheatre at Rosemary Farm, probably by Isadora Duncan dancers. Frances Benjamin Johnston, c. 1915. *Library of Congress Prints and Photographs Division, LC-USZ62-116034.*

known as Burrwood was located to develop descending garden rooms. The original mansion and grounds, designed by Carrère & Hastings around 1898, needed improvements, so in 1912 Thomas Hastings requested that Olmsted develop suitable new surroundings. To one side of the expanded house, assisted by Dawson, he placed an elegantly proportioned Italianate walled garden, replete with numerous sculptural features; on the other, he created a terrace to capture the distant views overlooking a ravine garden of native plantings, with steps and landings down the steep slope to a lower pool. The varied gardens, decoratively articulated by skilled craftsmen working in brick, metal, and other materials made Burrwood a landscape of interesting juxtapositions. The family retained the property after Jennings's death in 1933, with Olmsted horticulturist Hans J. Koehler providing planting advice until the 1950s, when Burrwood became the Industrial Home for the Blind. It survived as an institution for decades, until it was resold to a developer who demolished the house and subdivided the property, leaving only scattered garden artifacts.[10]

In contrast, the landscape patterning for Ormston, the property of the utilities magnate John Aldred, was a more subtle evocation of Olmsted creativity in developing a complex but unified country estate. Beginning in 1912, Percival Gallagher fashioned a 100-acre tract of shorefront, woods, and swampy fields in Lattingtown into a landscape of axially related, orchestrated spaces with specialized garden apartments. Acceding to his client's wish for an "American estate ... [with] the character ... of old England," Gallagher included, among other features, an intimate "Elizabethan" garden with topiary and a formal rose garden bounded by a pleached hornbeam allée, surrounded by a park of textured woodlands and expansive meadows. The periphery was defined by beachfront, walls, and ancillary buildings, linked by curving drives designed to heighten the sequential experiences.[11]

The build-out of the Ormston plan lasted well into the 1930s, by which time Gallagher had died. In a 1935 tribute to his colleague, Edward Clark Whiting, now in charge of completing the project, praised the Aldreds' commitment to Gallagher's consummate artistry to shape elements of land and sky into a cohesive and exceptional expression of the landscape art. In 1944, after the Aldred fortune waned, the estate was purchased in its entirety by a Ukrainian monastic order, the Basilian Order of St. Josephat, which continues to manage it today, adapting the buildings for worship and teaching, and maintaining with pride what they can of the once-grand landscape.[12]

Less landscape subtlety was required for Oheka, the grand château designed for Otto Kahn by Delano & Aldrich in 1915 specifically to surpass the grandeur of Clarence Mackay's Harbor Hill in Roslyn and echo the design of George W. Vanderbilt's Biltmore by Richard Morris Hunt in Asheville, North Carolina.[13] The immense house was constructed on an inland site atop a man-made hill built up to enable views to the Sound. In 1917 Rick Olmsted and associates Fred Dawson and Harold Hill Blossom were engaged to develop a formal landscape appropriate to such an imposing edifice. Rather than exercising their usual picturesque landscape language, the designers refined the proportions of formal terraces, crafted a water parterre with sculptural accoutrements close to the mansion, and installed mature trees and evergreens to provide enclosure and accents. Beyond that precinct they planned a more relaxed landscape: woodlands were thickened, threaded with bridle paths, more intimate gardens created, all surrounded by an 18-hole Seth Raynor-designed golf course. After 1919 landscape architect Beatrix Farrand further reconfigured many of these spaces. Although impressive, at a mere 423 acres, the Oheka environs provided few opportunities to integrate the mansion's architectural mass artistically into its setting, as had been the case with the 125,000 acres at Biltmore.[14]

Unable to sustain Oheka after her husband's death in 1934, Mrs. Kahn transferred the estate to New York City, which used it for a time as a retreat for city sanitation workers. After World War II, the property was sold to a military academy, which caused considerable damage to the building and grounds before going bankrupt. Kahn's private golf course was acquired by the Cold Spring Country Club, while much

Oheka, Huntington, New York. Aiglon Aerial Photo Company, c. 1925. *Courtesy of the National Park Service, Frederick Law Olmsted National Historic Site.*

Entrance to the main garden at La Selva. Mattie Edwards Hewitt, c. 1920s. *Courtesy of the National Park Service, Frederick Law Olmsted National Historic Site.*

of the remaining land was subdivided. The grand castle languished for decades, saved somewhat from squatter depredations by its fireproof construction. Its slow reincarnation to its present success as a resort destination is largely due to a determined businessman pursing his dream to restore this icon, respecting the historic fabric of building and grounds, while reanimating the grandeur for a commercial purpose.[15]

La Selva, directly across the road from Planting Fields, provides a more diminutive "gem" of Olmsted landscape artistry, this time in the Italianate mode requested by the clients, financier Henry Sanderson and his wife, Elizabeth. Here, beginning in 1915, a unified composition was crafted by Fred Dawson. Well versed in the Italian aesthetic, he offset the site's modest 25 acres with plantings to achieve a sense of greater spaciousness while retaining privacy around the stucco villa by Hunt & Hunt.[16] Along the curving entrance, tree groupings screened the garage-paddock complex and a decorative vegetable garden. Terraces overlooking rolling wooded terrain expanded vistas from the loggias of the Renaissance-style mansion. This private world was further enhanced by sequenced axial garden rooms on different levels, enclosed by high walls, enlivened by sculptural panels by Johan Selmer-Larsen, and textured by wisteria arbors. A walled garden extended southward from the living room loggia, across a four-square court garden, through a *tapis vert* with planted borders to a fountain centered within a colonnaded cirque, its entrance imposingly guarded by tall columns topped by figures of a mermaid and man.[17]

Sanderson sold the property in 1927 to Frederick Wheeler of the American Can Company, who renamed it Dellwood and consulted the Olmsted firm about inserting a swimming pool and bathhouses. The estate then became a Franciscan monastery, followed by years of problematic ownership until its purchase by its present stewards, who have taken extraordinary measures to recapture the essential character of the property.[18]

The Planting Fields commission presented a different set of challenges for the Olmsted firm. The property, first patterned by James L. Greenleaf for earlier owners to surround an eclectic Grosvenor Atterbury house, was subsequently refined by Guy Lowell and A. Robeson Sargent for the new owners, William Robertson Coe and his wife, Mai Rogers Coe. In 1918 following the destruction of the house by fire, the Coes turned to the firm of Walker & Gillette to insert a new Tudor-style mansion into the existing setting. Coe and his architect, Leon Gillette, then contacted Fred Dawson to continue planning the grounds.[19] Thus began a relationship between the designers and a demanding, periodically parsimonious, and often testy client with grand ideas, which would continue for more than a decade. The task was to transform the property into a uniquely balanced complex of primary and ancillary buildings and landscapes, some highly articulated, others seemingly "natural." While respecting the designs of the earlier professionals, Dawson and his colleagues had to subtly refine and expand upon what had been established and integrate new features, substantial new plantings, and new acreage into a cohesive example of the landscape art, while accommodating W. R. Coe's significantly developed horticultural interests.[20]

As was the Olmsted practice, the first task was to have a comprehensive survey made of the property. Initial projects involved siting a more graceful approach drive; developing several terraces to relate new house arcades with sequenced garden rooms and richly planted pathways; and improving circulation routes to link various areas and accessory structures, such as the new Camellia House built for W. R. Coe's extraordinary collection. Beyond the structured kitchen and cutting gardens with their espaliered fruit trees, formality relaxed into a more sylvan environment of shadowy wooded bays and headlands encircling large swaths of undulating fields, giving an illusion of expansive space for important vistas.

The camellias were a source of particular pride, pleasure, and pain to W. R. Coe. The collection was originally imported before World War I from Guernsey, probably with encouragement from the Coes' previous landscape advisor A. Robeson Sargent. Coe later involved the Olmsted firm in developing horticulturally suitable and attractively augmented greenhouses to display his sizable plants. Often photographed, including by Mattie Edwards Hewitt, or featured in exhibitions, the collection suffered several devastations, notably a greenhouse roof collapse in February 1920 and

Terrace study for Planting Fields by A. J. Scholtes, with a proposed tree sketched into the existing landscape, 1918. *Courtesy of the National Park Service, Frederick Law Olmsted National Historic Site, #06645-35 tp2.*

Yew tree delivered to Planting Fields by Faulk & Company, c. 1925. *Planting Fields Foundation Archives.*

Arrival of the beech trees from Mai Coe's family home in Fairhaven, Massachusetts, at Oyster Bay wharf, 1915. W. R. Coe is at right. *Planting Fields Foundation Archives.*

a destructive fire in January 1924. Dawson and Carl Rust Parker tried to put a value on the rare plants that had been destroyed and to get plant importation restrictions eased so that unusual species could be recollected from abroad.[21]

Ever the serious horticultural collector, Coe ordered plants by the carload, particularly rhododendrons, azaleas, and other ericaceous material in addition to his beloved camellias. Many were imported from foreign purveyors. In February 1919, he ordered 2,000 rhododendron from the noted John Waterer Nursery in Surrey, England, and in April had an order placed for azalea kaempheri and Japanese iris from the Yokohama Nursery in Japan.[22] He shepherded the installation of specimen trees, either purchased from Hicks or other Long Island nurseries, or from other estates, or found in the woodlands.

Dawson's own horticultural expertise made him a reliable advisor, augmented by the skills of Blossom, Koehler, and Sloet as they worked to texture the planted borders.[23] Dawson's tasks for Coe extended far beyond landscape advice to selecting capable property and farmstead managers and guiding Coe's acquisition of suitable sheep and cattle breeds.

Coe made other acquisitions as well, notably the eighteenth-century Carshalton Gates, which had once graced the entrance to an English park. Purchased in England in 1921, they were shipped to Oyster Bay, arriving in spring 1922. In order to respect the scale and stature of this sizable but delicately wrought ironwork, Dawson had to convince Coe to purchase more land to develop a spacious foreground at the chosen entrance rather than a "straightway approach." To further enhance this purchase, Coe authorized the construction of a new curving beech-lined approach drive and engaged Walker & Gillette to develop a gate lodge and walls, which they planned in Georgian style to match the gates rather than the Elizabethan house. It was not until 1927, three years after Mai Coe's death, that the Gates ensemble—the last major project that Dawson developed for Coe—was installed.[24]

In 1933, at the behest of Marion Taber of the New York State Charities Association, Fred Dawson wrote a narrative of the Planting Fields development to be used for a tour. He described the landscape as a "fairyland" of agricultural fields interspersed with a park of "velvet-like lawns bordered by flowering trees and plants;" of great terraces off the Elizabethan house with vistas and walks bordered by herbaceous plants, planned to a color scheme; of specialized gardens such as the Heather Garden, framed by trees and of the entrance through the "great gates" augmented by the "indescribable beauty" of the masses of flowering dogwoods and azaleas. Modestly noting his role in helping this development, he fully credits leadership of "Mr. Coe's own personal interest in things of beauty, his love for fine architecture and his rare and unusual love and knowledge of trees and plants."[25]

THE PRATTS AND THE DE FORESTS

Beginning in 1905, Rick Olmsted was engaged to develop a long-range improvement plan for Queens and Brooklyn.[26] It was this study that first brought him into the civic and philanthropic orbits of Robert de Forest—one of the original members of the Montauk Association—and Frederic Pratt, president of the Pratt Institute, both of whom then asked for his advice regarding their Long Island properties.

W. R. Coe in the Blue Pool Garden at Planting Fields. Mattie Edwards Hewitt, 1921. *Courtesy of Nassau County Photo Archive.*

The de Forest family clustered around Cold Spring Harbor, with speculative land ventures in Centerport. In 1906 Rick Olmsted gave planting advice for the surrounds of Wawapeck, Robert de Forest's picturesque Grosvenor Atterbury–designed house, set within a 600-acre family holding of woods and meadows. Today some of the landscape remains as a passive preserve of woodland trails.[27] At the same time, work began to improve the estate known as Nethermuir, belonging to Robert's brother, Henry. In 1906, evaluating the extant conditions, Rick Olmsted thought the existing formal garden "half-baked," the steep access roads problematic, and cluttered with entirely too many trees for such a small site. Together with Edward Clark Whiting and Harold Hill Blossom, he set about refining the disparate parts into an integrated artistic composition that better fit into its natural landforms. High stone walls retaining the wooded hillsides protected an elongated garden, which he redesigned to emphasize a forced perspective along its length to a terminal feature. Within this space he contrasted central grass panels against lush herbaceous borders intersected by axial paths, while at the edges the warmth of the walls encouraged rich displays of plantings and climbing vines. An elevated shelter, a teahouse, and arbors provided suitable places to view this flowery bounty. In the rest of the property, he integrated Henry de Forest's house and that of Henry and Robert's sister, Julia, with sweeps of mixed trees and shrubs. The Olmsted work on Nethermuir lasted into the 1930s.[28] Today, the property (the house is no longer extant), now incorporated into the Cold Spring Harbor Laboratory campus, has been subdivided into parcels, with Airslie, Julia de Forest's house, as well as a stable, a pumphouse, a few garden walls, and plantings remaining to affirm a previous form.[29]

The Pratt family holdings were vast, more than 1,000 acres encompassing Glen Cove and beyond, in an area that had been named Dosoris Park.[30] This land was originally owned in common by the six sons and two daughters of the petroleum pioneer Charles Pratt. Beginning in 1905, and for more than thirty years thereafter, Rick Olmsted and the firm advised the Pratt family on landscape shaping, management, and garden room designs for their extensive holdings and for their individual properties, several clustered along the shore.[31] Reflecting changing tastes, most of the original picturesque wooden houses owned by the Pratt siblings were replaced by grander brick or stone structures with new landscape surrounds, presumably obliterating much of the earlier Olmsted work. These large properties have now been variously repurposed as a school, a retirement home, even as a Russian diplomatic retreat. Welwyn, the estate of Harold and Harriet Pratt, survives, though significantly altered. The remnants of Olmsted planning can be seen in the approach drives and location of outbuildings, many now standing as graffitied skeletons. How much of the more extensive Olmsted work and tree plantings remains is unclear and in need of further study. The mansion itself is now occupied by the Holocaust Memorial and Tolerance Center of Nassau County, with 200 acres of woods and beachfront protected as a county preserve.[32]

Beyond the various landscape plans within individual Pratt estates, Rick Olmsted had been consulted as early as 1906 to advise the trustees on distribution of the commonly held property. While respecting views and landscape features, he was asked to offer recommendations on boundary modifications, equitable distribution of land parcels for future generations, and management of the joint undertakings, such as the farm and dairy. The Pratt holdings were a widespread complex of scenic pastures, woodlands, beachfronts, farmsteads, and workers' cottages, with newly added sports facilities, managed from an administrative core in an area known as The Oval. An early Olmsted project was to give dignity and grace to this elliptical collection of utilitarian staff buildings, workshops, stables, and offices for the head of each family grouping.[33] However, the more important goal was to guide the family toward practical and equitable decisions that would sustain wise management of real estate assets while protecting inherent values of harmony and unity in the landscape.

By 1934 the Pratt brothers had decided to give up the farm and administrative groupings and approached Olmsted Brothers to help to revise roads and entrances in their estates. On the land between Crescent Beach, Woolsey Avenue, and Dosoris Lane, Harriet Pratt instructed Carl Rust Parker to lay out house sites on 70 acres. She had purchased mature plant material from Hicks Nursery, removed from their fields due to the construction of the Northern State Parkway, and directed Parker to embellish the properties of the newly planned neighborhood.[34]

SUBDIVISIONS AND RESORTS

That the Olmsted firm was hired to plan a community of this sort—and at the behest of one of its wealthy residential clients—was far from unusual. There are twenty-six commissions for subdivisions and resorts in Nassau and Suffolk Counties. One of the first was in Montauk, following Frederick Law Olmsted's earlier work there.

With the death of Arthur W. Benson in 1889, his son Frank Sherman Benson took over the land development. A portion of the original 10,000 acres had previously been sold to Austin Corbin, then president of the Long Island Rail Road, who had a plan to dock transatlantic passenger ships at Fort Pond Bay, with the trip into New York City to be continued by train. In 1897–88, anticipating this LIRR proposal, Benson hired John Charles Olmsted to plan a subdivision for the property known as Wompenanit, stretching from the Island's tip to Lake Munchogue and along the south shore.

With surveyor Gordon Taylor, Olmsted tramped over the windy wild dunes to lay out lots and roads, working with topographic and other site features to place house plots without obstructing view corridors. This development scheme was short-lived, due primarily to the 1897 economic downturn, though the notoriety caused by Theodore Roosevelt's quarantining his returning Rough Riders on this isolated land to prevent the spread of yellow fever probably did not help.[35]

Returning in 1904 to plan another Benson residential enterprise farther along the south coast known as Hither Hills-Hither Woods, John Charles Olmsted wrote to his wife of regret to be planning for houses to interrupt the starkly beautiful sweep of natural meadows and shorefront dunes. As at Wompenanit, implementation of the Olmsted plan was beset by obstacles, including lawsuits brought by the indigenous people now protesting the original Benson acquisition.[36]

By 1924 much of the undeveloped acreage was condemned by Robert Moses as chairman of the Long Island State Park Commission to create the Hither Hills State Park and Montauk Point State Park. Around the same time, Carl Fisher, a successful Miami developer, purchased the remaining acreage to create a club and cottage colony for an anticipated sportsmen's resort. He quickly built a large hotel and some houses, the latter possibly along roads originally laid out by the 1904 Olmsted plan. This enterprise went bankrupt after 1929.[37]

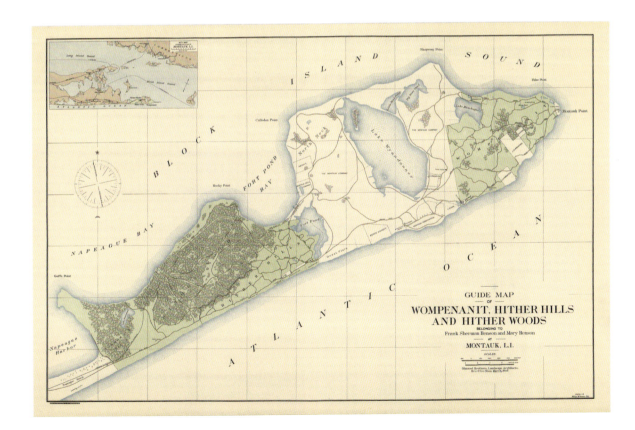

Guide Map of Wompenanit, Hither Hills and Hither Woods Belonging to Frank Sherman Benson and Mary Benson, 1905. *Courtesy of the National Park Service, Frederick Law Olmsted National Historic Site.*

Railroad and real estate interests again converged for another such venture, this time encompassing 2,700 acres on the isthmus between the Atlantic and Peconic Bay, also disputed indigenous land. This effort reunited childhood friends from Central Park days, John Charles and landscape architect Downing Vaux, the son of Calvert Vaux. Employed in 1906 by William C. Redfield of the Shinnecock Hills & Peconic Bay Realty Company, they planned curvilinear roads with diversely sized villa lots, as well as grounds for the Canoe Inn (still extant), on the scenic rolling terrain romantically depicted in the paintings of William Merritt Chase. Chase's Art Colony, the Shinnecock Golf Club (1892), and numerous private properties were encompassed by the scheme; among these was a large property belonging to the family of Grosvenor Atterbury, architect of the first house at Planting Fields. Although three Long Island Rail Road stations were included, the area did not yet have enough appeal for the intended middle-income families, and much of the land remained undeveloped until decades later. This was the last major involvement of John Charles Olmsted in Long Island projects, as he turned his focus toward building the firm's West Coast clientele.[38]

Over the succeeding decades, the Olmsted firm would plan approximately thirteen more subdivisions on Long Island, from Great Neck to Stony Brook to Fishers Island, of differing scales and complexity. Among these, the transformation of the 4,000 acres of Fishers Island, with its glaciated topography of hills, ponds, and salt marshes, and its jagged rock-strewn coastline, was the most complicated. Closer to the Connecticut shore than to New York, Fishers Island, a segment of the same terminal moraine that shaped Long Island's North Fork, had a complex territorial history, which was resolved in 1879, when it was administratively joined to the Town of Southold in Suffolk County. The Ferguson family had managed the island for generations, mostly for agriculture and fishing with some vacation cottages. In the fever of 1920s real estate speculation, they hired Frederick S. Ruth, a successful developer with Olmsted experience to create an exclusive resort club colony with Rick Olmsted as his land planner.[39] Beginning in 1924, Rick, together with his colleagues Henry Hubbard and Leon Zach and golf course designer Seth Raynor, explored the island, analyzing locations for a clubhouse with amenities, golf courses, a central dock, and diverse lot locations while emphasizing protection for the extensive and fragile natural moorland as an open wild common.

Incorporating infrastructure for this narrow island—roads, cables for electricity and telephone, pipes for fresh water and sewer systems, etc., all without damaging the land and viewsheds—required more than 1,500 plans, making this one of the largest projects in the Olmsted office.[40] This careful planning retained the distinctive picturesque blend of land and water, balancing individual property privacy with public spaces, characteristics that continue to be protected over the decades.

What is clear here, as in so many other instances, is that the advice of the firm's principals went beyond simple land-shaping. They had become very astute at assessing short- and long-term investment risks, understanding that working with, rather than distorting, natural conditions was economically productive and that following good design standards usually had future benefits for the greater community.

More modest in scale and complexity than Fishers Island, Munsey Park in Manhasset originated as a 700-acre property bequeathed by publisher Frank Munsey to the Metropolitan Museum of Art in 1926. This consisted of his estate and various abutting speculative acquisitions.[41] Robert de Forest, chair of the board of trustees,

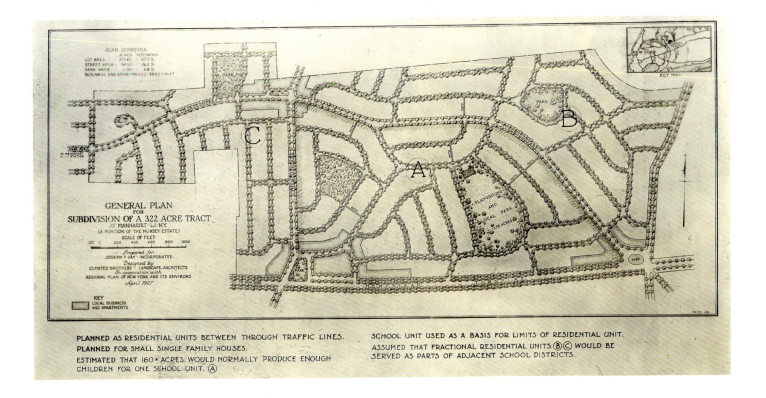

Plan for Munsey Park, a subdivision of "small single family houses" at Manhasset, New York, 1927. *Courtesy of the National Park Service, Frederick Law Olmsted National Historic Site.*

champion of progressive causes, and an Olmsted client, was determined to oversee the best use for this bequest, to make it an example of good planning principles then being espoused by the Regional Plan for New York and Environs, rather than having the land auctioned off to be gridded for maximum profit. To that end, in 1927 the museum engaged Edward Clark Whiting to develop a portion of the bequest into an affordable self-contained neighborhood of tree-lined streets curving around the topography, with many named for artists to reflect the museum affiliation. The road system was planned to connect to the major transportation arteries and the train station but to discourage cut-through traffic to retain privacy and safety within. Park and playground amenities with districts for schools and shopping augmented the plan. Heralded in its time as innovative, Munsey Park's thoughtful concept continues to sustain value, now managed as an incorporated village within Hempstead.[42]

Further east along the North Shore, well beyond the heralded Gold Coast, the Olmsted design pedigree also held allure for real estate developers serving a more modest clientele. In the historic Three Villages area (Old Field, the Setaukets, and Stony Brook), some of the fragile coastal land was initially utilized for sand and gravel extraction, crucial for all the island's building activity. With the aim of transforming the dredging-scarred shoreline and depressed area into prosperous yet affordable residential communities, the Melville family, with strong ties to these villages, sought to recapture their bygone charm.[43] In 1928 they hired Edward Clark Whiting to design Old Field South, a community intended to evoke a colonial village, in the same vein as the one John D. Rockefeller was constructing in Williamsburg, Virginia. The timing was unfortunate, however, as the economic dislocations of the Depression years disrupted the full build-out according to plans. Still, today the homeowners association acknowledges the Olmsted design heritage.[44]

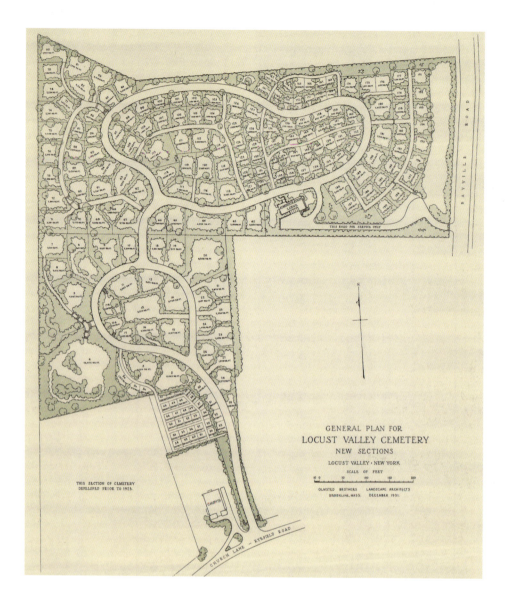

General Plan for Locust Valley Cemetery, New Sections, 1931. W. R. Coe and Caroline Coe are buried in Lot 125. *Courtesy of the National Park Service, Frederick Law Olmsted National Historic Site.*

THE CONTINUING OLMSTED/COE RELATIONSHIP

In a 1914 letter to Henry de Forest, Rick Olmsted noted that his controlling design motive was always to capture and preserve for his clients "a certain type of quiet, peaceful, beautiful landscape, self-contained and admirably secluded from outside distractions, sufficiently large and intricate to have some of the charms of mystery and variety yet thoroughly self-consistent and harmonious as a landscape type." Though he might easily have been writing about plans for a country estate, the commission in question was the design for a de Forest family burial site.[45] More than a decade later, in 1925, after the death of Mai Coe in December 1924, W. R. Coe also engaged the firm for such a project.[46]

The concentration of works under the typology heading "Cemeteries, burial grounds…" may be the most surprising aspect of Olmsted projects on Long Island.[47] There are some forty of these listings, of which two are for sizable additions to existing cemeteries, the Memorial Cemetery of St. John's Church in Laurel Hollow and the Locust Valley Cemetery. Some of these new areas to be designed by the firm were laid out in traditional rows of marked plots set amid swaths of lawn, but more than thirty-five of these commissions were for individual family "rooms." This was, in fact, a design modality that the Olmsted firm had mastered: specialized landscaped spaces intended to be contemplative and private, separated by enclosing decorative boundary plantings, yet interwoven into the surrounding terrain, and variously furnished with walls, steps, paving stones, and markers. Not only did their prominent clientele choose a thoughtful Olmsted surround for their dwellings, but they desired this aesthetic for their final resting places.

In its cemetery projects, as in all its undertakings, the Olmsted firm strove for subtle artistry, enhancing the innate beauty of the chosen sites and respecting the

Maquette for siting the Coe mausoleum in the Memorial Cemetery, Laurel Hollow, New York. *Courtesy of the National Park Service, Frederick Law Olmsted National Historic Site.*

Coe mausoleum, as built and planted. Carl Rust Parker, 1937. *Courtesy of the National Park Service, Frederick Law Olmsted Historic Site.*

integral land forms, while also endeavoring to dignify the personal wishes of each client. In both of the Long Island cemeteries greatly shaped by the Olmsted firm, the existing topography was an essential partner. A considerable amount of skillful regrading was required to develop level areas, with slopes retained by various wall forms, some of rustic fieldstone, others ashlar with bluestone coping, usually at a height to encourage seating for contemplation. Steps of all characters eased accessibility, some bluestone slabs built into walls, others as stepping stones more in keeping with woodland paths. The de Forest gravesite set a pattern of using a multilayered native plant palette, from ground cover to tree canopy. As dictated by site conditions and clients' tastes, some sites used headstones to establish the family setting; others used a central structure. Many followed the de Forests' early example of using flat stones as grave markers, allowing the landscape setting to dominate. For his part, W. R. Coe opted for construction of an elegant stone mausoleum, designed by Leon Gillette.

Olmsted Brothers generally produced models to illustrate their intentions, and this proved a very effective tool, given the complicated grading often needed. Such a maquette was essential to expedite the design and development process for the challenging plot W. R. Coe had purchased in the Memorial Cemetery. Rather than the ample valley plot he had first been offered, he had chosen a small, wooded lot on a downhill slope at the junction of two roads. Although Dawson wanted to lay out the site personally, Coe was too impatient to await his trusted designer's September 1925 return from Palos Verdes, California. The arrangements were managed in Dawson's place by Hans J. Koehler, the firm's knowledgeable plantsman, who had worked on many of the other memorial sites.[48]

Great diplomacy was required to adjust Coe's architectural and planting expectations to the realities of the difficult site. He wanted all decorative plant material, such as rhododendron, kalmia, and hemlocks, to come from Planting Fields, but he then grumbled that everything was planted too closely under the extant oaks. Ultimately, he was convinced that this approach created a sense of seclusion in the exposed setting. Gillette met the site's architectural challenges with a small temple completed in 1927, a graceful octagonal structure with Corinthian columns and the Coe name prominently incised over the door.[49]

While the firm provided landscape advice for W. R. Coe's acquisition in 1930 of Cherokee Plantation, an expansive property near Charleston, South Carolina, at Planting Fields the Olmsted Brothers involvement was winding down, largely limited in the 1930s to refining garden areas. Aided by Carl Rust Parker, Dawson advised on new greenhouse construction for hibiscus and acacia collections and on installing antique doorways, columns, and statues, mostly acquired from Howard studios in New York, to grace these structures. The problems of maintaining these decorative features filled much of the final 1930s correspondence.

Unlike the Pratts or the de Forests, Coe seems to have been uninterested in speculative development of Long Island real estate, though in late 1935, at an economic low point, he had the Olmsted firm produce a subdivision plan with about thirty-three sizable lots for the Planting Fields property. He did not pursue this venture when he realized the considerable expenditure he would be required to make to provide necessary infrastructure.[50] Instead, as his health declined in later years, he made other arrangements for his cherished estate. By time of Coe's death in March

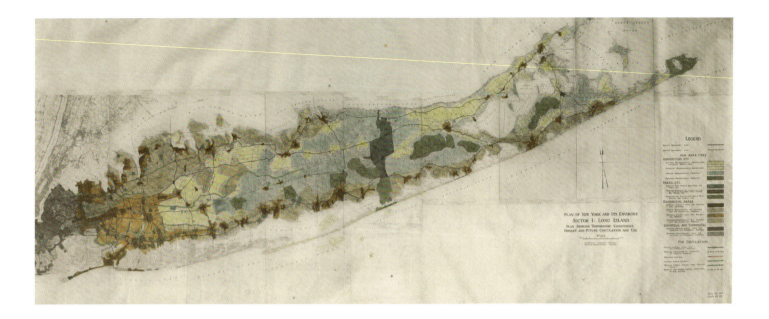

Plan of New York and Its Environs, Sector 1: Long Island, Plan Showing Topographic Conditions, Present and Future Circulation and Use, June 1923. *Courtesy of the National Park Service, Frederick Law Olmsted National Historic Site.*

1955, many of the other great Gold Coast estates had been dismantled, and his former Olmsted firm advisors were also gone. Gallagher had died early in 1934 and Dawson in 1941. Rick Olmsted had meanwhile retired to California, where he would die in 1957. It was Carl Rust Parker who replied to a 1955 request for plan copies from Planting Fields' next, if not final, occupant, the Long Island Agricultural Institute of the State University of New York. A new chapter had begun.

CONCLUSION

Over the course of their long practice from the late nineteenth century to the 1970s, Olmsted Brothers collaborated with numerous architects, some with great regularity, to design settings for diverse endeavors, whether for residential or institutional ventures. Architectural colleagues came to rely on the suitability of the Olmsted landscape aesthetic and advice by individual practitioners to appropriately settle and enhance their structures to serve their intended function without undue manipulation. Of the fifteen or so varied but distinctive Long Island projects designed by Walker & Gillette from around 1913 to the Depression, for example, a majority had Olmsted Brothers landscapes, either by Gallagher or Dawson, a remarkable record of design collaboration between architect and landscape architect that speaks to the Olmsted firm's stylistic versatility and ability to respond to diverse site demands—and to the demands of a distinguished roster of influential clients.

Many members of this coterie of politically powerful civic leaders, bankers, businessmen, and philanthropists were vital to the nascent regional planning efforts for New York. After becoming a city of five boroughs in 1898, New York, as the hub of a metropolis that included the Long Island counties, was beset by uncontrolled population growth, deplorable housing, chaotic transportation, immovable congestion, and fragmentary administration—all of which were unhealthy and certainly bad for business. In 1922 the Russell Sage Foundation, led by Robert de Forest, convened the most innovative thinkers from many disciplines to address these challenges.

From this gathering emerged a multivolume study, *Regional Plan for New York and Environs,* and a self-renewing organization, the still-influential non-profit Regional Plan Association, which celebrated its centennial in 2022 and issued its fourth regional plan in 2017.[51]

Rick Olmsted was among these "thinkers," following his father's work of sixty years earlier. For the senior Olmsted, the park innovations were always keystones in a more comprehensive scheme. He had intended them to be part of an armature upon which to build a more livable city without the mind-numbing, dominating rectilinear street layout. In New York, the grid was too powerful, though Olmsted's concept took root elsewhere.[52]

In 1922 planning at the regional level was an innovative effort. There were few experienced practitioners with such a broad scope, little cohesion about data collection and analysis, almost no political power to enforce, and minimal funding sources. Rick Olmsted brought to this challenge his landscape perspective, his strategic city planning expertise, and his knowledge of Long Island; he was assigned Nassau and Suffolk counties for the 1923 Report. His main concerns were transportation corridors to connect to the urban core; protection of the historic, ecological, and recreational assets of the island; and the development of necessary administrative and legal mechanisms to enable and support such planned endeavors.[53] Long-range environmental considerations and social equity were not yet on the agenda. Since the report did not recommend Long Island as a site for satellite industrial towns, residential planning was mainly to be for people of middle incomes, as was transportation. Enamored of the automobile, Olmsted thought in terms of parkway connectors rather than a future public transit network. The Regional Plan would eventually help facilitate the suburbanization of Long Island, as the changing economic realities brought about the dismantling of many great estates of the North Shore.

Though he frequently criticized the Regional Plan as elitist, Robert Moses, under the aegis of both the Port Authority and the Long Island State Park Commission, would later implement—and take credit for—many of Olmsted's ideas. Although the great estates themselves largely disappeared, the thoughtful planning by the Olmsted firm had, in fact, protected numerous special site features, many of which appealed to Moses for preserves—as long as he did not first decide to run a parkway through them.[54]

That Planting Fields did not suffer the fate that befell so many other Long Island estates is a tribute to W. R. Coe. Whether from pride of ownership, financial planning, or more philanthropic motives, Coe made a commitment to protect the multilayered landscape and architectural artistry that he and his creative advisors had developed over the decades. His 1952 transfer of the property to New York State for educational purposes was visionary; the 1972 recognition of the site's horticultural collections as the Planting Fields Arboretum State Historic Park and its 1979 listing on the National Register of Historic Places have enabled this carefully protected estate to educate the public about its design and historic significance, more than merely as a protected preserve.

Today, as a collaborative endeavor between the New York State Office of Parks, Recreation and Historic Preservation and the Planting Fields Foundation, the property provides a notable example of visionary stewardship management, planning, and outreach to a broad range of constituencies. In caring for the multiple aspects of its built and natural environments, the leadership has looked to educating audiences about the history, diversity, complexity, and significance of its holdings, while supporting the simple enjoyment of its landscape spaces. With its recent in-depth landscape evaluation by Heritage Landscapes, Planting Fields is actively addressing the climatic challenges to its arboricultural ecosystems, serving as a critical model for other institutions, public and private. And with the curation of its considerable and growing archive, it provides an inspiring opportunity for future scholarship to better understand the social, political, and environmental implications of Long Island's historic designed environments.[55]

Patricia M. O'Donnell

A Historic Landscape Evolving Sustainably

Planting Fields is a striking and nuanced historic designed landscape. It is naturalistic and yet highly contrived; it is a former private estate and an evolving public garden. It includes a remarkable collection of rare plant specimens along with increasingly important natural habitat. It embodies both the legacy and vision of W. R. Coe, his designers, and superintendents. The landscape of Planting Fields is both history and prologue, past and future.

This duality requires a balanced approach to the care and management of the landscape. Heritage Landscapes has provided a roadmap for such a balanced approach . . . that gives reasoned weight to preserving and enhancing the property's pre- and post-Coe era landscape features; and it is a roadmap that encourages us to carefully consider the property's natural heritage value as part of a contemporary and evolving urban landscape

—From the foreword to the *Planting Fields Cultural Landscape Report*.[1]

THE DESIGNED LANDSCAPE OF PLANTING FIELDS THAT WE KNOW TODAY BEARS witness to more than a century of continuity and change. Although the land itself has been inhabited and cultivated for millennia, the modern phase of Planting Fields starts in 1904 and evolves with Helen Macgregor Byrne and James Byrne's land purchases that reach nearly 378 acres of Oyster Bay real estate by 1912.[2] Helen Byrne developed the gardens around her newly constructed mansion with landscape architect James Greenleaf. The circular pool off what we now know as the Cloister Garden dates from this period. With the acquisition of the property by William Robertson Coe and Mai Coe in 1913, design of the landscape shifted to Andrew Robeson Sargent; the design of the sunken Blue Pool (or Italian) Garden is largely his work. The fruitful collaboration between Sargent and Coe, which continued until the spring of 1918, ended with Sargent's sudden death and the loss of the original house to fire just a few weeks later. From that point forward, and into the 1930s, Coe worked closely with the Olmsted Brothers, with James Frederick Dawson, principal, as the third set of landscape architects to be engaged to shape what had grown to a 409-acre estate.[3] W. R. Coe was a knowledgeable, enthusiastic plant aficionado and the Planting Fields grounds staff carried out much of the work under Coe's and Dawson's direction. The period in which an individual owner of Planting Fields acted as the primary custodian of continuity and change came to an end with the death of Coe in 1955 and the transfer of ownership to the State of New York. A clear 1955 aerial photograph viewing from the south captures the property as developed by Coe to this date. Coe's interest in education informed the addition of horticultural collections with the Synoptic Gardens educational collection and an expanded arboretum in the early years of New York stewardship.

In 2019 my firm, Heritage Landscapes, was engaged by the Planting Fields Foundation to work with them in collaboration with the New York State Office of Parks, Recreation, and Historic Preservation to develop a historically grounded landscape renewal plan for the future of the Planting Fields site. This was to be based in preservation, while recognizing that visitor experience, management, and sustainability needed to be important vectors moving forward. The *Planting Fields Cultural Landscape Report* (CLR) was crafted from a detailed study of the designed features and natural character of the historic landscape, and through the active engagement of the key stakeholders. This document lays the foundation and provides details for

Aerial image of Planting Fields at the close of the Coe era, c. 1955. *Planting Fields Foundation Archives.*

implementation of a series of sensitive, historically informed interventions to preserve and uplift this public place.

The plan intertwines concerns for heritage preservation and sustainability with contemporary best landscape practices. It recognizes both the cultural value of Planting Fields as a significant place and the necessity of situating it within a context framed by the three pillars of economy, environment, and society. The plan aligns with the agenda articulated in the United Nations Sustainable Development Goals adopted in 2015. This thoughtful work also recognizes that creativity, funding, and action are necessary to address biodiversity loss and the climate emergency crises.[4] Charting a course to reduce the carbon footprint advances the property toward net zero drawdown through a combination of green energy generation from solar power and carbon sequestration in woodland and fields.

The human and financial resources available to manage and maintain Planting Fields today are a fraction of those provided during the period of private ownership, and real-world capabilities have had to be factored into each recommendation. Still, each step forward can, to greater and lesser degrees, uplift the historic landscape, enhance habitat and ecology, welcome diverse visitors, tell inclusive stories, adjust for feasible maintenance, and integrate resilience and action in response to deepening environmental challenges both here and worldwide.

PLANTING FIELDS: PLANNING FOR PRESERVATION

Underlying every detail of the CLR is the recognition of the importance of Planting Fields as one of the very few surviving and essentially intact Gold Coast estates among the many that were shaped by the firm of Olmsted Brothers in the early twentieth century, when hundreds of such properties were created on the North Shore of Long Island. By the 1990s, the State of New York had begun assembling and assessing historical documentation for the site, and that preliminary work yielded draft historic narratives and landscape plans keyed to specific dates in the property's evolution. These served as a first step toward preparing the current CLR as a comprehensive planning document.

In developing any document like the CLR, the preservation landscape architecture team's process follows a logical course of tasks to gain deep understanding of the place, to build the required basis for recommendations, and to reach consensus on the way forward. These collaborative tasks include:

—Conduct research to document the historic landscape
—Detail current character and uses of the landscape and future objectives
—Analyze landscape integrity noting both continuities and changes
—Investigate the legibility of the historic landscape in the site as it now exists
—Select from the U.S. Secretary of the Interior four preservation treatment approaches
—Provide a landscape preservation vision and an implementation plan to meet objectives
—Advance recommendations for sustainable uses, ecology, and management at Planting Fields

Preservation is often considered a freeze frame, with a single moment in history as its taskmaster. Best preservation practices, however, insist on broad respect not only for what once was, but also for what we inherit today. Once identified and confirmed through research and field observation, the authentic contributing features of the landscape require protection, care, and integration with future actions. Changes to address current and future needs and goals are carried out within a context of respect for heritage. Although accurately rebuilding documented lost features may be feasible, preservation does not demand returning features that are missing or degraded or focusing on a particular moment in time.

Federal preservation standards define four approaches to undertake work in a historic landscape such as Planting Fields.[5] These entail varying degrees of intervention. It is important to note that the alternative treatments are not mutually exclusive. Although one overarching approach can be determined, certain areas or features within a landscape may warrant a focused intervention that varies from the overall treatment approach.

Preservation protects and stabilizes. It is the act or process of applying measures necessary to sustain the existing form, integrity, and materials of a historic property. Work generally focuses on the ongoing maintenance and repair of historic features to match the original, rather than on extensive replacement or new construction. Preservation is a modest intervention that emphasizes stabilization and repair. It is an appropriate choice for stewardship and sustainability when many original elements are intact, when interpretive goals can be met within the existing conditions, and/or when financial resources or staffing are limited. To conserve, maintain, and repair extant historic features, preservation is the treatment approach that underlies the three more intensive preservation treatments, *restoration, reconstruction,* and *rehabilitation*, which are often applied in combination.

Restoration is the act or process of accurately bringing back the form, features, and character of a property as it appeared at a particular time. A restoration approach seeks first to preserve, through stabilization and repair, all historic fabric remaining from the period of significance, and then to reinstate lost character or renew degraded materials and features. Restoration requires and is informed by a high level of documentation that supports a fact-based intervention with very limited speculation. Restoration treatment may also target the removal of contemporary landscape elements. While taking a restoration approach, functional issues such as visitor safety and service access are only accommodated as they originally were, or in the least conspicuous manner possible.

Reconstruction is defined as the act recreating, by means of new construction, the form, features, and detailing of a non-surviving site, landscape, building, structure, or object, for the purpose of replicating its appearance at a specific period and in its historic location. Reconstruction requires detailed documentation to construct an exact replica of a contributing landscape feature with limited speculation.

Rehabilitation is defined as the process of making possible a compatible use for a property through repair, alterations, and additions while preserving those portions or features of a site that convey its historical and cultural values. Rehabilitation adjusts for contemporary uses and takes account of diverse needs and goals, solves problems, addresses management, and considers sustainability while respecting the extant historic landscape and its remaining character-defining features. A rehabilitation approach, integrating respect for historic assets while tackling issues of maintainability, code compliance, safety, etc., is the most frequent approach applied to landscapes that have changed use and evolved.

Given the level of change to the Planting Fields landscape that had taken place over nearly a century, alongside our agreed-upon goals of respect for assets, the human and financial resources available to manage this public park and historic site, and the need, moving forward, for increased resilience, it was obvious that preservation alone would be insufficient to enhance the stewardship, renewal, and sustainability of Planting Fields.

In bequeathing the property to New York State, W. R. Coe himself had set Planting Fields on a path of both continuity and change. As an avid plant collector, he sought to establish an even more varied plant collection for educational purposes in his formerly private landscape. The Synoptic Garden, a diverse horticultural plant collection alphabetically organized and positioned to the north of the West Lawn, as well as a series of trees and shrub collections postdate Coe's residence and life, but they grew out of his wishes for the property. These valuable collections are a primary reason why neither restoration nor reconstruction of the Planting Fields landscape that Coe had created for his personal enjoyment could be recommended.

Of the four strategies, rehabilitation underlain with preservation is the one that aligned most closely and realistically with our ambitions for renewing Planting Fields. Combined with the restoration of select features, it would maintain the compatibility of cultural and natural resources while safeguarding, stabilizing, and enhancing surviving landscape assets, and it would be able to accommodate the changes imposed by the site's evolution from private estate to campus, public park, historic site, and arboretum. There was consensus among the representatives of the Planting Fields Foundation, Planting Fields Arboretum and New York State team, and Heritage Landscapes that rehabilitation, combining adaptation and respect, and preservation, stewarding remaining features, would serve effectively as the basis for future directions.

The outcome was the development of concrete and innovative recommendations for protection, intervention, adaptation, and accommodation at Planting Fields to suit this place, those who steward it, and its visitors for today and in years to come.

A SUSTAINABLE LANDSCAPE FOR PLANTING FIELDS

While the preservation approaches chart one course for the future of Planting Fields, ensuring the sustainability of this collaboratively stewarded property provides a second and equally important platform for planning and action. There is a widespread misconception that sustainability focuses on environmental concerns alone. True sustainability, however, must balance environmental, economic, and societal demands.[6]

An ongoing goal is to ensure that Planting Fields offers a robust model for how the three aspects of sustainability, coupled with heritage, can be instrumentalized as the drivers and enablers of action that builds on the past and enriches the future. In this, we found ourselves mapping individual projects at Planting Fields onto specific objectives set forth in the United Nations Sustainable Development Goals. These understand that "sustainable development everywhere must integrate economic growth, social well-being, and environmental protection." In shaping our recommendations, we drew, in particular, on five of the UN goals.[7]

Goal 3: To promote good health and well-being for all ages. What can the implementation of the comprehensive plan achieve to enhance health and wellness by engaging with the Planting Fields landscape?

Goal 11: To ensure a future in which cities and communities are inclusive, safe, resilient, and sustainable. How, at Planting Fields, can we advance landscape inclusion, perceived safety, universal access for people and greater resilience and sustainability to the landscape?

Goal 13: To take urgent action to combat climate change and its impacts. What projects and initiatives can focus on carbon sequestration and green energy generation and effectively communicate to the public what Planting Fields does to combat the climate emergency?

Goal 15: To sustainably manage forests, to halt and reverse land degradation, and to halt biodiversity loss. What effective protection and restoration of the terrestrial ecosystems can we advance that are aligned to the heritage of Planting Fields? How might healthy productive land at Planting Fields enhance biodiversity and enrich habitat?

Goal 17: To revitalize partnerships between governments, the private sector, and civil society. What effective collaborations can Planting Fields mobilize to share knowledge, expertise, technology, and resources in a way that uplifts the property?

United Nations Sustainable Development Goals. Numbers 3, 11, 13, 15, and 17 help shape the goals for Planting Fields. *United Nations with open permission to publish.*

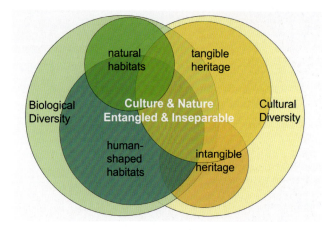

Biocultural heritage diversity integrates. With 75 percent of the earth deeply altered by humanity, we must take responsibility for resilience of the human-shaped landscape. *Patricia M. O'Donnell.*

Through implementation of sustainability goals targeted in the CLR, the existing partnership between the Planting Fields Foundation and the New York State Office of Parks, Recreation, and Historic Preservation and others is extended and made more effective; by aligning the goals of the report with the UN Sustainable Goals, we find multiple ways to think globally and act locally. Empowering this critical work is the recognition that the preservation of the historic landscape can and must be compatible with sustainability and biotic and cultural diversity (biocultural diversity), an interrelationship captured well in this diagram that depicts cultural landscape as the combined work of nature and humanity.

CULTURAL LANDSCAPE REPORT AND HISTORIC LANDSCAPE INVESTIGATION

In bringing contemporary best practices to preservation and sustainability concerns, the CLR provides visionary directions to achieve a vibrant future. It is no contradiction that the report itself is based in meticulous historical research.

The starting point of any such plan is building knowledge from documentary sources. To ensure accuracy, Heritage Landscapes applies a protocol that demands documentation by a minimum of two confirming sources, such as a drawing or plan and a photograph, that capture both what was intended at the design stage and what was built.

In the case of Planting Fields, we are fortunate to have hundreds of archival sources documenting the origins and evolution of the landscape. Among some 400 extant Olmsted Brothers documents for Planting Fields, for example, we have an annotated field inventory and sketch of the entry drive that reveal what existed and was intended, while historic photographs provide evidence for character.

Professional photography albums by Mattie Edwards Hewitt capture some 80 images of the estate through the 1920s, while more than an additional 100 Coe-era photos augment those in the albums. In all, more than 700 Coe-era documentary sources—correspondence, surveys, aerial and ground photographs—survive, augmented by several hundred additional records through the 1990s. Together, these offer a robust record of the design, construction, and evolution of the landscape.

The Olmsted design can be seen today in varying degrees by area, and it was verified through study and analysis. The records clarify the Olmsted Brothers design

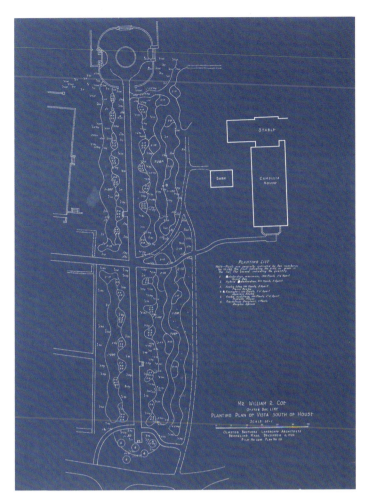

and shaping of the new Carshalton Gates entry and drive, the East and West Lawns, and the gardens and productive landscape spaces south of the Coe residence.

These works, which were carried out in the Coe years with James Frederick Dawson, were intact at the time of Coe's death and are captured in detail in a plan we created from numerous sources to document the 1956 landscape.

At W. R. Coe's death in 1955, the transfer to the State University of New York Long Island Agricultural and Technical Institute added an education-purposed structural layer to the property. Following Coe's wishes, the arboretum collections expanded in the Synoptic Garden and elsewhere; at the same time, elements of the Olmsted/Coe landscape began to age or were altered to meet new purposes. The Planting Fields Foundation and Planting Fields State Park and Arboretum have stewarded the property since 1971, when the use of Planting Fields as a temporary campus for SUNY Stony Brook, Westbury, and Farmingdale came to an end. The CLR brought these partners together to engage with the origins, evolution, and study of landscape as it was in 2019. From that basis, informed recommendations were advanced, shaping an actionable and historically informed framework plan. The Olmsted Brothers design is honored, and the important plant collections of the arboretum are equally privileged. These compatible principles were applied to the recommended actions, designed to uplift the core assets of Planting Fields.

Planting plan of Vista Path south of the house, (Azalea Walk), 1920, showing the density of understory massing. *Courtesy of the National Park Service, Frederick Law Olmsted National Historic Site.*

Azalea Walk as constructed, showing the density of planting that encloses views and screens the adjacent path. Mattie Edwards Hewitt, c. 1928. *Planting Fields Foundation Archives.*

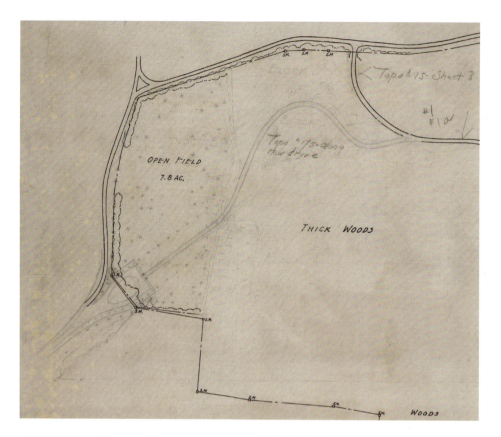

Detail of general plan for Planting Fields, 1920, with location of the new drive and the placement of the Carshalton Gates at lower left. *Courtesy of the National Park Service, Frederick Law Olmsted National Historic Site.*

View from the new drive toward Chicken Valley Road. Harry G. Healy, c. 1928. *Planting Fields Foundation Archives.*

OLMSTED BROTHERS LANDSCAPE DESIGN AT PLANTING FIELDS

Landscape design is about composing space, employing views, topography, circulation systems of drives and walks, water elements, structures, and objects as well as vegetation of all types, including lawns, shrubs, trees, fields, and woodlands. At Planting Fields, Olmsted Brothers incorporated all these features to choreograph a sequence of three-dimensional spaces through which visitors would move. The landscape architects also understood and designed for a fourth dimension, that of time, through which the landscape itself would move and mature to bring the full effect of the design forward.

As a contributor to the preservation and renewal of more than sixty Olmsted legacy places, I understand the firm's design style and details and their application. In the dominant naturalistic style, design draws on organic landscape forms and shapes and uses generally curvilinear circulation. Spiral curves are employed in convex and concave forms that instill grace and ease into scenery in balanced asymmetrical compositions. Close to a building or a group of buildings, the design shifts to a formal style in relationship to the built features. Olmsted landscape design forms envelopes of space that flow one to another, with some broad and others intimate and sequestered. At Planting Fields, the naturalistic landscape style shapes both principal entries to the property and the gently rolling East and West Lawns, while more formal axial and geometric relationships emerge in the context of the main residence, the barns, paddocks, crop rows, and pastures to the south.

The landscape spaces and related components at Planting Fields create a series of character areas. Crafted design shapes three-dimensional compositions that vary with movement: purposeful views fluctuate from close to distant and from focused to broad; topography combines native and altered elements to fulfill design intent; structures and plantings shape a layered vertical composition; and above, a tree canopy ranges from dense to open, allowing the visible sky overhead to alter the feeling

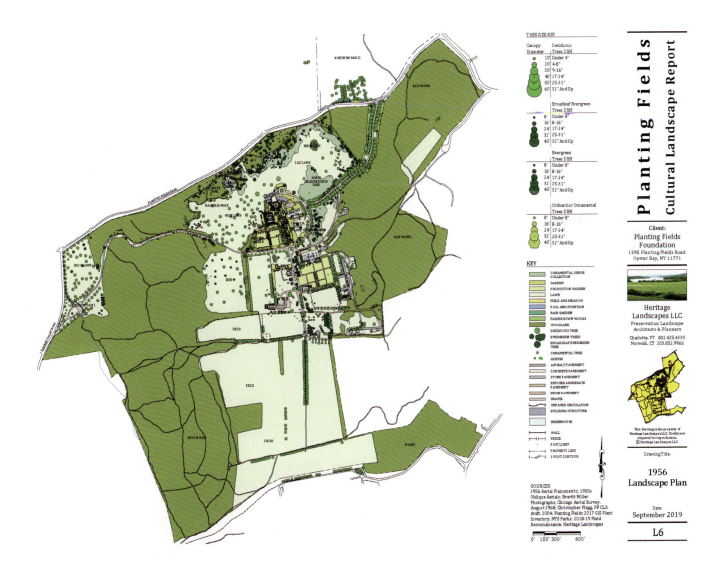

The reconstructed 1956 landscape plan. *Planting Fields Cultural Landscape Report,* Heritage Landscapes LLC, 2019.

Aerial view of Planting Fields, showing the Olmsted Brothers work in progress. Aiglon Aerial Photo Company, c. 1922. *Courtesy of the National Park Service, Frederick Law Olmsted National Historic Site.*

and perception of space and light with harmony and richness. The variable light in the landscape produces a *chiaroscuro* effect of contrasting bright and shadow, as dappled sunlight falls unevenly on the paths and plantings. The variety of the foliage's textures—from coarse to fine—and colors—from green, to yellow, to gray, to blue-green—enhances the visitor's experience.

Spatial extension and articulation within an area occurs in several places at Planting Fields, including the Azalea Garden walks and plantings. There, curved and straight paths are laid out in close proximity, with dense plantings between to offer differing characters and views in a loop walk. On the West Terrace walk, a gracefully curving route is framed by layered plantings and pedestals for pots of blooming plants; hidden below, the Surprise Pool exploits topographic change and introduces rustic materials, offering a contrasting space of stone, dark still water, and plants. Here, as is typical, Olmsted Brothers landscape design plays with a variety of scales and characters. Interconnected and diverse, the designed landscapes of Planting Fields are a varied composition, flowing from one area to the next in a planned choreography.

SHAPING INTEGRATED ACTIONS FOR A THRIVING PLANTING FIELDS LANDSCAPE

Taking a comprehensive approach, a range of appropriate landscape recommendations and actions emerged from the CLR:

—Restore the historic Coe/Olmsted Brothers designed landscape
—Expand and manage arboretum collections to promote biodiversity and horticultural science
—Present ecology and scenery by developing nature-based solutions for woodlands and fields
—Enhance visitor experience, learning, and services

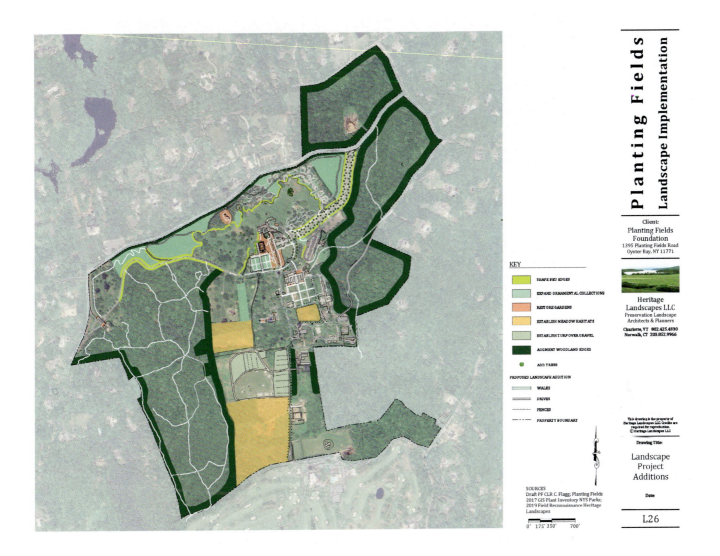

Color-coded landscape recommendations by primary objective for phased implementation. *Planting Fields Cultural Landscape Report, Heritage Landscapes LLC, 2019.*

—Pursue active functions to manage the landscape, considering maintainability in all initiatives

In truth, however, action to meet any of these five priorities invariably also engages others to some degree. If each of the five is thought of as a thread, we may imagine them not as separable, but as braided together into a stronger whole. The Planting Fields landscape combines inseparable cultural and natural heritage assets that we have chosen to address broadly and inclusively with multi-pronged efforts. With that caveat, let us explore the way each of these objectives unfolded in specific kinds of action for the notable landscape features.

RESTORE: RENEWING THE COE/OLMSTED DESIGN

Recognizing that the period of significance ended with the death of W. R. Coe in 1955, the CLR documented that landscape in detail, constructing a 1956 plan for knowledge and reference. That plan captures the form of the East and West Lawns and planted margins, the Beech Copse, the sequence of the Azalea and Sunken Gardens, and the Carshalton Gates and drive areas, all of which employ Olmsted naturalistic design principles and details.

The East and West Lawns: The expansive lawns exhibit an important spatial and visual aspect of Olmsted design, a complex edge planting that drops down, rises, and layers, presenting a series of sequentially unfolding rounded shapes. These graceful overlapping forms draw the stroller along the convex edges and into the concave arcs along the large lawns to see each successive planted margin. When viewed from the main house, this complex bed-edge design visually extends the space through its receding intricacy. Defining continuity and change through comparison of the 1956 and 2019 landscape plans and pairs of historic and current views, we were able to gain a thorough understanding of how that intended character has remained or been altered. The undulating margin of 1956, shown in orange, is a particularly interesting aspect of the West and East Lawns.

Our recommended changes follow the historic plan concept to recapture the character of that edge over time. The revised edge form will work around valued existing plantings and add new ones. It will shape space to restore the layered views that recede to extend perceived depth and will draw visitors walking on the lawn onward to explore the margins further.

Heather Garden: North of the West Lawn, the framed and enclosed Heather Garden is an excellent example of Olmsted design. One enters the narrow garden on high

Plan showing the variable 1955 Olmsted bed forms outlined in orange. The bed shapes were intended to extend the apparent distance and increase interest. *Planting Fields Cultural Landscape Report, Heritage Landscapes LLC, 2019.*

ground that drops into a topographic bowl, edged by flowering and evergreen trees, employing topography and enclosure for internalizing views. The experience of this garden proceeds along steppingstone paths in a gradual, circuitous descent to reach a small pool that reflects the sky.

By 2019, however, the Heather Garden had deteriorated significantly. When developing the early recommended projects, we identified this part of the landscape as one with a clearly defined scope. As the garden holds an edge position separate from the adjacent expansive East and West Lawns, remnant landscape rehabilitation could be undertaken with limited impact beyond the framed space. The combined evidence on site, with topography, stone paths, deteriorated pool masonry, and selected remaining plants, along with archival photographs of the garden as it once flourished, provided detailed data to restore the overall character. Soil percolation, pH, and nutrients would be critical to the renewed success of this sunny space. Given the difficulty of cultivating and sustaining heathers without constant care and replacement, they were supplemented with other more dependably maintained plants selected to mimic heathers in size, form, and texture. Supported by private funding, the Planting Fields Foundation team completed the Heather Garden renewal in April 2022 and opened it on Frederick Law Olmsted's two-hundredth birthday.

Heather Garden as constructed, showing the framed, enclosed hollow. Harry G. Healy, c. 1928. *Planting Fields Foundation Archives.*

The renewed Heather Garden captures the original form, enclosure, materials and details, while adapting for a more durable plant palette. David Almeida.

PROMOTE BIODIVERSITY: EXPAND AND MANAGE
THE ARBORETUM COLLECTIONS

The extensive collections of varied plant species at Planting Fields can be used for teaching purposes. This horticultural education mission, conceived in the 1950s by Coe and Carl Wedell, professor of ornamental horticulture at Long Island Agricultural and Technical Institute, is a robust feature of the property today.[8] This richness of horticulture is centered in the complex, thriving Synoptic Garden, where hundreds of labeled plants are displayed, and in the diverse tree arboretum. Other teaching collections are located in specific areas. The Taxus Field hosts varieties of yew, while the

Acer Collection offers a range of maples. These, and companion collections, can be expanded in specific locations going forward. The acreage to the north of the Synoptic Garden, as well as parts of the planted area west of the main lawns, can be transformed from remnant woodland with invasive species, to areas for expanded specialized collections. Continuing to steward these significant horticultural collections for casual and focused learning extends Coe's vision for landscape learning as a priority.

PRESENT ECOLOGY AND SCENERY: NATURE-BASED
SOLUTIONS IN WOODLANDS AND FIELDS

Augment Woodlands: At the same time it is essential to preserve and improve stewardship of the expanses of largely uninterrupted woodland. Limited woodland management in recent decades has permitted natural accumulation on the forest floor alongside natural growth and decay to support a biodiverse habitat. Invasive species of flora are present in woodland edges and some interior areas, requiring ongoing suppression and replacement with native species as well as the everegreen shrubs of laurel, rhododendron and azalea and flowering native trees that Coe favored to provide attractive, complex, layered edges along the face of the woodlands.

Some species of fauna inhabit only uninterrupted interior woodland, as defined as an area at least 100 meters (328 feet) from all edges. Conservation of the innermost areas of the larger west woods protects habitat for these sensitive species. A proposed plan for the west woodlands bolsters a continuous edge, removing incursions, to consolidate the interior woods. The proposal limits visitor use near the interior in the spring, as even passing foot traffic can dissuade nesting. A modified west woodland trail network would restrict access during nesting season and support use for guided bird-watching tours. Some trail removals from public use would consolidate interior habitat, with remaining trails connecting and circling the protected core.

Because of their size, the woodlands at Planting Fields have substantial ecological value. Together, the west woods of 115 acres and the east woods of 65 acres cover 44 percent of the total acreage. These 180 acres of woodland sequester carbon in standing trees, dead wood in decay, and soils. An estimate of sequestration for annual carbon offset is one to two USA tons of CO_2e (carbon dioxide equivalent) per acre.[9] In other words, the woodlands provide between 180 and 360 tons of carbon offset each year. This woodland carbon uptake will be a key element in bringing Planting Fields toward net zero carbon emission.

When the Carshalton Gates and related road grading and plantings were installed in 1927, W. R. Coe and Olmsted Brothers planted the entire disturbed and graded margin of the new drive through the woodlands with rhododendron, mountain laurel, azalea, ferns, and in a sunny area, with large drifts of spring bulbs. With the exception of a few remnants, these plantings are largely gone, with no movement to replace them. As invasive edge plants are suppressed, they must be replaced with desirable plants, or invasive species will infest the space. Returning Coe's plants, mixed with woodland edge natives, is proposed. Over time, the woodland margins can be sequentially improved by clearing out undesirable plants and adding native trees and shrubs that provide the edge character desired without intensive maintenance. A focused and limited management approach aligns with the goal of fostering woodlands as a vibrant natural resource asset.

Transform Fields: While temperate meadow would have been present in the Long Island landscape prior to colonization, there was little meadow habitat at Planting Fields during the Coe years. Fields were planted with crops and mown for hay, with tall grass and wildflowers present prior to haying. Today, meadow as a valuable habitat resource is under even greater pressure from urbanization than woodland, and its reintroduction at Planting Fields is desirable.

In bringing open meadow landscapes back to Planting Fields, we can foster increased pollinator populations and diverse flora and fauna, providing an essentially new asset that coexists with the historic designed landscapes and collections. Restoring former agricultural fields to their historic functions does not align with the contemporary uses of a public landscape, but open meadows can engage visitors with new views of the land and vibrant habitats. In the coming years, we plan to turn the pastures and hay fields over to native grass and wildflower meadows, providing pollinator and field bird habitats while preserving broad views of land, sun, and sky. As Planting Fields is located along the Atlantic flyway, migrating birds and butterflies may also use these areas for refueling and sheltering.

The environmental impact will be great. Research suggests that grasses can accumulate and deposit carbon into the soil, sequestering 1,000 pounds or more of carbon per year per acre. Sources comparing woodland and meadow observe that native grasses and wildflower meadows can uptake even higher levels of carbon dioxide than woodlands and can be established more quickly.[10] When a meadow is cut or grazed, new growth sequesters carbon; by not plowing or tilling, we encourage the generation of carbon-rich soil. Were solar panels to be placed in the southern areas of the former fields, they would add a direct source of electrical energy to the property, providing renewable power while decreasing fossil-fuel uses.

Even undisturbed lawns sequester carbon. We plan to add a light layer of topsoil over the large gravel parking areas in the former fields and to seed these areas with mixed species turf. The literature on lawn sequestration varies widely in projected values, with a lower limit of 200 pounds of carbon per acre per year.[11] Even so, this is another path toward carbon reduction. Together, the potential of the woodlands, lawns, and meadows of Planting Fields combines to reduce the site's carbon footprint significantly.

ENHANCE INCLUSIVE VISITATION WITH A UNIVERSAL ACCESS WALK

Whether there for casual exploration, a walk with friends or family, to attend an event or a program, or to take a guided tour, every visitor to Planting Fields should have ease of access to all public areas of the site and effective and informative wayfinding and interpretive tools. Indeed, as a twenty-first century landscape welcoming a broad public, providing universal access to people of all abilities is not only desirable, but required by federal law.[12]

A new walk now provides a clear barrier-free route from the parking lots that were created after 1956 in a former woodland margin to the main house to the southwest and the Synoptic Garden to the northwest. In planning this new walk, we studied and discussed both federal guidelines and the original Olmsted design for drives and walks at Planting Fields. Several potential construction materials were considered before we selected an exposed aggregate concrete for the cast-in-place paving. While concrete has a generally high carbon footprint due to the extreme temperatures required to make Portland cement, additives can drop carbon inputs and the anticipated 50-year-plus lifespan of the well-detailed walk provides a long-term benefit, albeit one with an extended timeline to achieve carbon neutrality.[13] This material selection also avoids the migration of petrochemicals into the soils that accompanies asphalt paving. The same project brought the entry drive back to its original configuration, removing the guard booth, island, and lay-bys. The amount of impervious paving removed from the drive balanced the paving of the new walk, avoiding a net increase to stormwater runoff.

The new pedestrian route traverses a graded slope with a 10-foot elevation change across slightly more than 200 feet. This concrete walk achieves universal access of 5 percent maximum grade change through careful elevation control during construction. This graceful curving uphill accessible walk replaces a tangle of gravel paths that included steps and steep grades. Extending to the west of the entry drive, the approximately 925 feet of additional gently curvilinear walk ranges from 1 to 4 percent gradient, well within universal access limits. This walk is positioned west of a new entrance drive allée of 102 trees for pedestrian comfort and a landscape experience.

The Olmsted approach to grading walks and drives drops the pavement into the landscape with swales and slight mounds to one or both the sides. We were able to emulate this technique in the new walk on the west side of the entry drive, giving visual prominence to the surrounding landscape with only portions of the walk visible at any one time. This Olmsted grading detail also manages drainage beside the walk.

MANAGE THE LANDSCAPE FOR EFFECTIVE FUNCTIONS

The historic landscape at Planting Fields must also support essential management and maintenance services required for this public property. At a designed historic landscape and arboretum such as Planting Fields, improvement of water supply and irrigation is essential. Without ready access to water, it is impossible to support the plant collections, historic gardens, and ongoing planting work that make Planting Fields the special place that it is. Ensuring water availability, whether with quick-couple hose connections or durable automatic irrigation systems, will be ever more crucial as we face the increasing challenges imposed by climate change. Roof water capture, cisterns, and other ways of conserving and reusing water are also important to consider going forward.

Meeting this and other functional needs is a paramount concern for the stewards of Planting Fields, and these goals may be of interest to visitors as an element of overall sustainability. Functional concerns, however, should not be the first thing about which a visitor thinks upon entry. Indeed, one might argue that the more effectively Planting Fields is managed, the less obvious the staff, tools, and machinery that make everything run smoothly will be. With a goal of achieving separation, distinct routes for maintenance can often be somewhat removed from visitor drives and walks. To reduce staff and visitor conflicts, maintenance vehicle movements can take place at times with fewer visitors.

The formal Beech Drive in its prime, with consistent tree massing and rhythm. Harry G. Healy, c. 1928. *Planting Fields Foundation Archives.*

An aerial photograph shows no discernible allée remaining. John Pacini, 2021.

The Heather Garden and the renewed entry serve as highly visible markers of early implementation, while many more initiatives for gardens, woodlands, and meadows will come forward in phases. Over time the fabric of Planting Fields will strengthen and cohere, resulting in a more uplifting landscape, the parts of which will flow seamlessly into one.

BRINGING IT ALL TOGETHER: THE ENTRY DRIVE ALLÉE

From 1918 on, an allée of European beech trees (*Fagus sylvatica*) flanked the entry drive to Planting Fields. In earlier times, these large canopy trees had extended along the entire length of the roadway in four rows aligned across the drive in triangular offsets with geometrical precision.

By 1955 this monoculture of beech trees was already in decline, a victim to age, pests, and disease; by 2019 the formal character of the feature was unrecognizable in the ragtag mix of unevenly spaced trees of varying size and vintages. Considering preservation alone, the first choice would have been to replace the entire feature to match what had once flourished. The fact was, however, that the allée's decline was due to virulent diseases that were ravaging the beech tree monoculture and that the original tight spacing caused the branch conflicts and entangled roots that helped speed the spread of disease. It was failure that brought forward the question of how better to choose and plant viable replacements to the beeches.

Tree monocultures are generally no longer in favor, precisely because pests and disease can readily affect an entire planting, and we recognized the need to avoid making the same mistake again. In redesigning the allée, we acknowledged as well that the Planting Fields property provides a highly diverse plant community in which native trees play an important part. Oaks are one of the best genera to support insect and bird life, among other landscape benefits. After considering a range of native canopy trees, we settled on two distinct but compatible oak species. Both are long-lived trees, with a canopy similar in form to beech. We positioned Chinquapin oaks

Rendering of the new Oak Allée. *Heritage Landscapes LLC.*

(*Quercus muehlenbergii*) at the drive edge and white oak (*Quercus alba*) in the outer rows. The spacing between the trees was enlarged, with an eye toward the specimens' eventual thirty- to thirty-five-foot spread at maturity. The margin between the trees and the drive was also increased to fifteen feet to promote long-term tree and soil health. As these trees mature, the Chinquapin oak will reach a height of around 50 feet while the white oak, behind the Chinquapin to each side, can gain 70 feet, restoring an effective drive framing and stature at two heights. The ground below the trees was planted in no-mow fescue, a hybrid turf grass that requires limited, if any, mowing, thereby reducing the need for ongoing care and contributing to our goal of reducing the carbon footprint. Two new irrigation lines were installed along the length of the allée to provide water to the newly planted trees and turf.

The recently completed rehabilitation of the allée included not only the removal of the diseased beech trees and their replacement, but also the careful insertion of the new walk, graded to meet guidelines for full handicap access without ramps or handrails. For the visually impaired, detectable pavers in contrasting colors warn people each time a path abuts a drive so that crossing can be carried out safely.

Removal of so many venerable trees might have caused an uproar had we not communicated news of the poor health of the remaining beeches and their intended replacement through website notices and on-site signs that provided simulated images and additional information. These efforts helped build support for the project and lessen the shock of tree removal. Visitors and supporters learned that as the new oak trees mature, they will help to improve air quality, provide shade, and aid in stormwater absorption and carbon sequestration. Supporters were even encouraged to donate a tree and choose its location from an on-line map (no on-site markers were used to clutter the landscape and create maintenance issues). These efforts helped to build community, even sparking the development of an Oak Circle donor group, offering annual benefits to supporters.

The replanting of the entrance allée was completed in 2023, and it exemplifies the ways in which, at Planting Fields, the renewal of one of the signature features of the Coe/Olmsted landscape could enhance sustainability, provide education, and elevate visitor experience. None of this happened by accident. Everything was planned. All of it provides a model for future efforts to uplift this remarkable place.

New Oak Allée. David Almeida, 2024.

MOVING FORWARD

W. R. and Mai Coe had an immense fortune at their disposal. It is important to remember that the extraordinary levels of staffing and funding that created and maintained this landscape for private use between 1913 and 1955 were far greater in real terms than what is available for the public park of today and tomorrow. For every change that is proposed moving forward, we must consider the costs in terms of maintenance demands, human resources, skills, and equipment. These constraints make thoughtful planning critical, but success is already visible. As a public property, a state park, an Olmsted landscape, an arboretum, woodlands, and gardens adjacent to a historic house museum, Planting Fields offers many tangible reasons to visit, learn, enjoy. The potential is even greater and richer as the landscape we have been privileged to inherit is renewed through the informed and visionary actions of its current guardians. The path forward for Planting Fields is preservation-based and firmly rooted in the past yet coupled with innovation and adaptation to meet current and future needs and issues by acting locally and thinking globally. The future of this heritage landscape is vibrant and sustainable.

NOTES

A Country Place and Its Makers

1. Norman T. Newton, *Design on the Land: The Development of Landscape Architecture* (Cambridge, Mass.: Belknap Press, 1971), 427.
2. Geoffrey Scott, *The Architecture of Humanism: A Study in the History of Taste* (New York: W. W. Norton & Co., 1999), 32.
3. F. Scott Fitzgerald, *The Great Gatsby* (New York: Penguin Books, 1994; orig. pub. 1926), 11.
4. Carter B. Horsley, "More Mansions on Long Island's 'Gold Coast' Fall," *New York Times* (June 16, 1974) section 8: 1.
5. "More Mansions": 10.
6. *Long Island Estate Gardens* (Brookville, NY: Hillwood Art Gallery, Long Island University, 1985), 15.
7. John A. Strong, *The Algonquian Peoples of Long Island from Earliest Times to 1700* (Interlaken, NY: Empire State Books, 1997).
8. *Long Island Country Houses and Their Architects, 1860–1940*, Robert B. MacKay et al, eds. (New York: W. W. Norton & Co., 1997), 33.
9. George Whitney Martin, *Causes and Conflicts: The Centennial History of the Association of the Bar of the City of New York 1870–1970* (New York: Fordham University Press, 1997), 203.
10. John Oller, *White Shoe: How a New Breed of Wall Street Lawyers Changed Big Business and the American Century* (New York: Dutton, 2019), 175.
11. *Causes and Conflicts*, 204.
12. Helen Byrne's name is the only one on the property deeds. Her central role in running the house is underlined by a later letter from the Ralph B. Carter Co. who serviced the pumps and water system: "We wish to state that our relations with Mrs. Byrne have always been of the most pleasant sort." Ralph B. Carter Co. to William Robertson Coe, January 19, 1914. Planting Fields Foundation Archives.
13. Peter Pennoyer and Anne Walker, *The Architecture of Grosvenor Atterbury* (New York: W. W. Norton & Co,, 2009), 57.
14. Grosvenor Atterbury, "The Former Residence of Mr. James Byrne at Locust Valley, L.I.," *Country Life* (November 1919), 34.
15. John Taylor Boyd Jr., "The Residence of William R. Coe, Esq., Oyster Bay, L.I.," *The Architectural Record* (March 1921), 196.
16. Mark Alan Hewitt, *The Architect and the American Country House, 1890–1940* (New Haven: Yale University Press, 1990), 108.
17. *The Architecture of Grosvenor Atterbury*, 47.
18. Wilkie Collins, *My Miscellanies* (London: Sampson & Low, 1863).
19. "The Former Residence of Mr. James Byrne," 34.
20. "House at Locust Valley, Long Island, N.Y." *The Brickbuilder* 17 (January 1908), 13–14.
21. June Byrne Spencer, undated memorandum. Planting Fields Foundation Archives.
22. "The Former Residence of Mr. James Byrne," 34.
23. *Causes and Conflicts*, 204.
24. Charles A. Birnbaum and Robin Karson, eds., *Pioneers of American Landscape Architecture* (New York: McGraw-Hill, 2000), 146.
25. *Pioneers*.
26. "Locust Valley Property Rented," *Brooklyn Daily Eagle* (May 8, 1911), 15.
27. The rent for Planting Fields was substantial, $1,000 a month, about $30,000 today. "William Robertson Coe reminisces with Everitt L. Miller" (taped c. 1954), 1. Planting Fields Foundation Archives.
28. Helen Macgregor Byrne to William Robertson Coe, November 2, 1914. Planting Fields Foundation Archives.
29. Helen Macgregor Byrne to Mai Rogers Coe, March 29, 1914. Planting Fields Foundation Archives.
30. "Bracelet Costing Thousands Is Lost," *Washington Times* (September 19, 1915).
31. Peter Messent, *Mark Twain and Male Friendship: The Twichell, Howard, and Rogers Friendships* (New York: Oxford University Press, 2009), 160–61.
32. Michael D. Coe, *Final Report: An Archaeologist Excavates His Past* (New York: Thames & Hudson, 2006), 13; "Three Noted Men Left $79,196,371," *New York Times* (July 23, 1914).
33. "Distinguished architects who have made a specialty of designing successful country houses," *Country Life* 37 (April 1920), 142.
34. "William Robertson Coe reminisces," 1. Planting Fields Foundation Archives.
35. Eran Ben-Joseph, Holly D. Ben-Joseph, and Anne C. Dodge, "Against all Odds: MIT's Pioneering Women of Landscape Architecture" (Cambridge, Mass.: Massachusetts Institute of Technology School of Architecture and Planning, November 2006).
36. Guy Lowell, *American Gardens* (Boston: Bates & Guild, 1902), 8.
37. *Long Island Estate Gardens*, 19.
38. Guy Pène du Bois, "An Eighteenth-Century Revival: The Work of Everett Shinn, Revivalist," *Art & Decoration* (1910–1915), Vol. 6, No. 2 (December 1915), 79.
39. *Art & Decoration*.
40. Elsie de Wolfe, *The House in Good Taste* (New York: The Century Company, 1913), 273.
41. Rebecca Van Houghton, "Mrs. William R. Coe's Hand-Made Tea House," *Town & Country* (July 1, 1916), 20.
42. Everett Shinn to William Robertson Coe, May 17, 1915. Planting Fields Foundation Archives.
43. "William Robertson Coe reminisces," 2.
44. "Coe House Burned with $700,000 Loss," *New York Times* (March 27, 1918).
45. Noel McVickar to Robert Douglas Coe, March 29, 1918. Planting Fields Foundation Archives.
46. "Coe House Burned."
47. "William Robertson Coe reminisces," 2.
48. *The Architect and the American Country House*, 77.
49. "William Robertson Coe reminisces," 2.
50. "The Residence of William R. Coe, Esq., Oyster Bay, L.I.," 224.
51. Jacques Seligmann to William Robertson Coe, June 9, 1922. Planting Fields Foundation Archives.
52. Jacques Seligmann to E. Furmont, May 25, 1923. Planting Fields Foundation Archives.
53. Jacques Seligmann to William Robertson Coe, May 25, 1923. Planting Fields Foundation Archives.
54. Walker & Gillette to William Robertson Coe, July 23, 1920. Planting Fields Foundation Archives.

55. Lauren Drapala, "Building the House of Fantasy," in *Robert Winthrop Chanler: Discovering the Fantastic*, Gina Wouters and Andrea Gollin, eds. (New York: Monacelli Press, 2016), 64.
56. Walker & Gillette to William Robertson Coe, May 21, 1920. Planting Fields Foundation Archives.
57. John C. Olmsted to William Robertson Coe, October 15, 1918. Planting Fields Foundation Archives.
58. Charles E. Peterson, "Historical Notes on the Camellia House." Undated report, 64. Planting Fields Foundation Archives.
59. William Robertson Coe to James Frederick Dawson, June 19, 1921. Planting Fields Foundation Archives.
60. Ibid.
61. William Robertson Coe to Natalie Coe, January 23, 1924. Planting Fields Foundation Archives.
62. William Robertson Coe to A. Stewart Walker, February 20, 1924. Planting Fields Foundation Archives.
63. "W. R. Coe, Sportsman, Weds Suddenly at 57; Bride Mrs. Slaughter, 49, Recently Divorced," *New York Times* (December 5, 1926).
64. *Final Report*, 22.
65. *Final Report*.
66. William Robertson Coe to Frederick Law Olmsted Jr., October 18, 1926. Planting Fields Foundation Archives.
67. J. Starkie Gardner, *English Ironwork of the XVIIth and XVIIIth Centuries: An Historical and Analytical Account of the Development of Exterior Smithcraft* (London: Read Books, 2013; originally published 1911).
68. Dawson was misremembering—there was an orangery at Carshalton Park but no house. James Frederick Dawson to William Robertson Coe, April 6, 1926. Planting Fields Foundation Archives.
69. John David Myles, "Cherokee," unpublished report, Chip Hall Plantation Services, Charleston, S.C., 2017.
70. William Robertson Coe to James Frederick Dawson, October 23, 1935. Planting Fields Foundation Archives.
71. "Remarks by Mr. William Rogers Coe, Chairman of the Board of Trustees of the Planting Fields Foundation at Dedication of Planting Fields Arboretum, Oyster Bay, New York—May 24, 1952." Planting Fields Foundation Archives.
72. "Last Will and Testament and Codicil of William Robertson Coe." Planting Fields Foundation Archives.
73. Map, c. 1960, State University College on Long Island, Planting Fields. SBU Special Collections & Archives.
74. Ibid.; *Specula 1962* (State University of New York Long Island Center, 1962).
75. *The Secretary of the Interior's Standards for the Treatment of Historic Properties with Guidelines for the Treatment of Cultural Landscapes*, Charles A. Birnbaum and Christine Cappella Peters, eds. (Washington, D.C., 1996), 5.

Before the Gold Coast: The Early History of Planting Fields

1. The first human migrations to Long Island are estimated to have occurred from 10,000–12,000 years ago. Patrick J. Lynch, *A Field Guide to Long Island Sound* (New Haven: Yale University Press, 2017).
2. David J. Bernstein, "Patterns in the Prehistoric Use of Non-agrarian Botanical Resources in the Long Island and Block Island Sound Region of Eastern North America," in *Hunter-Gatherer Archaeobotany: Perspectives from the Northern Temperate Zone*, ed. Sarah L. R. Mason and Jon G. Hather (New York: Routledge, 2016); Anne-Marie E. Cantwell and Diana diZerega Wall, *Unearthing Gotham: The Archaeology of New York City* (New Haven: Yale University Press, 2003), ch. 5.
3. Peter Nabokov and Robert Easton, *Native American Architecture* (London: Oxford University Press, 1989), ch. 1; Dennis A. Connole, *The Indians of the Nipmuck Country in Southern New England, 1630-1750: An Historical Geography* (Jefferson, NC: McFarland and Co. Publishers, 2007), 7.
4. Kathleen J. Bragdon, *Native People of Southern New England, 1500-1650* (Norman: University of Oklahoma Press, 1999), 123.
5. Natalie A. Naylor, *Women in Long Island's Past: A History of Eminent and Everyday Lives* (Mount Pleasant, SC: Arcadia Publishing, 2012); Robert S. Grumet, "Sunksquaws, Shamans, and Tradeswomen: Middle Atlantic Coastal Algonkian Women During the 17th and 18th Centuries," in Mona Etienne and Eleanor Leacock, ed., *Women and Colonization: Anthropological Perspectives* (New York: Praeger, 1980); Trudie Lamb Richmond and Amy E. Den Ouden, "Recovering Gendered Political Histories: Local Struggles and Native Women's Resistance in Colonial Southern New England," in Colin Calloway and Neal Salisbury, ed., *Reinterpreting New England Indians and the Colonial Experience* (Boston: The Colonial Society of Massachusetts, 2003).
6. Betsy McCully, *City at the Water's Edge: A Natural History of New York* (New Brunswick, NJ: Rutgers University Press, 2007), 55–57.
7. Jean M. O'Brien, *Dispossession by Degrees: Indian Land and Identity in Natick, Massachusetts, 1650-1790* (Lincoln: University of Nebraska Press, 2003), 21.
8. Connole, *The Indians of the Nipmuck Country*, 19.
9. William C. MacLeod, "The Family Hunting Territory and Lenape Political Organization," in *American Anthropologist*, 24, no. 4 (October–December, 1922): 448–463.
10. Penelope Myrtle Kelsey, *Reading the Wampum: Essays on Hodinöhsö:ni' Visual Code and Epistemological Recovery* (Syracuse, NY: Syracuse University Press, 2014); Clara Sue Kidwell, "Native American Systems of Knowledge," in *A Companion to American Indian History*, ed. Philip J. Deloria and Neal Salisbury (New York: John Wiley & Sons, 2008): 87–102; Tom Arne Midtrød, *The Memory of All Ancient Customs: Native American Diplomacy in the Colonial Hudson Valley* (Ithaca, NY: Cornell University Press, 2012), 36–39; Lynn Ceci, "The Value of Wampum among the New York Iroquois: A Case Study in Artifact Analysis," *Journal of Anthropological Research* 38, no. 1 (1982): 97–107; Marc Shell, *Wampum and the Origins of American Money* (Urbana: University of Illinois Press, 2013).
11. William A. Ritchie, *The Archaeology of New York State* (New York: Knopf Doubleday, 2014).
12. John A. Strong, "Wyandanch and the Dispossession of Indian Land on Long Island, New York: Grand Sachem, Puppet, or Cultural Broker?" *Long Island History Journal* 30, no. 1 (2022).
13. Paul Otto, "Henry Hudson, the Munsees, and the Wampum Revolution," in *The Worlds of the Seventeenth-Century Hudson Valley*, ed. Jaap Jacobs and Lou Roper (Albany: SUNY Press, 2014), 4.
14. Van Tienhoven's description specifically refers to land extending from Oyster Bay to Matinecock Bay (or Martin Gerritsen's Bay as the Dutch sometimes called it) and Schout's Bay. Cornelis Van Tienhoven, "Information Relative to taking up land in New Netherland," March 4, 1659, transcribed in John Demos, *Remarkable Providences: Readings on Early American History* (Hanover, NH: University Press of New England, 1991), 21–22.
15. Van Tienhoven, "Information Relative to taking up land in New Netherland," 1650.
16. Paul Kelton, *Epidemics and Enslavement: Biological Catastrophe in the Native Southeast, 1492-1715* (Lincoln: University of Nebraska Press, 2007), xvii; Daniel K. Richter, *Facing East from Indian Country: A Native History of Early America* (Cambridge, MA: Harvard University Press, 2009), 59–62; Russell Thornton, *American Indian Holocaust and Survival: A Population History Since 1492* (Norman: University of Oklahoma Press, 1987), 64, 71; Catherine M. Cameron, Paul Kelton, and Alan C. Swedlund, eds., *Beyond Germs: Native Depopulation in North America* (Tucson: University of Arizona Press, 2015).
17. Neal Salisbury, *Manitou and Providence: Indians, Europeans, and the Making of New England, 1500-1643* (New York: Oxford University Press, 1984); Richter, *Facing East*; David Silverman, *Thundersticks: Firearms and the Violent Transformation of Native America* (Cambridge, MA: Harvard University Press, 2016).
18. David Graeber, *Toward an Anthropological Theory of Value: The False Coin of Our Own Dreams* (London, UK: Palgrave Macmillan, 2001), 119.
19. David Murray, *Indian Giving: Economies of Power in Indian-White Exchanges* (Amherst, MA: University of Massachusetts Press, 2000), ch. 5; Otto, "Henry Hudson," 8.
20. January 15, 1639 Agreement between by the Director and Council of New Netherlands and Mechowodt,

recorded by Cornelis Van Tienhoven, Secretary for New Netherland, *Documents Relative to the Colonial History of the State of New-York*, vol. 14, 15.

21. Strong, "Wyandanch and the Dispossession."
22. Strong, "Wyandanch and the Dispossession."
23. Martin Gerritsen's Bay was the Dutch name for a bay of Long Island Sound, located adjacent to Shouts Bay and Oyster Bay. Sometimes, as here, it was used to refer to the entire area around the three bays, causing some confusion for the English (and later historians). "Indian deed to the Directors of the West India Company for land on Long Island," Fort Amsterdam, New Netherland, January 15, 1639, Dutch Colonial Council Minutes, 1638–1665 (series A1809), New York State Archives, scan NYSA_A1880-78_VGG_0028. Documents available online at the New York State Archives (NYSA) are hereafter cited by scan number.
24. "Instructions to Secretary Van Tienhoven to proceed to Martin Gerritsen Bay, on Long island, and arrest a number of English strollers, who had intruded on lands there, purchased by the Dutch from the great sachem, Penhawits," Dutch Colonial Council Minutes, May 13–15, 1640, scan NYSA_A1809-78_V04_p062
25. "Protest against certain parties who have settled without authority at Matinnekonck, or Martin Gerritsen's bay," Dutch Colonial Council Minutes, March 23 1655, scan NYSA_A1809-78_V06_0025a
26. Frederick Van Wyck, *Keskachauge: Or the First White Settlement on Long Island* (New York: G.P. Putnam's Sons, 1924), 479, 484–85.
27. The deed, although signed in 1653, was not entered in the official records for New York until March 27, 1667. More specifically, it stated that the purchase included all "Land Lyeing and Scitiate Oyster Bay & bounded by oyeter River to ye East side & Papaquatunck river on ye west side with all ye woods rivers marshes uplands ponds and & all other the appurtenances lyeing between the bounds aforementioned with all ye Islands lyaing to ye Sea war, excepting one Island commonly called Hog Island, & bounded neere Southward by a point of trees called Canteaiog." J. D. Perrine, *The Wright Family of Oysterbay* (New York, 1923), 28.
28. Perrine, *The Wright Family of Oysterbay*, 28.
29. Accounts of Oyster Bay land purchased by Nicholas Simkins, December 20, 1683 and Samuel Titus, October 24, 1684, transcribed in Townsend book, 12–15.
30. For more on conflicting English and Indian land uses, see Strother E. Roberts, *Colonial Ecology, Atlantic Economy: Transforming Nature in Early New England* (Philadelphia: University of Pennsylvania Press, 2019).
31. Letter from the Director and Council of New Netherland to Governor of Connecticut, October 26, 1654, Dutch Colonial Council Minutes, scan NYSA_A1809-78_V05_0394

32. "Minutes of Council," January 19, 1655, Dutch Colonial Council Minutes, scan NYSA_A1809-78_V06_0006
33. "Appointment of commissioners to settle some difficulties in the English towns on Long Island," March 16, 1655, Dutch Colonial Council Minutes, scan NYSA_A1809-78_V06_0023a
34. Cornelis Van Tienhoven, "Protest against certain parties who have settled without authority at Matinnekonck, or Martin Gerritsen's Bay," March 23, 1655; Cornelis Van Tienhoven, "Power of Attorney of the fiscal to the court messenger, authorizing him to serve a protest against Mr. Leverit and others," April 2, 1655, Dutch Colonial Council Minutes, scan NYSA_A1809-78_V06_0025a; scan NYSA_A1809-78_V06_0026a
35. Strong, "Wyandanch and the Dispossession."
36. Strong, "Wyandanch and the Dispossession."
37. Margaret Ellen Newell, "The Changing Nature of Indian Slavery in New England, 1670–1720," in *Reinterpreting New England Indians and the Colonial Experience,* ed. Colin Calloway and Neal Salisbury (Boston: The Colonial Society of Massachusetts, 2003), 126–27.
38. Perrine, *The Wright Family of Oysterbay*, 33–34, 45; *Oyster Bay Town Records,* vol. 1, 43–44, 47, 64–65.
39. John A. Strong, *The Unkechaug Indians of Eastern Long Island: A History* (Tulsa: University of Oklahoma Press, 2013), 74–75, 81–82.
40. Record of land grants for 1672, *Oyster Bay Town Records*, vol. 1, 78–79.
41. Deed of sale, Job Wright to Robert Townsend, January 19, 1686; Deed of sale, Adam Wright to John Townsend, July 30, 1686; Deed of sale, Job Wright to John Townsend, September 6, 1686, *Oyster Bay Town Records*, vol. 1, 361–368, 435–436.
42. *Oyster Bay Town Records*, 315–316.
43. Andrea C. Mosterman, *Places of Enslavement: A History of Slavery and Resistance in Dutch New York* (Ithaca, NY: Cornell University Press, 2021).
44. Jonathan Olly, *Long Road to Freedom*, (Stony Brook, NY: Long Island Museum, n.d.), 18.
45. Will of Alice Crabbe, Oyster Bay, dated Feb. 22, 1685; proved Oct. 13, 1685, transcribed in *Abstracts of Wills on File in the Surrogate's Office 1665-1707*, vol. 1 (New York: New-York Historical Society, 1892), 472–473.
46. Will of Nathaniel Coles, Jr., Oyster Bay, Queens, Sept 25, 1705; proved June 6, 1706, transcribed in *Abstracts of Wills on File in the Surrogate's Office 1665-1707*, vol. 1, 423.
47. Edmund Wright, Will, Dec. 2, 1731, transcribed in Perrine, *The Wright Family of Oysterbay*, 150–151.
48. Will of Wright Frost, yeoman, Matinecock, Oyster Bay Town, dated March 18, 1738; proved Aug. 19, 1738, transcribed in *Abstracts of Wills on File in the Surrogate's office, City of New York, 1730-1744*, vol. 3 (New York: New-York Historical Society, 1895), 253–255.

49. Cited in Shane White, *Somewhat More Independent: The End of Slavery in New York City, 1770–1810* (Athens: University of Georgia Press, 2012), 22.
50. *Boston Gazette & Country Journal*, March 27, 1766, transcribed in Olly, *Long Road to Freedom*, 29.
51. Graham R. Hodges, *Root and Branch: African Americans in New York and East Jersey, 1613–1863* (Chapel Hill: University of North Carolina Press, 2005), 118.
52. Revolutionary War Claims submitted by John Sammis, December 1, 1776 and by Silas Sammis and Jeremiah Wood, December 12, 1777; Account of John Sammis with Col. Thomson, March 1, 1783. Huntington Town Clerk's Archives, Huntington, NY (NYHeritage.com).
53. Document recording birth and manumission status of Rachel, by Ephenetus Sammis, February 17, 1804. Rachel later appeared in the records of the Overseers of the Poor, January 1, 1807. Manumission document for Hannah, certifying her fitness with Overseers of the Poor, June 27, 1823. Huntington Town Clerk's Archives, Huntington, NY (NY Heritage.com).
54. "A Farmer Wanted," *The Evening Post*, March 21, 1827, 1.
55. *History of Queens County, with illustrations, Portraits & Sketches of Prominent Families and Individuals* (New York: W.W. Munsell & Co., 1882).
56. "A Solid Citizen of Oyster Bay. The Prosperous Career of John M. Sammis," *Times Union* (Brooklyn), May 25, 1901, 21.
57. *Brooklyn Daily Eagle,* January 11, 1892 and April 8, 1884.
58. "A Big Fuss over a Little Road," *Brooklyn Daily Eagle,* September 11, 1889; "Audry Avenue Decided on," *Brooklyn Daily Eagle,* October 12, 1890 and December 3, 1891; *Times Union* (Brooklyn), November 6, 1891; and "James M. Sammis Innocent," March 16, 1893.
59. "The Way They Do It on Long Island," *Sunday Eagle-News* (Poughkeepsie, NY; reprinted from the *Brooklyn Sunday Eagle*), October 28, 1890.
60. "A Solid Citizen of Oyster Bay."
61. Helen Macgregor (1869–1945) was born in Indiana and, in 1896, married lawyer James Byrne (1857–1942), who became the first Catholic member of the Harvard Corporation. See short biography in R. J. Hutto, *Their Gilded Cage: The Jekyll Island Club Members* (New York: Henchard Press, 2006); Peter Pennoyer and Anne Walker, *The Architecture of Grosvenor Atterbury* (New York: W. W. Norton & Company, 2009), 84–87.
62. "McCoun Farm Sold for $40,000," *Brooklyn Daily Eagle,* June 1, 1905; "Big Deal Near Oyster Bay," *New York Times,* June 3, 1905.
63. Helen Byrne became an honorary member of the Nassau County Horticultural Society. "Many Wealthy People Exhibit in Flower Show," *Brooklyn Daily Eagle*, October 25, 1911, 6; *Times Union* (Brooklyn), November 11, 1911.

64. *United States Census of 1910*, New York Enumeration District 1137, sheet 13A.
65. "Country Lanes Offering New Phase of Club Life. The Members of the North Shore Colonies are Exploring New Paths and Getting Away from Macadam Motor Highways," *Brooklyn Daily Eagle*, September 15, 1912.
66. "New Hunting Grounds in Locust Valley Hills," *Brooklyn Daily Eagle*, October 14, 1906, 18.
67. "Newcomers on North Shore," *Brooklyn Daily Eagle,* March 19, 1913; "Suburban Leases," *New York Times*, March 15, 1913, 19; "Many New Colonists Along North Shore. Well-Known Country Estates of Nassau County Leased to Prominent People. Charms of Long Island Prove Strong to Residents of Distant Inland Cities," *Brooklyn Daily Eagle,* April 30, 1913, 4; "Billings at Oyster Bay," *Brooklyn Daily Eagle,* May 29, 1913, 4; "Mr. and Mrs. Billings Entertain," *Times Union* (Brooklyn), July 7, 1913, 8.
68. "Coe Buys Byrne Estate. Manhattan Man to Live at Planting Fields in Oyster Bay," *Brooklyn Daily Eagle,* October 21, 1913; for sale price, see *Brooklyn Daily Eagle,* February 20, 1915, 4. A later article about real estate transactions in the area states that the Coes paid Mrs. James Byrne the sum of $650,000 for 355 acres. *Brooklyn Daily Eagle,* February 7, 1915, 47.
69. "With Famous Natural Attractions and the Modern Business and Home Making Facilities the Section Attracts the Most Discriminating," *Times Union* (Brooklyn), May 4, 1912, 20.
70. "World's Greatest Nesting Place of the Multi-Millionaires," *San Angelo Evening Standard*, July 22, 1913, 3. This article also listed "Prominent Men" residing on the North Shore, including James Byrne (just three months before he sold Planting Fields to William Coe).
71. "World's Greatest Nesting Place."

On Planting Fields and the Making of Place

1. John Phibbs, *Place-making: The Art of Capability Brown* (Swindon, UK: Historic England, 2017) also seized on that Brownian term, though it plays a small part in his analyses.
2. David Leatherbarrow, *Topographical Stories: Studies in Landscape and Architecture* (Philadelphia: University of Pennsylvania Press, 2004), 4.
3. Thomas Whately, *Observations on Modern Gardening* (1770), 156–7.
4. *The Moralists, A Philosophical Rhapsody* (1709), Part III, section 1.
5. Olmsted Job #06645-tp2, March 7, 1921.
6. These gates, elaborately carved on the park side, came from Carshalton Park, in Surrey, an eighteenth-century seat belonging to Thomas Scawen, the nephew of Sir William Scawen, a founding member of the Bank of England. The lead statues on the outer pillars have been attributed to John Nost II.
7. Henry B. Joyce, *Guidebook to Coe Hall* (Oyster Bay, NY: Planting Fields Foundation, 2018), 67. My analysis and catalogue of his designs, *William Kent* (London: A. Zwemmer, 1987), show that he designed a few temples and a "ruined hermitage" at Stowe, but no plans for Stowe exist; in fact there is only one unique plan among all Kent's drawings: a crude layout of a garden with boathouse (see my catalogue no. 94).
8. Margaret Jourdain, *The Work of William Kent: Artist, Painter, Designer and Landscape Gardener* (New York: Charles Scribner's Sons, 1948) and Michael Wilson, *William Kent: Architect, Designer, Painter, Gardener, 1685–1748* (London: Routledge & Kegan Paul, 1984).
9. See pp. 25, 26, and 31 in Isabel Wakelin Urban Chase, ed., *Horace Walpole: Gardenist: An Edition of Walpole's "The History of the Modern Taste in Gardening"* (Princeton, NJ: Princeton University Press, 1943).
10. *Planting Fields Cultural Landscape Report* (Charlotte, VT: Heritage Landscapes, 2019), ix.
11. Susan Owens, *Spirit of Place: Artists, Writers and the British Landscape* (London: Thames & Hudson, 2020). But the concept of "the spirit of place" has been used carefully about Planting Fields by Gina Wouters in her introduction to David Brooks and Mark Dion, *The Great Bird Blind Debate* (Oyster Bay, NY: Planting Fields Foundation, 2020).
12. Avi Friedman, *The Nature of Place: A Search for Authenticity* (New York: Princeton Architectural Press, 2011); Edward S. Casey, *Representing Place: Landscape Painting and Maps* (Minneapolis: University of Minnesota Press, 2002).
13. *Planting Fields Foundation Strategic Plan 2020–2023* (September 10, 2020), 3.
14. Bonfadio and Taegio's versions of the phrase and its origins, in 1541 and 1559 respectively, have proved a useful way of placing gardens in the large landscape. I have used the idea on several occasions, but explained it most fully in "The Idea of a Garden and the Three Natures" in my *Greater Pefections: The Practice of Garden History* (Philadelphia: University of Pennsylvania Press, 2000). For a visual and lively exploration of the three natures in French and English by modern designers, see Christine and Michael Péna, *Pour une troisième nature: For a Third Nature* (Paris: ICI Interfaces, 2010).
15. Joyce, *Guidebook to Coe Hall*, 62.
16. I have used the paperback edition of *Italian Villas and Their Gardens* with introductions by Arthur Ross, Henry Hope Reed, and Thomas S. Hays (New York: Da Capo Press, 1976). I quote page 7 on the "subtle transitions" of spaces; page 184 for Tuckermann; page 139 on Villa Lante; and page 85 on Percier and Fontaine. See also Vivian Russell, *Edith Wharton's Italian Gardens* (Boston: Little Brown, 1997).
17. "Il faut toujours dire ce que l'on voit, surtout il faut toujours, ce qui est plus difficile, voir ce que l'on voit." Quoted here in the English translation by Anthony Eardley of *The Athens Charter* (New York: Grossman Publishers, 1973).

Planting Fields and the Olmsted Brothers on Long Island

The Olmsted Brothers firm was established in 1898, after the retirement of Frederick Law Olmsted Sr. From his earlier professional involvement with his father, John Charles Olmsted had developed a methodology to keep track of the widespread and growing practice with a system of Job Numbers assigned to its clients. These Job Numbers were consistently applied to all relevant documents for each client, whether correspondence, reports, plans, or photographs. Currently, the concentration of these files is found in either the Manuscript Division of the Library of Congress, Washington, D.C., or at the National Park Service, Frederick Law Olmsted National Historic Site, Brookline, Massachusetts.

Files from the Series B (business correspondence files), Olmsted Associates Records, Manuscript Division, Library of Congress [OAR/LC] are cited with the relevant Job Number and may include specific references to individual correspondence or file folders. Documents from the Series A (business correspondence letter-press books) will be similarly referenced as OAR/LC, series A and will include volume and page number.

Files from the Frederick Law Olmsted National Historic Site [NPS/FLONHS] are cited with the relevant Job Number and may include specific correspondence references. Additonally, the digitized plans and photographs at FLONHS, also organized by Job Number, will be identified though their Flicker website.

Documents published in the *Papers of Frederick Law Olmsted* series are indicated by PFLO followed by the volume and page number (PFLO, 3:221).

Documents published in the *Papers of Frederick Law Olmsted Supplementary Series* are likewise indicated PFLO, SS followed by the volume and page number (PFLO, SS1:page number).
1. Ralph Henry Gabriel, *The Evolution of Long Island* (New Haven: Yale University Press, 1921), *passim*; Evan T. Pritchard, *Native New Yorkers: The Legacy of the Algonquian People of New York* (Chicago: Council Oaks Books, 2007), 268–202 and *passim*.
2. Beginnning with the 1858 partnership of Frederick Law Olmsted Sr.[FLO] and Calvert Vaux when they began their work on Central Park, a firm involving FLO, his progeny, and their successors, under various names, practicing landscape architecture and later urban planning, continued until about 1980, when the Olmsted office in Brookline, Massachusetts, was acquired by the National Park Service to become The Frederick Law Olmsted National Historic Site [FLONHS]. At that time, the last remaining partner, Artemas Richardson, retained the name The Olmsted Office and moved his practice to New Hampshire, where he died in 2015. Olmsted and Vaux dissolved their New York partnership in

1872 when John Charles Olmsted [JCO] joined his stepfather in the practice, becoming a full partner in 1884 after Olmsted Sr. had moved his home and practice from New York to Brookline in 1882. Olmsted Sr. officially retired in 1897 and in 1898 Frederick Law Olmsted Jr. joined his brother to form Olmsted Brothers. As the client list grew in numbers, in geographic range, and in diversity of project types, even before there were programs to teach this new profession, the Olmsted office became an atelier to train young men in the aesthetic, environmental, and social principles of design on the land, working with nature and for the benefit of the greater public wherever possible, which the Olmsteds espoused. Innovative systematized procedures, mostly set up by JCO, enabled the female staff (many of whom were recent college graduates) to manage a national and eventually international practice. The firm also set up systems of temporary satellite offices in the various areas where a concentration of projects evolved. The various skills required by such a burgeoning practice involved designers, draftsmen, engineers and surveyors, plantsmen, architects, and many other subspecialities that developed as the practice diversified. Several of these men were foreign-born, coming from Great Britain, Holland, and Germany, among other countries. At the busiest point of its practice in the 1920s, the Olmsted firm had as many as 60 in professional staff. The Depression years, followed by World War II, diminished the practice, with the profession greatly changing focus after the war. By that time, there were many more competing firms.

3. The years before World War I were particularly busy as the firm's client roster had expanded with municipalities, institutions, and private clients all demanding attention. By 1917 America's engagement in the war limited both available staff and laborers as well as building supplies. Several of the firm's principals were engaged in wartime planning for military cantonments and housing for war-time industries. In the postwar years, after the death of JCO in 1920, many of the Olmsted principals were also involved in major West Coast planning, particularly for the subdivision originally covering the entire 26 square miles of the Palos Verdes peninsula, south of Los Angeles, where their contract required their on-site presence for lengthy periods. For its time, this was the largest such undertaking of its kind. It involved complex engineering on the steep shifting, earthquake prone hillsides to design for roads, houses, and institutions, and to develop the infrastructure systems needed to service these several newly planned communities, such as transportation, schools, and other municipal services.

4. Over its lengthy practice, the Olmsted firm developed various lists of its projects, grouped by types such as parks, institutions, and residences. Over the decades, with the complexity of the practice, these lists became inconsistent. In the 1990s, FLONHS working in partnership with the National Association for Olmsted Parks [NAOP], with initial funding from the National Center for Preservation Technology and Training, developed Olmsted Research Guide Online [ORGO] to begin to systematize the numerous record categories at FLONHS, and make this a publicly accessible database. Of the several groupings of records supplied, one was labelled 'Project Type' and included 15 separate categories such as "parks, parkways . . ;" "subdivisions and suburban communities;" "grounds of public buildings;" "cemeteries, burial lots . . . etc." into which the more than 6,000 project entries were catalogued. While this system provided some order, inconsistencies remain to complicate the categories. For example, while retaining the same job number, a project begun as a private estate might then be subdivided into multiple dwellings which even later might contain a park. Thus, interpreting these typologies remains a research task in progress.

5. For Planting Fields, Olmsted Job #06645 OAR/LC, over the period of active work (1918–37), about 395 plans were generated. Only for neighbor Henry Sanderson at La Selva, Olmsted Job #06218 OAR/LC, on smaller acreage but for very complicated designed spaces, were more plans produced (about 640 plans).

6. Coe's complaints were particularly strident at the stressful time around Mai Coe's death, the development of her mausoleum and the delivery and installation of the Carshalton Gates. Coe to Dawson, April 12, 1926; Dawson to FLO Jr., October 20, 1926; FLO Jr. to Coe, November 3, 1926, all found in correspondence file #5, in Olmsted Job #06645 OAR/LC.

7. PFLO, 8:435; PFLO SS3 pp.248-254. Cynthia Zaitzevsky, "William Bayard Cutting Estate, 'Westbrook'" in Robert B. MacKay, Anthony Baker, and Carol A. Traynor, eds. *Long Island Country Houses and Their Architects 1860–1940* (Cold Spring Harbor, NY and New York: Society for Preservation of Long Island Antiquities and W.W. Norton, 1997), 317–18. Also Olmsted Job #01047, OAR/LC, *passim*.

8. FLO, Sr. to Cornelius Rea Agnew, [c. June to October 1881], PFLO, 8:555-557. Raymond W. Smith, Montauk Association Historic District, National Register of Historic Places Nomination Form (Washington, D.C.: U.S. Department of the Interior, National Parks Service, 1976), *passim*. Historic Resources Policy #23, Section VIII, Town of East Hampton, *passim* [https://dos.ny.gov/system/files/documents/2019/04/section-viii.pdf].

9. Olmsted Job #05526 OAR/LC, *passim*. See also Zaitzevsky, "Roland Ray Conklin Estate, 'Rosemary Farm'" in MacKay, et al., *Long Island Country Houses*, 320. Zaitzevsky notes how unusual it was for an amphitheater to be designed for a private client. For renewed interest in this site, see North Shore Land Alliance [https://northshorelandalliance.org/category/2021-spring-conservation-news]

10. Olmsted Job #06287 OAR/LC, *passim*. Zaitzevsky, "Walter Jennings Estate, 'Burrwood'" in MacKay et al., *Long Island Country Houses*, 326; "Industrial Home buys L. I. Estate," *New York Times*, December 8, 1950; George Goodman Jr., "A Stately Home for the Blind," *New York Times*, November 27, 1977. Among the scattered garden artifacts, a wrought-iron gazebo from Burrwood is installed in the Elizabeth Street Garden in Manhattan. [https://untappedcities.com/2020/11/10/elizabeth-street-garden-gilded-age-olmsted-gazebo/] .

11. Edward Clark Whiting, "The Gardens at Ormston: A Country Seat in the English Manner," *Landscape Architecture Magazine* 28 (July 1938): 192 and *passim*. Olmsted Job #05578 OAR/LC, *passim*.

12. See Whiting, "The Gardens" and Zaitzevsky, "John E. Aldred Estate, 'Ormston'" in MacKay et. al., *Long Island Country Houses*, 321–23; Terry Winters et al, "John E. Aldred Estate (Ormston) [aka St Josephat's Monastery]," National Register of Historic Places Nomination Form (Washington, DC: U.S. Department of the Interior, National Parks Service, 1979).

13. Delano & Aldrich designed numerous notable houses on Long Island, many for Olmsted Brothers' clients. See Richard Guy Wilson, "Delano & Aldrich, 1903–1940" in MacKay et al., *Long Island Country Houses*, 127–43.

14. Olmsted Job #06499, OAR/LC *passim*.

15. James Warren, "Oheka," National Register of Historic Places Nomination Form (Washington, D.C.: U.S. Department of the Interior, National Parks Service, 2004); Megan Johnson, "Oheka Castle: Everything You Need to Know about the Long Island Mansion," *Architectural Digest*, December 25, 2023; "A Rich and Vibrant History" [https://www.oheka.com/history.htm]

16. The sons of Richard Morris Hunt, Richard Howland Hunt and Joseph Howland Hunt, had been in partnership since 1901 and were responsible for several large Long Island houses. Their opening letter to Olmsted Brothers of July 9, 1915, regarding the Sanderson property notes that "One of Mr. Sanderson's partners, Mr. Jay Cooke of Philadephia has spoken very highly of your Mr. James F. Dawson." Noting that they would like to consult with him, they continued "It is a pleasure to renew the relations begun so delightfully by the friendship of Father Olmsted and Father Hunt at Biltmore." Olmsted Job #06218, OAR/LC. See also Richard Chafee, "Hunt & Hunt, 1901–1924" in MacKay et al., *Long Island Country Houses*, 223–32.

17. Olmsted Job #0618, OAR/LC *passim*. Sculptural components of all sorts by Johan Selmer-Larsen graced both public and private Olmsted Brothers projects for nearly three decades. Coming from Norway in 1912, he settled in Marblehead, Massachusetts, where he and his wife were active members of the artists' community. With great

versatility, he designed freestanding figures, wall plaques, fountains, pedestals, benches, and jardinieres at all scales. See "Garden Sculptures of Johan Selmer-Larsen" [https://www.nps.gov/frla/learn/historyculture/larsen-sculptures.htm]

18. Zaitzevsky, "Henry Sanderson Estate, 'La Selva'" in MacKay et al., *Long Island Country Houses*, 325.

19. The Olmsted firm frequently collaborated with Walker & Gillette on such residential projects. During this period, the two firms were collaborating on design for at least seven other Long Island clients, including a major project in Southampton for H. H. Rogers, Mai Coe's brother (Olmsted Job # 06042 OAR/LC).

20. Olmsted Job #06645, OAR/LC *passim*. See *Planting Fields Cultural Landscape Report* (Charlotte, VT: Heritage Landscapes, 2019), *passim*.

21. Olmsted Job #06645 OAR/LC correspondence folders 3–5, *passim*.

22. J. F. Dawson to Gomo Waterer, February 14, 1919; J. F. Dawson to W. R. Coe, April 18, 1919, correspondence folder 2, Olmsted Job #06645, OAR/LC and *passim*.

23. Writing to Coe from California about renovating the herbaceous borders, Dawson remembered that William Robinson, the noted English horticulturist, had told him that "whenever you plant a herbaceous border, you ought to use enough plants of each variety to make that particular variety of plants count." J. F. Dawson to W. R. Coe September 9, 1925, correspondence folder 6, Olmsted Job #06645, OAR/LC.

24. J. F. Dawson to W. R. Coe April 6, 1926; W. R. Coe to J. F. Dawson, April 12, 1926; Walker & Gillette to Olmsted Brothers, June 23, 1927. Olmsted Job #06645 correspondence folders files 5-6, *passim*, OAR/LC. Coe purchased more than three acres from H. Lee Anstey along Glen Cove-Oyster Bay Road in May 1922, but the exact location of the gates was still under discussion in an August 1924 letter from Dawson to Coe. Mai Coe's death in December 1924 and planning her mausoleum, among other factors, delayed the gate decisions. By April 1926, Coe and Dawson discussed making a model to ease the process (though it is unclear if this was ever accomplished); by fall 1926, grading was underway, and by March 1927, construction of the lodge and walls began. Charles E. Peterson, "Progress Report, Supplement One," September 12, 1979 [unpublished manuscript], 8 and *passim*.

25. J. F. Dawson to Marion Taber, May 2, 1933, correspondence folder 8, Olmsted Job #06645, OAR/LC.

26. In January 1905, the NYC Improvement Commission requested advice from Frederick Law Olmsted Jr. for comprehensive park planning for the city's recently acquired boroughs, even before there was adequate administrative structure in place to carry out such planning. By September 1905, Olmsted, assisted by George Gibbs Jr., a landscape architect at Olmsted Brothers, began an assessment of the Borough of Queens for opportunities for parks, parkways, and main thoroughfares to serve present and future populations anticipated for this borough. The lengthy illustrated report of 1906 noted the impact that developing rapid transit lines were having, making accessible considerable new territory and the need for sound planning to avoid chaotic congestion. Olmsted Job #00521 and #00522 correspondence OAR/LC, *passim*.

27. Only 32 acres of the larger holding remain as the Wawapek Preserve on Mowbray Lane, Cold Spring Harbor. Today, the rest seems to be in houselots, some sizable. [https://northshorelandalliance.org/nature-preserves/wawapek-preserve/]. The former property on Shore Road of W. A. W. Stewart and his wife, Frances, who was Robert de Forest's daughter, also had some Olmsted firm planning. Job #4087 OAR/LC, *passim*.

28. Olmsted Job #03175 OAR/LC, *passim*; with plans and photographs from FLONHS https://www.flickr.com/photos/olmsted_archives/sets/72157659982967211 /https://www.flickr.com/photos/olmsted_archives/sets/72157647222238757/

29. Zaitzevsky, "Henry W. de Forest Estate, 'Nethermuir,'" MacKay et al., *Long Island Country Houses*, 318–19. Kathleen LaFrank, "Cold Spring Harbor Laboratory Historic District," National Register of Historic Places Nomination Form (Washington, D.C.: U.S. Department of the Interior, National Parks Service, 1994) details some of the remnants from the Henry de Forest estate extant on the Laboratory campus, 19, 24–26 and *passim*.

30. According to a publication compiled by Dave Nieri in 2017 for the 350th Anniversary of the Founding of Glen Cove and the 100th Anniversary celebrating the City of Glen Cove, in the mid-eighteenth century, Rev. Benjamin Woolsey applied the name of "Dosoris," from the Latin "dos uxoris," to the farm his wife inherited. The land called Dosoris Park was purchased by Charles Pratt in the 1890s and distributed among his children for their estates, including an administrative center for the whole property. Dave Nieri, *Glen Cove History: Origins of Place Names and Public Parks*, 2017, 8 https://www.glencovelibrary.org/wp-content/uploads/2018/04/Origin-of-Place-Names-Public-Parks.pdf.

31. By the 1930s, the Pratt family compound consisted of at least 21 separate residences and 61 ancillary structures. Robert B. MacKay, "Introduction," in MacKay et al., *Long Island Country Houses*, 29. Olmsted Job #03120 OAR/LC, *passim*. [Note that work for all the Pratt properties, from estates to the cemetery are contained under Job #03120 OAR/LC.] See also Benjamin Goodrich, "A Country Life Community: Dosoris Park. L.I." *Country Life in America*, vol XXIX (January 1916): 19–23.

32. Today the Pratt family estates have been repurposed. The mansion, designed by Charles Platt for John Teele and Ruth Pratt is now the Glen Cove Mansion Hotel and Conference Center; Poplar Hill, for Frederic B. Pratt, is now the Glengariff Rehabilitation & Healthcare Center; The Braes, for Herbert L. Pratt, is now the Webb Institute of Naval Architecture; Killenworth, for George D. Pratt, is now the country retreat of the Russian delegation to the United Nations; and Welwyn, the Harold I. Pratt estate, has become a nature preserve containing the Holocaust Memorial & Tolerance Center of Nassau County.

33. As noted by Robert MacKay, "The Pratt Oval stands apart in the Long Island country-house experience—housing the services that have been found in an entire manorial village in the English countryside." At its height, more than 400 employees were engaged in support services for the family compound. MacKay, "Introduction," in MacKay, et al., *Long Island Country Houses,* 29.

34. Planning for this land subdivision is detailed in correspondence between Carl Rust Parker and Mr. and Mrs. Harold Pratt from June 13 through December 1934 and in Carl Rust Parker to E. H. Crawford, Superintendent of Dosoris Park, November 2, 1936, correspondence folder 3, Olmsted Job #03120, OAR/LC. Additionally this subdivision planning is illustrated on Plans #03120-167, 169, 196, FLONHS, https://www.flickr.com/photos/olmsted_archives/sets/72157678666229142/]

35. Olmsted Job file #02635 OAR/LC, *passim*.; "Roosevelt's Rough Ride Led to Montauk," *New York Times,* May 17, 1898; Dan Rattiner, "Our Amazing History: Teddy Roosevelt at Montauk" [https://www.danspapers.com/2021/07/our-amazing-history-teddy-roosevelt-at-montauk/].

36. Olmsted Job #02636 OAR/LC, *passim.* "Indians Bring Suit to Possess Montauk," *The Brooklyn Daily Eagle,* July 12, 1907. "Montauk Point Land Claim," Wikipedia Foundation, last modified July 13, 2023 at 10:15. [https://en.wikipedia.org/wiki/Montauk_Point_land_claim].

37. Historic Resources Policy #23, Section VIII, Town of East Hampton, *passim* [https://dos.ny.gov/system/files/documents/2019/04/section-viii.pdf]; David Laskin, "History at the tip of Long Island," *New York Times,* August 27, 1989; Ellen Fletcher Russell and Sargent Russell, "Carl Graham Fisher and Montauk Beach," in Robert B. MacKay, ed., *Gardens of Eden: Long Island's Early Twentieth-Century Planned Communities* (New York: W. W. Norton, 2015), 148–67.

38. Olmsted Job #03094, OAR/LC, *passim*. Writing to his wife in April 1906, JCO notes, "I like the wild open landscape very much and I only regret to be planning to spoil it with roads and houses and stables. It would be fine if one man would buy the whole of it and just keep it as is." JCO to Fidie [Sophia White Olmsted], April 4, 1906, Box 11A, folder 79. *Papers of John Charles Olmsted*, Frances Loeb Library Special Collections, Graduate School of Design, Harvard University. See also Robert B.

MacKay, "From Flatbush to the Shinnecock Hills," in MacKay, ed., *Gardens of Eden,* 62–63.

39. Between 1914 and the early 1930s, Rick Olmsted and the firm advised Frederick Ruth on the development of elite resort colony projects in Lake Wales, Florida; in Bermuda; and in several other New York locations in addition to Fishers Island.

40. In addition to the planning for the main corporation at Fishers Island, Olmsted Brothers was engaged by forty individual island property owners to site their houses or plan their landscape. There are voluminous records at the Library of Congress Manuscript Division or at FLONHS. Since 1960, the Henry L. Ferguson Museum has become the repository of information and artifacts concerning the island, including remarkable photographs of early construction following the Olmsted planning.

41. Olmsted Job #07348, OAR/LC *passim*. This estate—the mansion, supposedly inspired by the Petit Trianon, and about fifty acres—was purchased by Mrs. Graham Fair Vanderbilt, the ex-wife of W. K. Vanderbilt II. "Mrs. W. K.Vanderbilt Buys Munsey Mansion,"*New York Times*, May 28, 1927. The property ultimately became part of the Strathmore holdings of William Levitt, the developer, with the mansion preserved as the Strathmore-Vanderbilt Country Club. See https://manhassetlibrary.org/site/wp-content/uploads/Strathmore-Vanderbilt-CC.pdf

42. Olmsted Job #07435, OAR/LC, *passim*. See also Virginia L. Bartos, "Robert Weeks de Forest: Forest Hills Gardens and Munsey Park," in MacKay, *Gardens of Eden,* 193–97. See also http://www.munseypark.org/village-history.

43. Frank Melville Jr., founder of the multifaceted Melville Corporation, and his wife, Jennie, vacationed in the Stony Brook area beginning in late nineteenth century. In 1902 he created the Old Field Improvement Association to become the Suffolk Improvement Company to develop roads, house lots, parks, and open spaces in Old Field South and Stony Brook. His son, Ward Melville, joined the business and is credited with developing the successful Tom-McAn brand of mass-produced practical shoes, sold through their own store chain. He became a major landowner in the Three Villages area, concerned with restoration and conservation. In 1957 he gave the significant land to become the State University of New York (SUNY) at Stony Brook. Leonard Sloane, "Ward Melville, 90, Shoe Magnate, Dies" *New York Times* (June 6, 1977). "Ward Melville," Wikipedia Foundation, last modified April 1, 2024. [https://en.wikipedia.org/wiki/Ward_Melville].

44. Olmsted Job #09019 OAR/LC, *passim*. Richard F. Welch, "Old Field South," in MacKay, ed., *Gardens of Eden,* 240–45. "History of Old Field South" [https://oldfieldsouth.org/history.html].

45. Frederick Law Olmsted Jr. to Henry de Forest, September 23, 1914. Olmsted Job #05571 OAR/LC, and *passim*.

46. Olmsted Job #07403 *passim*.

47. There are more than 280 listings for the Project Type 08 in the Olmsted Research Guide Online [ORGO] which includes cemeteries, burial sites, memorials, and monuments. The majority of these are in Massachusetts (81), followed by New York (67, 40 on Long Island). Two are abroad, one in Ontario, Canada and the other the post–World War II American Military Cemetery in Cambridge, England.

48. Olmsted Job #07403 OAR/LC, *passim*. The correspondence reveals that Coe admired the Fairhaven, Massachusetts, mausoleum built for his father-in-law, H. H. Rogers; but after an inspection visit to Fairhaven, Koehler suggested to Leon Gillette that that such a structure was inappropriate for the small sloped lot. Hans J. Koehler Reports of Visit, June 15, 1925; August 4, 1925. Olmsted Job #07403 OAR/LC.

49. See #07403 plans and photographs: https://www.flickr.com/photos/olmsted_archives/sets/72157646472399277/ https://www.flickr.com/photos/olmsted_archives/albums/72157672170093263/ While three of the four children of W. R. and Mai Coe would choose to be buried in the elegant mausoleum with their mother, Coe and his third wife, Caroline, selected Locust Valley, the Olmsted-designed cemetery in Lattingtown instead.

50. Dawson advised Coe in October of 1935 that if subdivision was to be considered, the plan must consider lotting in relation to the main residence and its approaches. Plan #06645-287 retained 53 acres around the mansion and its greenhouses, while providing other lots ranging from 2 to 23 acres. Olmsted Job #6645 OAR/LC, correspondence folder 8. See also: https://www.flickr.com/photos/olmsted_archives/33517568154/in/album-72157681990246115/

51. David A. Johnson, *Planning the Great Metropolis: The 1929 Regional Plan of New York and Its Environs* (New York: E & FN Spon, 1996), *passim*. See https://rpa.org/centennial-exhibition and https://rpa.org.

52. Johnson, chapter 3. The senior Olmsted made several attempts in his early regional and town planning to loosen the grid. See also Charles E. Beveridge, Lauren Meier, and Irene Mills, eds., *Frederick Law Olmsted: Plans and Views of Communities and Private Estates*, The Papers of Frederick Law Olmsted Supplementary Series, vol. 3 (Baltimore: Johns Hopkins University Press, 2020), 70–130.

53. There are several Olmsted Job numbers associated with greater New York City planning, particularly Olmsted Job #00536 concerned with the New York Regional Plan and #00536a concerned with the Sage Foundation and Rockefeller property, both beginning in 1922. Even earlier, in 1905, Rick Olmsted was approached by the New York Improvement Commission (Olmsted Job #00521 OAR/LC) concerning park development through the city and the newly attached boroughs. Work for these inquiries expanded to become park planning for the borough of Queens, Olmsted Job #00522 OAR/LC.

54. Robert A. Caro, *The Power Broker: Robert Moses and the Fall of New York* (New York: Alfred A. Knopf, 1974), *passim*. Olmsted Job #09037 OAR/LC for the Wheatley Hills Parkway relocation in 1928–29 is a good example of Moses's tactics to disrupt the great estates land ownerships by attempting to take property for a parkway. Much of the disruption, in this example, was somewhat thwarted by persuasive planning. See correspondence and plans for Olmsted Job #09037 *passim*.

55. The wise plan at Planting Fields to retain, curate, and expand the significant archival collection is much to the credit of the State and the Planting Fields Foundation and its Board. In this period of devastating climatic change, the documents, plans, and photographs retained on site are enabling such studies as the *Planting Fields Cultural Landscape Report* to better care for its landscape, to evaluate conditions over time, and to develop sound future procedures for this remarkable property. Additionally, such documents provide scholars with a window into the past, to better understand the views and values of the leaders and their families of earlier eras, as well as the workers and craftsmen.

A Historic Landscape Evolving Sustainably

1. Gina Wouters, Christopher Flagg, & Vincent Simeone, "Foreword," *Planting Fields Cultural Landscape Report* (Charlotte, VT: Heritage Landscapes, 2019), i–ii.

2. Between December 1904 and May 1906, Helen MacGregor Byrne purchased five contiguous lots within the upland flats southwest of Oyster Bay Harbor, and added a sixth lot of 70 acres in September 1912, bringing the total to a bit over 377 acres. *Planting Fields Cultural Landscape Report,* chapter 2.

3. Andrew Robeson Sargent, (1876–1918), the son of Charles Sprague Sargent, director of the Arnold Arboretum, was a plantsman and a landscape architect. Henrietta Sargent, his sister, married architect Guy Lowell, and A.R. Sargent was a professional in Lowell's office.

4. "Transforming Our World: The 2030 Agenda for Sustainable Development, A/Res/70/1" (New York: United Nations, 2015). The interlinked climate and biodiversity crises require action. The 2022 Kunming-Montréal Global Multidimensional Biodiversity Framework, adopted during the fifteenth meeting of the Conference of the Parties (COP 15) supports these goals and seeks to increase the area, quality and connectivity of existing protected lands to increase benefits in the face of the biodiversity and climate crises.

5. U.S. Secretary of the Interior's "Standards for the Treatment of Historic Properties with Guidelines for the Treatment of Cultural Landscapes." See www.nps.gov/crps/tps/landscape.

6. "Report of the World Commission on Environment and Development: Our Common Future," 20 March 1987, 39, "Paragraph 51. No single blueprint of sustainability will be found, as economic and social system and ecological conditions differ widely among countries. Each nation will have to work out its own concrete policy implications. Yet irrespective of these differences, sustainable development should be seen as a global objective."

7. Transforming Our World: the 2030 Agenda for Sustainable Development (UN, 19 September 2015).

8. According to research conducted by Christopher Flagg, Carl Wedell encouraged Coe to consider the potential for Planting Fields to become a laboratory for training and education in horticulture.

9. Pennsylvania State University forest carbon accounting research, downloaded March 3 2024 [https://extension.psu.edu/carbon-accounting-in-forest-management].

10. Miles King, Director of Conservation, The Grasslands Trust, indicates that grasslands lock-up carbon in plants and soils to a significant degree, and if maintained, rank higher than woodlands with active forestry and removals. [https://www.brightseeds.co.uk/carbon-offsetting-with-wildflowers/].

11. [https://www.thelawninstitute.org/environmental%20-benefits/carbon-sequestration/].

12. Americans with Disabilities Act of 1990 and subsequent access laws and guidelines provide details required in construction to provide universal access for persons of all abilities.

13. Accounting of carbon in construction is focusing on concrete carbon footprint reduction as global use of concrete is considerable. Additives in concrete, such as fly ash and recycled glass reduce the footprint. Low carbon concrete is becoming more readily available and will be used whenever possible.

INDEX

Italicized page numbers indicate illustrations. An asterisk (*) after a page number indicates a footnote at the bottom of the page while "n" and "nn" are used to indicate endnotes. Unless otherwise indicated, all locations are in New York state.

Acer Collection, 190
African Americans, 71, 76
    See also slavery and slave trade
Airslie (Cold Spring Harbor), 163
Aldred, John, 158
Algonquian peoples, 61–63, *62*, 66, 152
Al Hadid, Diana: *The Outside In*, *130–31*
American Revolution, 75–76
American Society of Landscape Architects (ASLA), 30, 153
Americans with Disabilities Act of 1990, 206n12
The Architectural Record on Coes' rebuilt house (1921), 43
Arnold Arboretum (Harvard University), 37, 47, 50, 144, 205n2
Arts and Crafts movement, 25
Asahroken (Matinecock sachem), 70
Ashcan School, 39
Assiapum (Matinecock sachem), 68–71
Astor, William Waldorf, 38
Athelhampton (Dorset, England), 41
Atterbury, Grosvenor
    background of, 24–25
    as Gold Coast property owner, 166
    as Planting Fields architect of Byrnes, 25–30, *26*, 35, 42, 56, 79, 160
    See also Byrnes' development of Planting Fields
Azalea Walk/Garden, 48, *104*, 141, *183*, 186, 188

Basilian Order of St. Josephat, 158–59
Battle of Long Island (1776), 75
Bayard Cutting Arboretum State Park, 154
bedrooms, 45, *46*, 52, 56, *92–93*
beech trees and Beech Drive, 48–50, 162, *162*, 193–94, *193*
Benson, Arthur W., 155, 164
Benson, Frank Sherman, 164–65
Big Tree Farm (Oyster Bay), 46

Billings, Cornelius K. G., 32, 36, 40, 80
    yacht *Vanadis*, 80, *80*
Biltmore House (Asheville, NC), 46, 47, 159
biodiversity concerns, 178, 181, 182, 186, 189–90, 191, 205n4
Black Point (Southampton), 40, 46, 47–48, *156*
Blenheim Palace (England), 141
Blossom, Harold Hill, 153, 159, 162, 163
Blue Pool (sunken or Italian) Garden, 37–39, *38*, 47, 48, *50*, 56, *86*, *112*, *134–35*, 138–41, *139*, 145, *147*, 163, 176
Bonfadio, Jacopo, 145, 202n14
The Braes (Glen Cove), 30
    See also Dosoris Park
Bridgemen, Charles, 142
British Army, occupation under, *75*, 75–76
Brooks, David: *The Budding Bird Blind*, 140, *140*
Brown, Lancelot "Capability," 18, 136, *137*, 141, 143
Burrwood (Cold Spring Harbor), 157–58
Burtis, T. W., 76
Byrne, James and Helen Macgregor, *23*
    Helen's background, 24, 201n61
    James' background, 24, 201n61
    land purchase for Planting Fields, 22, 23–24, 78, 176, 205n2
    sale of Planting Fields to Coe, 32–33, 80, 202n68
    West 59th Street townhouse, 24, *33*
Byrnes' 1904–13 development of Planting Fields (with Atterbury and Greenleaf), 22–33, 78–81
    Atterbury's architectural plans, 25–30, *26*, 35, 42, 56, 79, 160
    bedrooms, 27, 29
    billiard room, 27, *28*
    Coe on, 36
    drawing room, 27, *29*
    entrance hall, 27
    Greenleaf's garden and landscaping, 30–31, *31*, 37, 160, 176
    Helen's role and influence, 56, 81, 199n12
    interior furnishings and decoration, 30
    long hall, 27, *28*
    playhouse and cottages, 31, *32*, 40, 50
    purchase of land, 22, 23–24, 78
    rental in summer, 32, 80, 199n27
    sale to Coe family, 32–33, 80, 176, 202n68

    service wing, 27
    stable, 29–30, *37*
    Vista Path (north-south walk), 31, *31*
    west wing, 25

Camellia House, 47, 48, *50*, 51, *106–9*, 161
carbon footprint, reduction of, 190–91, 194, 206n10, 206n13
Carlhian, André, 45
Carshalton Gates and gatehouse, 52–53, *53*, *84–85*, 140, *141*, 162, *174–75*, 183, *184*, 190, 202n6, 204n24
Carshalton Park (Surrey, England), 52, 200n68, 202n6
Casey, Edward S.: *Representing Place*, 144
Caumsett (Horse Neck) sale to English settlers, 70
Caumsett mansion of Marshall Field III (Long Island), 47
cemeteries, burial grounds, etc., designed by Olmsted Brothers, 51, 168–69, 205n47
Chanler, Robert Winthrop, 44–45, *45*–46, 52, 57, *98*
Chase, William Merritt, 25, 166
Cherokee Plantation (Yemassee, SC), 53–55, 170
    Cusachs as architect, 54
    Olmsted as landscape designer, 53–54
Cheshire, William E., 77
Cicero, 145
Circular Pool Garden (Greenleaf's), 27, 30, 42, 48, *49*, *120–21*
Claude Lorrain, 143
climate change, 178, 181, 192, 205n4
Cloister Court and Garden, 48, *49*, 56, 57, *102–3*, 176
Cocks, W. Burling, 23
Cody, William F. "Buffalo Bill," 34
Coe, Caroline Graham Slaughter (third wife), 51–55, *51*
    burial plot with W. R. in Locust Valley Cemetery, 55, *168*, 205n49
    death of, 56
    disliked by children of W. R. and Mai, 52, 55
    first marriage to E. Dick Slaughter, 51*, 51–52
    home on southern part of estate during SUNY era, 56
    influence of, 52
Coe, Mai (Mary Huttleston Rogers, second wife), *34*
    background of, 33–34

Byrne letter to, 33
death of (1924), 51
French design and, 43–44, *44*, *45*, *46*, 141
mausoleum in Laurel Hollow Cemetery, 51, 55, 168–70, *169*, 205n49
Coe, William Robertson, 34–35, 51, 162–63
   background of, 33–34
   burial plot in Locust Valley Cemetery for himself and wife Caroline, 55, *168*, *169*, 205n49
   Cherokee Plantation (Yemassee, SC) home, 53–55, 170
   Cody, Wyoming, ranch home, 35, *35*
   Dawson and, 19, 52, 54, 154, 161, 170, 176, 203n6
   death of (1955), 55, 177, 183
   as defining vision of Planting Fields, 17, 18
   first marriage to Janie Hutchinson Falligant, 34*
   goal to keep Planting Fields intact, 17, 55, 56, 172
   health concerns, 54
   horticulture and, 50, 52, 54, 57, 161–63, 176, 180, 189–90, 205n8
   ornithology and, 55, 140, *140*
   as outdoorsman and hunter, 43, 141
   Palm Beach, Florida, home, 55
   purchase of Planting Fields (1913), 32–33, 80, 176, 202n68
   second marriage to Mai Huddleston Rogers, 34
   third marriage to Caroline Graham Slaughter, 51
   transferring of Planting Fields to State of New York, 55, 177, 183
   will of, 56
Coe children of W. R. and Mai (William, Jr., Robert, Henry, and Natalie), 34, *34–35*
   dislike of stepmother Caroline Coe, 52, 55
   Henry (son), 34, *34–35*, 54
   Natalie (daughter), 34, *34–35*, 54, 141, *142*
   Robert (son), 34, *34–35*, 40
   unlikely to maintain Planting Fields, 54
   William, Jr. (son), 34, *34–35*, 54
   William, Jr., Robert, and Natalie interred in Laurel Hollow mausoleum with Mai, 55*
Coes' development of Planting Fields 1913–18 (Mai and W. R. Coe with Walker & Gillette and Lowell), 33–40
   Blue Pool (sunken or Italian) Garden, 37–39, *38*
   farm buildings, 34–5, *36*
   fire (1918), 40, 176
   front door entrance, 35
   greenhouse and palm house, 37
   Hay Barn, 34, *36*, 40
   murals by Shinn, 39
   palm house, 37
   Sargent's landscaping, 37–38, 47, 160, 161, 176
   Teahouse design and murals by Shinn, 32, 39–40, *39*, 57, *114–15*
   Vista Path (north-south walk), 37
Coes' development of Planting Fields 1918–24 (Mai and W. R. Coe with Walker & Gillette and Olmsted Brothers), 40–51
   Azalea Walk/Garden, 48, 141

   beech copse, 48–50
   Blue Pool (sunken or Italian) Garden, 47, 48, *50*
   breakfast room with murals ("Buffalo Room"), 44–45, *45*, *98*
   Camellia House, 47, 48, 51
   Cloister Court, 48, *49*, 56, 57, *102–3*
   Dawson as Olmsted Brothers principal in landscaping, 17, 46–50, *49*, 84–85, 153–54, 158–62, 176, 183
   Dawson's expanded role, 50–51, 162
   den of W. R. Coe, 43, *96*
   entrance hall, 43, *44*
   French design favored by Mai, 43–44, *44*, *45*, *46*, 141
   Gothic and Doric features, 43
   Heather Garden, 48
   Hewitt's photographs documenting, *41*, 44–45, 48, *49*
   inscription over front entrance, 43, 60, *61*
   landscape design features intact after fire, 47, 48
   Living Room and Gallery, 43
   Mai's bedroom, 45, *46*, 52, *92–93*
   Mai's reception room, 43–44, *44*, 56, *97*
   palm house, 47
   reconstruction completed by 1920, 43
   rose garden, *51*
   second fire (1924), 51, 162
   stable, *42*, 43
   Surprise Pool, 48
   Tudor/Elizabethan style, 41, 43, 46
   Vista Path, 47, 48, *105*, 141
   Walker & Gillette's design of new residence, 40–51, *41–42*
   West Lawn, 48, *49*
Coes' development of Planting Fields 1924–55 (Caroline and W. R. Coe with Walker & Gillette and Olmsted Brothers), 51–55
   aerial photo (c. 1955), 177, *177*
   Carshalton Gates. *See* Carshalton Gates and gatehouse
   Dawson's continued involvement, 54
   dining room, 52, *94*, *99*
   estate managers' changes (1930–40), 54
   film of completed grounds (1928), 53
   Olmsted Brothers' end of work (1930s), 53, 170
   palm house enlargement, 53
   proposed subdivision of property, 54, 170, 205n50
   remodeling by Caroline, 52
Cold Spring Harbor, 163
   See also specific properties by name
Cold Spring Harbor Laboratory, 163
Cole family, 71
Coles, Nathaniel, Jr., 74
College of Old Westbury, 56, 183
Collins, Wilkie, 27
colonial era, 18, 64–71, *68*
   See also Dutch settlers and New Netherland; English settlers; indigenous peoples *for relations with settlers*

Colony Club, 24, 45
Conklin, Roland Ray, 157
Corbin, Austin, 165
cottages and playhouse, 31, *32*, 40, 50, *117*
country houses, 23, 25, 27, 35, 38, 41, 46, 81, 141
Country Place Era, 22, 31, 55, 57
Cox, Gardner, 30
Crabbe family, 71
   Alice, 74
   Richard, 74
Cravath, Paul D., 23, 24
Cusachs, Philip Alain, 53–55
Cutting, Bayard, 154, *155*

Dawson, James Frederick "Fred," 18–19
   advice from William Robinson to, 204n23
   background of, 47
   completing work of Sargent and Lowell, 46–50, *49*, 160–62
   death of, 171
   expanded role at Planting Fields, 50–51, 162
   Hewitt and, 48
   horticultural expertise of, 162
   La Selva and, 160
   narrative of Planting Fields development by, 162–63
   Oheka and, 47, 159
   as principal of Olmsted Brothers working on Planting Fields, 17, 46–50, *49*, 54, *84–85*, 153–54, 158–62, 176, 183
   proposed subdivision of Planting Fields, 54, 170, 205n50
   relocation to California, 52, 170
   W. R. Coe and, 19, 52, 54, 154, 161, 170, 176, 203n6
   Walker & Gillette collaboration with, 171
de Forest family
   family burial site, design for, 168, 170
   Henry, 155, 163, 168
   Julia, 163
   Robert, 155, 163, 166–67, 171
Delano & Aldrich, 35, 45, 47, 159, 203n13
den of W. R. Coe, 43, *96*
Depression, 22, 54, 167, 171, 203n2
de Wolfe, Elsie, 45
   The House in Good Taste, 39
   Town & Country article on Teahouse (1916), 39
dining room
   in Byrnes' Planting Fields, 27
   in Caroline Coe's Planting Fields, 52, *94*, *99*
   in Mai Coe's Planting Fields, 44
   stained-glass window, *99*
   in SUNY era, 56, 57
Dion, Mark: *Posh Blind* (2020), 129, 140, *140*
Dosoris Park (Glen Cove), 164, 204n30
Du Bois, Guy Pène, 39
Duke's Law (1665), 71
"Dutch gardens" (English name for geometrical flower gardens), 38
Dutch settlers and New Netherland, 64–70, *65*, 67–68, 74, 200–201n23

Dutch West India Company, 64, 74
Duveen, Charles J. (Charles of London), 45–46, 52, 141

East Lawn, 183, 185, 188, *196–97*
   view of Main House from, *91*
Elizabethan style. *See* Tudor/Elizabethan style
English influence, 38, 141–42
   See also country houses
English settlers
   arrival on Long Island, 64
   conflicts with indigenous peoples, 69, 70
   encroaching on Dutch lands, 67, 70
   first community at Oyster Bay (1653), 68–69
   founding families' ownership of Oyster Bay land, 71–72, 77–78
   inheritance practices ensuring land ownership by, 73
   map of English takeover from Dutch, 68, *68*
   peace agreements with Native peoples, 66
entry drive, 161–62, 182, 183, *184*, 190, 192–94, *193–95*
   See also Carshalton Gates and gatehouse
equestrian and hunt clubs, 78–80
European colonization of Long Island, 64–68, *68*
   See also Dutch settlers and New Netherland; English settlers
Eyre, Wilson, 157, *158*

Faber, Denison, 1st Baron Wittenham, 52
Farnsworth, 35, 36, 37, 55
Farrand, Beatrix, 159
Fatio, Maurice, 55
Ferguson family, 166
Field, Marshall, III, 47
fields, transformation into open meadow, 191
fire (1918), 40, 176
fire (1924), 51, 162
Fisher, Carl, 165
Fishers Island, 166, 204–5n40
Fitzgerald, F. Scott, 22
Fontaine, Pierre, 146
Forest Hills Gardens, 25
Friedman, Avi: *The Nature of Place: A Search for Authenticity*, 144
front door entrance, 35, 43, 60, *61*, *90*
Frost family, 71
   Wright, 74

Gall, Tom (né Owah, free Black man), 74
Gallagher, Percival, 47, 153, 158, 171
Gallery
   in Caroline Coe's remodeling, *95*
   in Mai Coe's rebuilding, 43
   in SUNY era, 56
   W. R. Coe's outdoors sports interests reflected in, 43, 141
The Garden on W. R. Coe's camellia collection, 51
Gauwarowe (Massapequa sachem), 66
"genius loci" (genius of the place), 137, 141, 144
Georgian revival, 25, 27, 35, 36, 41, 47, 162

Gillette, Leon N., 35, 40, 160, 170
   See also Walker & Gillette
Gold Coast estates, 18, 22, 30, 55, 77, 141, 171, 178
Goldwyn, Samuel, 39
Goodhue, Bertram Grosvenor, 41, 43, *156*, 158
Gradual Manumission Law (NY, 1799), 76
Great Bird Blind Debate (Oyster Bay, 2020), 140, *140*
The Great Gatsby (Fitzgerald), 22, 57
Grecian Temple and Valley at Stowe (England), 136–37, *137*
greenhouses, 37, 48, 56, 161
   entrance to Main Greenhouse, *122*
   new construction (1930s), 170
   roof collapse (1920) and fire (1924), 161–62
   See also Camellia House
Greenleaf, James Leal, 30–31, 37, 47, 48, 56, 160, 176
Gugler, Eric (Gugler & Kimball), 56

ha-ha to define garden space, 144–45, *145*
Haight, Charles Coolidge, 155
Harbor Hill (Roslyn), 36, 37, 55, 159
Hartford Treaty (1650), 68
Hastings, Thomas, 158
Hay Barn, 34, 36, 40, 56
Heather Garden, 48, *125–26*, 139, *140*, 163, 188–89, *189*, 193
herbaceous garden with hedges, *119*
Heritage Landscapes, 176, 177–78, 180
   See also Planting Fields Foundation *for CLR*
Hever Castle (Kent, England), 38
Hewitt, Mark Alan, 27, 41
Hewitt, Mattie Edwards, *41*, 44–45, 48, 49, *87*, *94–95*, *118–19*, *148*, *160*, 161, *163*, *182*, *183*
Hibiscus House, 53, *123*, 170
"Historic Designed Landscape," 56
Hither Hills-Hither Woods (Long Island), 165, *165*
Hither Hills State Park (Long Island), 165
Hog Island (later, Centre Island), 69, 72
Hovingham (Yorkshire, England), 141
Hubbard, Henry V., 153, 166
Hudson Valley, 30, 74
Hunt, Richard Morris, 159, 203n16
Hunt & Hunt, 160

indigenous peoples, 152, 200n1
   contagious diseases and mortality rates, 65
   conversion to Christianity, 68
   disputes and suits over land transfers, 66–68, 70–71, 166
   European mischaracterization of, 64–65
   real estate dealings with, 66
   wampum and trade with Europeans, 63, 65–66
   See also Algonquian peoples; Matinecock people
Italian gardens as influence, 38, 138–39, 142, 145–47, 160
   See also Blue Pool (sunken or Italian) Garden

Jennings, Walter, 157–58
Johnson & Higgins, 34, 54

Johnston, Frances Benjamin, 38, 39, *158*
John Waterer Nursery (Surrey, England), 162
Jourdain, Margaret, 142
Joyce, Henry B.: *Guidebook to Coe Hall*, 141–42
Kahn, Otto, 47, 159
Kensington Palace (London), 38
Kent, William, 18
   Stowe (England) landscape design and, 141–43, *143*
Killenworth (Oyster Bay), 30, 41
Koehler, Hans J., 153, 158, 162, 170

L. Alavoine & Cie., 44, *44*
labor force, 62–63, 74, 76
   household staff of Byrne family, 27*, 79
   household staff of Coe family, 43*
   See also slavery and slave trade
"landscape architecture"
   Lowell's influence in emerging field of, 36
   as profession, 153
   use of term, 18, 136, 144
"landscape design," use of term, 184
La Selva (later Dellwood, Long Island), 160, *160*
Laurel Hollow, Coe mausoleum at Memorial Cemetery, 51, 55, 55*, 168–70, *169*, 205n49
lawn games, 31, 31*
Leatherbarrow, David, 136
Le Corbusier, 18, 149
Leverich, William, 68–72
Livingston, Robert, 32, 80
Locust Valley, 23, 27, 76
Locust Valley Cemetery, 55, *168*, 169–70, 205n49
Long Island
   divided into Nassau and Suffolk Counties, 152
   geomorphic background of, 152
   hurricane (1938), 54
   land sale/purchase (1653), 69
   map (1671), *68*
   map (1776), *75*
   Olmsted's estates and communities, 154–55
   suburbanization plan, *171*, 172
   transformation of land usage of, 152
   See also North Shore; Oyster Bay
Long Island Rail Road, 76, 77, 165–66
"Long Island, 'where cooling breezes blow'" (promotional book), *81*
Long Island State Park Commission, 154, 172
Lowell, Guy, 36–38, 46, 56, 160
   American Gardens, 36
   English influence on, 38
   Italian influence on, 145
   Olmsted Brothers' work building upon original landscape of, 47, 144, 145
   Smaller Italian Villas and Farmhouses, 38
Loyalists, 75–76

MacFadden, Mary, 157
Mackay, Clarence H., 36, 159
making of place, 135–49, 202n11

maps and plans
    Atterbury's floor plans, *26*
    British troops stationed on Long Island during American Revolution, *75*
    colonial Long Island (1671), *68*
    landscape plan (1920), 182–83, *183–84*
    landscape plan (1955/56), *185*, 187–89, *188*
    Locust Valley Cemetery, *168*
    Long Island (1776) with locations of British troops, *75*
    Munsey Park (Manhasset), *167*
    Plan of New York and Its Environs (1923), *171*
    Planting Fields archival sources of, 182–83
    Planting Fields general plan (1920), *184*
    Scholtes' Terrace study (1918), *161*
    Vista Path planting plan (1920), *183*
    Walker & Gillette's floor plans, *42*
    Wompenanit and Hither Hills-Hither Woods (Long Island), *165*
Massapequa people, 66–67, 152
Matinecock people, 17, 18, 23, 60–71
    crops and planting fields, 60, 62, 77
    disagreements with English settlers, 69, 70
    Dutch assertion of dominion over lands of, 64
    English land transactions with, 68–69
    gendered labor, 62–63
    governance, 63, 64, 70
    marginalization by Dutch and English division of Long Island, 68
    migration patterns, 62
    peace negotiations with the Dutch, 66
    sale of lands to English settlers, 69, 70–71
    wampum and, 63, *63*, 65–66
Mayhasit (Glen Cove), 46
Mayo, Samuel, 68–71
McCoun, Sidney, 78
McKim, Mead & White, 25, 30, 37*, 56, 155, *155*
McVickar, Noel, 40
Meadow Brook Club, 78
Mechowodt (Massapequa sachem), 66
Melville family, 167, 205n43
Montauk Association Houses, 154–55, *155*, 163, 164
Montauk people, 61, 152, 155
Montauk Point State Park (Long Island), 165
Moses, Robert, 165, 172, 205n53
Mott, Joseph Cooper, 33
The Mount (Lenox, MA), 38
Moyns Park (Essex, England), 41, *41*
Muir, John, 37
Munsey, Frank, 166
Munsey Park (Manhasset), 166–67, *167*, 205n41
murals
    by Chanler, 44–46, *45–46*, 52, 57, *98*
    by Shinn, 39–40, *39*, *114–15*

Nassau County, 152, 164, 172
    Horticultural Show, 79
National Historic District, Montauk as, 155
National Register of Historic Places, 17, 56, 172
naturalistic landscape design, 47, 136, 142, 157, 176, 185, 188
nature, explanations of, 136, 145, 202n14
Nethermuir (Cold Spring Harbor), *157*, 163
New Amsterdam, 64–65, *65*
    coats of arms, *67*
New Netherland. *See* Dutch settlers and New Netherland
New York (colony), 18, 68, *68*
    See also Dutch settlers and New Netherland; English settlers
New York City
    consolidation (1898), 152
    Improvement Commission, 204n26, 205n53
    Oheka used by, 159
    Regional Plan for New York and Environs (1922), 167, *171*, 172
    See also Moses, Robert
New York State
    historical documentation of Planting Fields compiled by, 178
    Office of Parks, Recreation & Historic Preservation, 18, 56, 172, 177, 182
    Parks system, 17
    W. R. Coe deeding Planting Fields to, 55, 177, 183
    See also SUNY
North Shore, 18, 22, 32, 36, 47, 76–81, 157, 167, 172, 178
    See also Gold Coast estates; Oyster Bay

Oak Allée to replace beeches, 193–94, *194–95*
Oheka (Huntington), 46–48, 55, 159–60, *159*
Old Field South (Long Island), 167
Olmsted, Frederick Law, 153–54, 202n2
    Biltmore House gardens and, 46
    Cutting and, 154, *155*
    Long Island estates and communities designed by, 154–55, 164, 205n52
    park innovations and livable cities concept of, 172
Olmsted, Frederick Law, Jr. "Rick"
    Arnold Arboretum, 37
    Atterbury collaboration with, on Forest Hills Gardens, 25
    background of, 153–54
    creativity of, 138
    de Forests and, 163–64
    design motive of, 168, 172
    Fishers Island resort and golf course development, 166
    Long Island estates with landscaping by, 157–59
    as member of Olmsted Brothers, 46–47
    New York City park planning and, 204n26, 205n53
    Pratts and, 164
    retirement and death of, 171
    signage to orient visitors from, 149
    specializing in town planning projects, 47, 153
    varied styles of, 47, 145
    See also Olmsted Brothers
Olmsted, John Charles, 46–47, 153, 202–3n2
    death of, 47
    Long Island subdivisions and, 165–66, 204n38
    as member of Olmsted Brothers, 46, 202
    See also Olmsted Brothers
Olmsted Brothers, 17, 18–19, 46–51, 152–73
    adapting to changing aspects of Planting Fields, 140–41, 144, 145, 183, 184–86
    background of, 46–47, 152–54, 202, 202–3nn2–4
    cemeteries, burial grounds, etc., 51, 168–69, 205n47
    as collaborator with Walker & Gillette, 154, 160, 171, 203–4n19
    elements *de rigeur* in work of, 147, 156–57
    historical documentation available for work at Planting Fields, 182–83
    influence of, 171
    Long Island oeuvre of, 156–62, 178
    models and maquettes as illustrations of proposed work, 170
    Planting Fields and. *See* Coes' development of Planting Fields *(by time periods)*
    residential projects overseen by Dawson and Gallagher, 47
    signage to orient visitors from, 149
    subdivisions and resorts planning by, 164–67
    Yemassee plantation landscaping, 53–54
    See also Dawson, James Frederick; Oheka; Olmsted, Frederick Law, Jr.; Olmsted, John Charles
Ormston (Lattingtown), 41, 48, *156*, 158
Owah (boy in bondage of Crabbe family), 74
Owens, Susan: *Spirit of Place, Artist, Writers & the British Landscape*, 144
Oyster Bay
    colonial history of, 18, 64–71, *68*
    economic struggles of small farmers, 76, 77
    equestrian and hunt clubs, 78–80
    high society estates in, 22, 76–77, 80–81
    labor shortages in, 76
    land sales and profits of founding families, 77–78
    name of, 64
    in nineteenth century, 76–81
    private clubs, proliferation of, 78
    reputation as home of rich and famous, 88
    riding trails, 29
    sale of Matinecock land to English settlers, 69, 70–71
    Shore Road (c. 1906), *79*
    transportation options and accessibility, 22, 76–77
    unpaved roads, preservation of, 79, *79*
    See also Gold Coast estates; Planting Fields

Paleo-Indians, 61
palm house, 37, 47, 53
Parker, Carl Rust, 153, 162, 164, *169*, 170–71
parklands, history of, 143
Patzig, August H., 25, 29, 30, 31, *31*
Percier, Charles, 146
picturesque design, 27, 29, 31, 41, 57, 146–47, 149, 152, 155, 157, 159, 163, 164, 166

Piping Rock Club (Matinecock), 79
place-making, 135–49, 202n11
Planting Fields, history of development of, 2–12
    adapting to changing aspects of, 140–41, 144, 145, 176, 180, 183
    aerial views of, *50*, *54*, *88–89*, *125–26*, 144, *158*, 177, *177*, 182, *186*, *193*
    Brown's influence on, 136
    Byrnes and. *See* Byrnes' development of Planting Fields
    Coes and. *See* Coes' development of Planting Fields *(by time periods)*
    cost considerations for the future, 195
    division among Oyster Bay's founding families, 71, 77
    evolution of, 138–40
    as exemplary model of preservation practices, 154, 172–73, 178–80
    historical background of, 17
    historical documentation available for, 182–83, 205n55
    as intact estate, 55, 56, 172, 178
    legacy of W. R. Coe and his designers, 176
    making of place, 135–49
    on National Register of Historic Places, 17, 56, 172
    in Olmsted Brothers' oeuvre, 17, 160–62, *161*
    Olmsted Brothers' records and design for, 182–83, 187–89
    SUNY era, *54*, 55–56, 57, 183
    terrace study (1918), *161*
    variety in gardens and landscaping of, 48, 138, 147, 156–57, 162, 180
    See also Planting Fields today and in the future
"Planting Fields" (name), 17, 43, 60, 79, 138
Planting Fields Arboretum State Historic Park, 56, 172, 180, 183
Planting Fields Foundation, 18, 55–56, 172, 180, 182–83, 189, 205n55
    Cultural Landscape Report (CLR, in conjunction with Heritage Landscapes and NY State Office of Parks, Recreation, and Historic Preservation), 17, 143–44, 173, 177–78, 182–83, 185, 186–87, *187–88*
    Strategic Plan of 2020–2023, 144
Planting Fields today and in the future
    integrated actions and priorities, 186–93
    maintenance routes, 192
    stewardship, 17–19, 172–73, 177, 179–80, 183, 190
    sustainability, 180–82, *181–82*, 194
    universal access walk to enhance inclusive visitation, 191–92, 206n12
    water supply and irrigation, 192
    woodlands and fields, augmentation and transformation of, 190–91
Platt, Charles A., 35
    Italian Villas and Their Gardens, 38
playhouse. *See* cottages and playhouse
Pope, Alexander, 18, 137–38
Pope, John Russell, 35, 47
Poussin, Nicolas, 143
Pratt family, 204nn31–33
    Charles, 164, 204n30
    Frederic, 163
    Harold and Harriet, 164
preservation practices, 154, 172–73, 178–80
    federal standards for preservation, restoration, reconstruction, and rehabilitation, 179–80
    integrated actions and priorities going forward, 186–93
private clubs and resorts, 78–80, 165, 166
Processional Arts: *Follies* performance (2024), *128*

Quakers, 67, 74

Raff (enslaved Black man), 74
Raynor, Seth, 159, 166
reception room, 43–44, *44*, 56, 97, 141
Redfield, William C., 166
Regional Plan Association, 172
Regional Plan for New York and Environs (multivolume study 1922), 167, *171*, 172
Renaissance-style gardens and structures, 145, 160
Repton, Humphry, 18, 143, *143*
Robinson, Thomas, 52
Robinson, William, 204n23
Rockefeller, John D., 33, 167
rococo, 39, 45
Rogers, Henry, 40
Rogers, Henry Huttleston, 33–34, 203–4n19
    See also Black Point
Roosevelt, Theodore, 79, 165
Rose Arbor, *16*, 31, 37, *118*
rose garden, *51*, 56
Rosemary Farm (Huntington), 157, *158*
Ruskin, John, 146
Russell, Benjamin B. F., 37
Russell Sage Foundation, 25, 171
Ruth, Frederick S., 166, 204n39

Sadler, Hammond, 153
St. Catherine's Court (Somerset, England), 41
St. John's Memorial Cemetery. *See* Laurel Hollow
Sammis family, 71
    Epenetus, 76
    John Merritt, 23, 75, 77–78, 81
    Silas, 75
Sanderson, Henry and Elizabeth, 160
Sargent, A. Robeson, 37–8, 40, 47, 56, 144, 145, 160, 161, 176, 205n3
    See also Coes' 1913–18 development of Planting Fields
Sargent, Charles Sprague, 37, 144, 205n2
Scawen, Thomas, 52, 202n6
Scholtes, A. J., *161*
Scott, Geoffrey, 22
The Secretary of the Interior's Standards for the Treatment of Historic Properties, 56
Seligmann, Jacques, 43–44
Selmer-Larsen, Johan, 160, 203n17

Shaftesbury, 3rd Earl (Anthony Asley Cooper): *Characteristics of Men, Manners, Opinions, Times in Three Volumes*, 137, *138*
Shinn, Everett, 39–40, *39*, 45, 57, *114–15*
Shinnecock Golf Club, 166
Silas, John, 75–76
Slaughter, E. Dick, 51*, 51–52
slavery and slave trade
    Dutch importation of enslaved Africans, 74
    English slave codes, 74
    manumission, 74, 76
    NY law phasing out, 76
    ownership transferred with other property in will, 74
    Quaker opposition to, 74
    runaways, 74–75
Sloet, Jacob, 153, 162
stable
    Atterbury development, 29–30, 37
    first fire (1918) and, 42, *43*
    Sargent's greenhouse and, 37
    second fire (1924) and, 51
stained-glass window in dining room, 99
State Historic Park designation, 56
stewardship, 17–19, 172–73, 177, 179–80, 183, 190
Stony Brook University (temporary location at Planting Fields), 55–56, 183
Stowe Gardens (England), 136–37, *137*, 141–43, *143*, 144–45, *145*
Suffolk County, 152, 164, 172
sunken garden. *See* Blue Pool Garden
SUNY (State University of New York) period (1955–70), *54*, 55–56, 57, 183
    Center for International Studies and World Affairs, 56
    Long Island Agricultural Institute, 171, 183
Surprise Pool (Dawson's circular pool), 48, *116*, 147, 186
Suscaneman (Matinecock sachem), 72
sustainability, 180–82, *181–82*, 194
    See also United Nations Sustainable Development Goals
Switzer, Stephen, 142
Synoptic Garden, 57, *124*, 177, 180, 183, 189, 191

Taber, Marion, 162
Tackapousha (Massapequa sachem), 67, 71
Taegio, Bartolomeo, 145, 202n14
Taxus Field, *132–33*, 189
Taylor, Gordon, 165
Teahouse, 31, *32*, 39–40, *39*, 57, *113–15*
Temple, Richard (Viscount Cobham), 144
theater/stage designs, 142, *143*, 145, 157, *158*
Three Villages area (North Shore), 167, 205n43
Tiffany, Louis Comfort, 79
Town & Country on Shinn's Teahouse (1916), 39
Townsend family, 71–73
    deed of sale from Wrights to, 73, *73*
    George, 74
    John, 72–73

Rebecca, 77
Robert, Jr., 72, *73*
Trowbridge & Ackerman, 41
Tuckermann, Herman, 146
Tudor/Elizabethan style, 29, 41, 43, 46, 154, 158, 160, 162–63

Underhill, John, 66
United Nations Sustainable Development Goals, 19, 178, 181–82, *181*
universal access walk to enhance inclusive visitation, 191–92, 206n12
University of Wyoming, Coe Library, 55
Upper Planting Fields Farm, 23, 24, 77, 78

Vanadis (yacht), 80, *80*
Vanderbilt, Frederick W., 30
Vanderbilt, George W., 159
    See also Biltmore House
Van Tienhoven, Cornelis, 64, 67–68, 70, 200n14
Van Wyck, Doris, 74–75
variety in gardens and horticultural collection, 48, 138, 147, 156–57, 162, 180
Vaux, Downing, 166
Veraton, 23, 36, 37, 55
Versailles, 138, 147
Villa Lante (Bagnaia, Italy), 146
Vista Path, 31, *31*, 37, 47, 48, 56, *105*, 141, *183*
Vitetti, Leonardo (Italian count), 54, 141, *142*
Vizcaya (Miami, FL), 45

Wait, Charles R. (Chick), 153, 157
Walker, A. Stewart, 35, 44, 46, 51
Walker & Gillette, 37, 39, 40–41, 53, 160
    background of firm, 34–35
    new residence for Planting Fields (1918–24), 40–51, *41–42*, 56, 162
    Olmsted Brothers as collaborator with, 154, 160, 171, 203–4n19
    other architectural jobs, 46–48
    Wyoming ranch home of W. R. Coe designed by, 35, *35**
Walpole, Horace: *History of the Modern Taste in Gardening*, 142–43
Washington, George, 75
Wawapeck (Cold Spring Harbor), 163
Wedell, Carl, 189, 205n8
Welwyn (Glen Cove), 164
Westbrook (Cutting house), 154, *155*
West Lawn, 48, *49*, *110–11*, *127*, 183, 185, 188
West Portico, *14*, *87*, *148*
West Terrace walk, 186
Wharton, Edith
    A Backward Glance, 146
    Italian Villas and Their Gardens, 38, 139, 145–47
Whately, Thomas, 137
Wheeler, Frederick, 160
White, Stanford, 24, 36
Whitehead, Daniel, 70
Whiting, Edward Clark (Ted), 153, 158, 163, 167
Whitney, Gertrude Vanderbilt, 45

Wilson, Michael, 142
Wompenanit (Long Island), 165, *165*
Wood, Jeremiah, 75
Wood, John Walter, 35*
wooden rooster (second floor), *101*
Woodland epoch (1000 BCE–1500 CE), 62
woodlands, augmentation of, 190
Wren, Christopher, 43
Wright family, 71–73, 201n27
    Adam, 72–73
    Anthony, 72
    Caleb, 72
    deed of sale to Townsend (1686), 72–73, *73*
    Edmund, 72, 74
    Job, 72, *73*
    John, 72
    Nicholas, 72
    Peter, 68–72
Wyandanch (Montauket sachem), 66–67, 70
Wyoming
    University of Wyoming, Coe Library, 55
    W. R. Coe's ranch home in Cody, 35, 35*

Yellin, Samuel, *100*
yew trees, *162*, 189
Yokohama Nursery (Japan), 162

Zach, Leon, 153, 166

CONTRIBUTORS

Jennifer Anderson is an Associate Professor of History at Stony Brook University who advised on the Long Island Museum's groundbreaking exhibition, "Long Road to Freedom: Surviving Slavery on Long Island." Her current scholarship focuses on changing land uses and labor relations on Long Island from the late seventeenth to the early twentieth century. She is the author of *Mahogany: The Costs of Luxury in Early America*, about the social and environmental history of the tropical timber trade.

John Dixon Hunt is Emeritus Professor of Landscape Architecture at the University of Pennsylvania. Originally trained in English literature, he has devoted himself to the study of landscape design since 1988. Among his many books are *Garden and Grove: The Italian Renaissance Garden in the English Imagination, 1600–1750*, *Greater Perfections: The Practice of Garden Theory*, *The Afterlife of Gardens*, and *The Making of Place: Modern and Contemporary Gardens*. In 2000 he was named a Chevalier of the Order of Arts and Letters by the French Ministry of Culture.

Arleyn A. Levee is a landscape historian and preservation consultant specializing in the work of the Olmsted firm. She has advised municipalities and private clients on the history and rehabilitation of their Olmsted-designed landscapes. In addition to various articles concerning Olmsted projects and firm members, she is the author of *The Blue Garden: Recapturing an Iconic Newport Landscape* and of *Experiencing Olmsted: The Enduring Legacy of Frederick Law Olmsted's North American Landscapes* (with Charles Birnbaum and Dena Tasse-Winter).

Patricia M. O'Donnell is founding partner of Heritage Landscapes LLC, Preservation Landscape Architects and Planners. She has led more than six hundred heritage-based landscape planning and implementation projects and has contributed to the continued vitality and resilience of sixty Olmsted legacy landscapes. In 2021 she received the Louise du Pont Crowninshield Award, the highest honor of the National Trust for Historic Preservation.

Witold Rybczynski is an architect and Emeritus Professor of Urbanism at the University of Pennsylvania, who has been described as "one of our most original, accessible, and stimulating writers on architecture" (*Library Journal*). He is author of twenty-two books, including the best-selling *Home: A Short History of an Idea*, *A Clearing in the Distance: Frederick Law Olmsted and North America in the Nineteenth Century*, *The Story of Architecture*, and most recently, *The Driving Machine: A Design History of the Automobile*.

David Almeida is a Long Island-based photographer with twenty years of professional experience in the heritage sector. He has worked in the photography departments of the Museum of Modern Art (MoMA), Wolfsonian-FIU, and University of Miami. His photographs have been published in journals and magazines including *Architectural Digest* and *Antiques and Fine Art* and in exhibition catalogues for MoMA, Wolfsonian-FIU, Vizcaya Museum and Gardens, Planting Fields Foundation, and The Cultural Landscape Foundation.

Jerome E. Singerman is Senior Humanities Editor emeritus at the University of Pennsylvania Press. His writing has appeared in *The Magazine Antiques* and *Mittelweg 36*. He is author (with Ruth K. Westheimer) of *Myths of Love: Echoes of Greek and Roman Mythology in the Modern Romantic Imagination*.

Gina J. Wouters is President and CEO of Planting Fields Foundation. In a career centered on the preservation and revitalization of historic sites, she has been Curator of Vizcaya Museum and Gardens in Miami and Vice President of Museum Affairs and Chief Curator at Cheekwood Estate and Gardens in Nashville. She is editor (with Andrea Gollin) of *Robert Winthrop Chanler: Discovering the Fantastic*.

The Robert David Lion Gardiner Foundation has generously provided major funding for this publication.

Copyright © 2025 The Monacelli Press and Planting Fields Foundation
Color photographs copyright © 2025 David Almeida
"A Country Place and Its Makers" copyright © 2025 Witold Rybczynski
"Before the Gold Coast: The Early History of Planting Fields" copyright © 2025 Jennifer L. Anderson
"On Planting Fields and the Making of Place" copyright © 2025 John Dixon Hunt
"Planting Fields and Olmsted Brothers on Long Island" copyright © 2025 Arleyn A. Levee
"A Historic Landscape Evolving Sustainably" copyright © 2025 Patricia M. O'Donnell

First published in the United States by The Monacelli Press. All rights reserved.

Library of Congress Control Number: 2024922323
ISBN: 9781580936828

Pages 2–3: View to the West Portico with cherry trees in bloom.
Pages 4–5: The Cloister Court. Mattie Edwards Hewitt, c. 1920. *Planting Fields Foundation Archives.*
Pages 6–7: View to the Blue Pool Garden from the Teahouse.
Pages 8–9: Path to the Blue Pool Garden. Mattie Edwards Hewitt, c. 1920. *Planting Fields Foundation Archives.*
Pages 10–11: Tree-lined pathway in North Border.
Page 12: Samuel Yellin gates in Blue Pool Garden.
Page 14: View from the West Portico. Mattie Edwards Hewitt, c. 1920. *Planting Fields Foundation Archives.*
Page 16: Rose arbor in bloom.
Pages 20–21: North facade of the Main House.
Pages 58–59: East Lawn forest edge in late summer.
Pages 134–35: View to the Blue Pool Garden with lilacs in bloom.
Pages 150–51: Walkway in the Vista Path with azaleas in bloom.
Pages 174–75: Carshalton Gates.

Design: Yve Ludwig

Printed in China

Monacelli
A Phaidon Company
111 Broadway
New York, New York 10006